Local Elites in Western Democracies

URBAN POLICY CHALLENGES
Terry Nichols Clark, Series Editor

Cities are critical. From the Los Angeles riots of 1992 to the Hong Kong reversion of 1997, cities represent in microcosm the problems and potentials we face at all governmental levels.

Focusing on cities can help clarify our most challenging issues. Most key decisions affecting our lives are made locally. Although national governments collect the majority of funds, most welfare state programs around the world are provided by local governments. Urban leaders play key roles in encouraging economic development, maintaining quality public services, and mandating reasonable taxes.

And they are pressed to do more: provide attractive physical environments, improve amenities such as bike paths, help encourage recycling, assist disadvantaged groups to achieve broader acceptance and access to public facilities, keep streets safe, and fill the gaps in health and social services.

Books in the *Urban Policy Challenges* series will explore the range of urban policy problems and will detail solutions that have been sought and implemented in cities from around the world. They will build on studies of leadership, public management, organizational culture, community power, intergovernmental relations, public finance, citizen responsiveness, and related elements of urban public decisionmaking.

These approaches to urban challenges will range from case studies to quantitative modeling. The series will include monographs, texts, as well as edited volumes. While some works will target professional and student audiences, many books will elicit attention from thoughtful public leaders and informed citizens as well.

BOOKS IN THE SERIES

The Los Angeles Riots: Lessons for the Urban Future, edited by Mark Baldassare

Local Elites in Western Democracies: A Comparative Analysis of Urban Political Leaders in the United States, Sweden, and The Netherlands, Samuel J. Eldersveld, Lars Strömberg, and Wim Derksen

Local Elites in Western Democracies

A Comparative Analysis of Urban
Political Leaders in the U.S.,
Sweden, and The Netherlands

Samuel J. Eldersveld,
Lars Strömberg,
and Wim Derksen

Westview Press

BOULDER • SAN FRANCISCO • OXFORD

Urban Policy Challenges

Copyright © 1995 by Westview Press, Inc.

Published in 1995 in the United States of America by Westview Press, Inc., 5500 Central Avenue, Boulder, Colorado 80301-2877, and in the United Kingdom by Westview Press, 36 Lonsdale Road, Summertown, Oxford OX2 7EW

A CIP catalog record for this book is available from the Library of Congress.
ISBN 0-8133-8880-5

Printed and bound in the United States of America

 The paper used in this publication meets the requirements
of the American National Standard for Permanence of Paper
for Printed Library Materials Z39.48-1984.

10   9   8   7   6   5   4   3   2   1

Contents

Preface

Much insightful scholarship has been devoted to the elaboration of the nature and functions of elites in modern societies. The theories and paradigms which have emerged have evoked both strong support as well as considerable criticism. Two key elements in the controversy are the inevitability of hierarchical control, on the one hand, and the inherent need in a democracy for elite public responsiveness, on the other hand. The early classical scholars (Mosca, Pareto, and Michels) emphasized the former more than the latter. In recent decades it is responsiveness which is identified and operationalized as a critical requisite. Lasswell stated years ago that in democratic societies the "essential condition to be fulfilled (for elites) is accountability" (Lasswell, Lerner and Rothwell, 1952, 21). Pitkin's conception of representative democracy went further, insisting that democracy required leaders "acting in the interest of the represented, in a manner responsive to them" (Pitkin 1967, 209). The authors of a recent book with an "elitist paradigm" admit that the problems elites face today require responsible management and "non-elite support" (Field and Higley, 1980, 95, 35).

This emphasis on the public responsiveness of elites underlies the analysis in this book. In operationalizing responsiveness, beyond the electoral involvement of elites, we join with other scholars in emphasizing certain key components. If elites are to be responsive in the cities they govern, there must be a two-way flow of interactions between them and the group infrastructures of their communities (parties, interest groups, media, citizens). Second, such contacts and relationships should make elites aware of the problems facing their communities and concerned about the resolution of these problems. Without genuine concern elites are unlikely to act in the public good. Further, such concern should be linked to a sense of responsibility to act as well as an acceptance of the power to act. Hopefully, this level of concern and this sense of responsibility will be embedded in a set of democratic values, principles and beliefs conducing them to action. Finally, however, this is not enough for elites to play a significant role in their communities. Concern, awareness, feelings of responsibility, impulses to be in touch with and responsive to community groups, and well-articulated values need to be supplemented by a will to take effective action, and, beyond that, the initiation of action. In the last analysis the real test is effective action. Some scholars have long recognized this operationalization of elite responsiveness (Verba and Nie 1972).

Testing this conception of the role of elites is a primary goal of the analysis presented here. We investigate in great detail in these three democratic systems the level of elites' concern for their problems, their sense of responsibility (and power) to act, their relations with community groups and the public, and their values. And throughout the analysis we keep in mind the question of "effective action." In the conclusion we present a set of models which suggest what types of factors seem to be associated with effective action, as these elites perceive it in their communities. Earlier research has been somewhat negative in its evaluation of the responsiveness and democratic orientations of elites in Western societies (for example, Eulau and Prewitt 1973, 426-427). The basic question still remains— under what conditions can and are local elites operating effectively in their communities? Our data may shed some light on that key problem.

This study both builds on and diverges from the early comparative research on local elites. The two most outstanding of these earlier comparative studies were: The 1966-67 study of 82 San Francisco Bay Area cities, directed by Heinz Eulau and Kenneth Prewitt (Eulau and Prewitt 1973), and the 1966 study of 120 cities (or their equivalents), thirty in each of four countries (the U.S., Poland, Yugoslavia, and India) by an international team under the direction of Philip Jacob (Jacob 1971). These pioneering works made significant contributions to our knowledge of the variance in local elite attitudes and behaviors. While using many of the same design features and questions of the four nation "values" study, our focus is quite different. We are exclusively engaged with three Western democracies (the U.S., Sweden, and the Netherlands), and substantively our emphasis is on the characteristics of elites, and their perceptions of the politics of their communities. That is, our emphasis is on a description and analysis of the social and political backgrounds of local leaders, their problem and conflict perceptions, their strategies for mobilizing support, their personal influence structures, and their political values. Our analysis is relevant to understanding differential patterns of leadership in communities in these three democracies, keeping in mind the differing conditions and contexts in which democracy functions in these systems. In doing this we seek to describe local elite political cultures and how they vary across systems and within systems.

The research reported here, with such antecedents, is now part of a new international program of comparative research called "The New Democracy and Local Governance." This program coordinated by a steering committee headed by Henry Teune (University of Pennsylvania) and Krzysztof Ostrowski (Kelles-Krauz Foundation, Warsaw) has expanded the interest in the study of local elites to other systems, particularly to former Soviet and Eastern European countries. These included Poland, Lithuania, Ukraine, Belarus, Slovenia, Kazakhstan, Russia, Uzbekistan, the Czech and Slovak Republics and Hungary. Also joining this program are Austria, Germany, Norway, Finland, Switzerland, Spain and Turkey. In Asia studies are being done in Taiwan, Mainland China, Korea and Japan. Hence, a truly international research program in the study of local elites is in place, of which the present study is the first major report for Western systems. Most of the design specifications and questions in this study have been adopted by the countries in this program now planning or conducting studies. In addition, many new questions have been pre-tested and used that are specifically relevant to the democratization process and the economic and social changes occurring in these countries. It is hoped that our study will constitute a type of "Western" benchmark for the "new democracy" studies.

We pay tribute here to the work of the late Philip E. Jacob, whose energy and intellect contributed so much to the 1966 "values" study. We also remember our colleague, Thomas Watts, whose untimely death prevented him from completing his work on this book. Many people have been involved in the data-collection and the preparation of the analysis for this book: Cecilia Bokenstrand and Stephen Szucs in Sweden; Judith Kullberg, Ricardo Rodriguiz, Anne Bennett, and Shen Mingming in the U.S.; Jeanet Pronk, Yoka van Eck, Hermine Rietman in the Netherlands. We are also very grateful to our secretaries who helped type and retype the many versions of this manuscript: Mary Breijak, Kris Moga, Tanya Hummels, Michelle Newton, Holly Bender, and Thelma M. Perry in Ann Arbor. In addition we appreciate the financial support we have received in the three countries: the Horace H. Rackham School of Graduate Studies and the Department of Political Science at the University of Michigan; the University of Leiden in the Netherlands, and the University of Göteborg in Sweden. Obviously without this support and assistance our work would never have been completed. The authors are alone responsible, however, for the analysis and interpretations.

It is our fervent hope that scholarly interest for comparative research on local government and particularly on urban political leadership is now again reviving and that this book may play an important part in such inquiry.

S. J. Eldersveld
Lars Strömberg
Wim Derksen

1

The Comparative Study of Local Political Elites

Our knowledge of the nature of local political leadership in modern democracies based on systematic comparative scholarship is limited. This makes it difficult to generalize across political systems. There are special studies of local leaders in particular countries which are frequently well done and have extended our knowledge of local government in one system. However, truly comparative (cross-national) studies of local political elites based on empirical research are few.[1] No doubt there are many reasons for this: lack of interest in city level politics, lack of useful comparative theory, unavailability of financial resources, difficulties in putting a comparative research team together, and other reasons also. Political scientists just have been more interested in their own political system, and in interviewing *national* politicians than in comparative studies of *local* leaders. Whatever the reasons, we have very little solid research to go with if we wish to theorize across nations about the backgrounds, beliefs, and behavior of local elites.

This book seeks to help fill that gap. It focuses on the nature of leadership in local governments in three different systems: the U.S., Sweden and the Netherlands. Such a study is important, not only to fill a void in research, but to help us understand how our respective political systems function. These three countries are democracies. In a sense ours is a benchmark study of what western democratic elites at the local level of government are like, who they are, what they believe, how they see their problems, and their views on their power and responsibility to deal with their problems. Further, we are interested in their assessment of whether effective action on these problems is being taken, and their personal influence role in policy making. By using the same methodology in all three countries, we have collected a comparable body of data which we hope can help explain the nature and variations in local elite democracy in the "West." That is our first objective. However, secondly, our aim is to explore in a preliminary way, the extent to which system differences in these three democracies may affect local elite attitudes and behavior. Sweden and the Netherlands are "strong" or maximal welfare state democracies, compared to the U.S. where the welfare state ideology is "weak" and mixed. How do the roles of local elites differ in these contrasting welfare state and ideological milieus?

Further, Sweden and the Netherlands are "unitary" systems and local government's relationship to the central government in Stockholm and Amsterdam is quite different, much more directly controlled (theoretically), than is the case in the "decentralized" American system where cities have no similar direct control relationship with Washington. Another difference is of course the party system—multi-party in Europe, a mix of partisan and nonpartisan at the local level in the U.S. And there are often organizational differences in local government among these three countries. The question posed throughout our study, then, is how do systemic ideological, institutional, and organizational differences affect local elites and local government?

The third focus we are committed to in this study is that of elite political cultures, because of the comparative approach we use here. We search for evidence that we do indeed have such elite cultures, peculiar to systems or transcending them. There are two aspects of our approach. We work with propositions which transcend particular political systems, particular countries, to see whether these propositions are empirically defensible across systems. And, second, we deal with explanations of phenomena in the context of a particular system or culture. In a sense we are exploring the position of scholars like Wildavsky who argue that "leadership is a function of regime or political culture"(Wildavsky 1989, 98). Long ago, Lasswell, emphasized these two perspectives. He said "we must examine . . . broad hypotheses which apply horizontally throughout the world," and at the same time these propositions "must be analyzed in terms of the web of cultural and historical factors which shape the character of the elite within a given country . . . "(Lasswell 1952,2). This is precisely our point of departure. We search for the uniformities and differences in local governing elites in these democratic societies. If there is an "interdependence" of cultures today, to what extent do we find that manifest in local political elites?

Most of the people living in these three countries are affected as much, if not more, by the decisions made by local authorities as by national (or state) governments. And the interest in the study of local government has been increasing, both as a special field of inquiry as well as to understand nation systems better. This is not true everywhere in the world, certainly not in all developing and non-democratic systems. But in our three "Western" democracies it is. It is quite true that local government in all these systems has considerable power and/or responsibility for dealing with their own problems.

There is a rich tradition of local self-government in all three countries. For European countries, this could be traced back to the Middle Ages, but the modern movement toward local self government dates from the early 19th century, after the French Revolution. There was considerable debate at that time over the functions, powers, and size of municipalities. In the U.S., also, the "home rule" movement for cities acquired momentum in the latter part of the 19th century and many cities adopted their own charters of government having been given considerable autonomy by state legislatures. Hence, it makes sense to study political leadership in cities, and the conditions under which that leadership functions, if we are to understand the nation system itself. Many of the problems of modern democratic societies are urban problems, not exclusively but certainly in large part. What types of elites are coping with these problems, operating from what types of backgrounds, perceptions, beliefs, and values, should be of great interest.[2]

The Meaning of Elite Political Culture

As already stated, this is in a sense a study of "elite political cultures". Our meaning and objectives may require a bit of explication. "Culture" is an elusive concept, yet widely used. The way it is often used, it appears to be an empty, catch-all, vague concept. Sometimes, it is used as a meaningless predictor or explainer—as when we are challenged to explain a finding and reply "it is because of the culture". It is probably better as an organizing concept, than as a predictor, although our ultimate hope is that "culture" can be so precisely operationalized and systematically studied as to be usefully linked to attitudes and behaviors. One objective in our study is to identify, describe, and begin to explain the components of elite political cultures at the local level of government.

Almond gave us the early definition of political culture as "a particular pattern of orientations to political action" (Almond 1956, 396). He referred particularly to attitudes, beliefs, values, and skills. He accepted the three components of Parsons and Shils, which were: perception (cognition), affect (preference), and evaluation (choice). Other scholars have elaborated on various ideas related to this or advanced new ideas (Knoke 1981, 204). One major emphasis recently is that culture is a product of "collective", human associations, of institutional life, of different types of structures. Barnes emphasizes culture as "shared assumptions and meanings"(Barnes 1988, 2). Thompson, Ellis, and Wildavsky take the explicit position that "political culture is shaped by structure" (Thompson et al. 1990, 218). Cultural meanings it is argued, can change over time in response to the changes in human structures, conditions, associations. There is some opposition, however, to "the fusion of culture and structure"(Lasswell and Kaplan 1950, 47; Thompson et al. 1990, 218). There is also some controversy as to how "culture" is linked to "behavior". Finally, it should be pointed out that students of culture emphasize the existence of subcultures or communities with their own cultures, or "special propensities", as Almond referred to them.

Although there are many controversies about the meaning of political cultures and the research which has been done has not cleared up the ambiguities, the scholarly discussion has been useful in setting the stage for our research. We will focus here on three basic components of elite political culture:

1. *Elite perceptions.* How do leaders view the political world, particularly their own community which they are leading? What are the public problems they face, how serious are they? To what extent can they deal with these problems—do they have the power and resources? What conflicts do they recognize in their communities? What pressures are there from groups, citizens, other leaders?
2. *Elite Evaluations.* How effective in their opinion is the action which is being taken in the solution of community problems? How do they evaluate the effect of community conflicts on the development of their communities? How much influence do they feel they have, and in which policy areas, on decisions in the community?
3. *Elite Values and Preferences.* In which policy areas do they feel they have or should have the responsibility to act, and in which areas no responsibility? With which types of groups do they work in order to get things done—i.e., what is their preferred strategy for mobilizing support? (Note: on both of these questions there is both a perceptual and a preferential component). Above all, what type of governmental system do they value? Do they believe in much citizen *participation* or little, *innovative* or traditional orientations to leadership, local *autonomy* from national control or the priority of national interests, *conflict* as a way to achieve progress (or consensus); and an economic *egalitarian* approach to decision-making or are they unconcerned about equity and economic opportunity for the "underclass"?

We are not only interested in *whether* elite political cultures differ, but *why*. A variety of theories can be advanced. Do elite cultures differ because of certain basic features of the political, economic, or social *system* in which leaders are reared and trained? Are the differences attributable to the social origins and status of elites? Or the process by which these leaders are recruited? Is the education system a critical factor? Or, the type of party system in which they learn about politics and to which they are attached? Are there perhaps community subcultures (the city, the commune) which are relevant because of differential norms and social conditions? These are difficult queries, and we shall attempt to deal with them in our analysis.

We would emphasize here that we study the components of cultures, in the plural. We expect to find within-system cultural differences among elites as well as inter-system differences. These are democracies, but elites do not all learn, nor believe in, the same norms about how their democratic systems work. We also emphasize here the idea of elite cultures interacting with the social and political context. Elites are in a sense constrained by the cultural expectations of their systems, as they perceive and understand them; but elites also contribute to the development and maintenance of their cultures.

Three Systems of Government

Although all three of our countries are democracies, the differences in their national systems of government are great and may have important consequences for the attitudes and beliefs of local elites. Sweden and the Netherlands are parliamentary systems, with unitary and national-local power relationships, and multi-party systems. This contrasts with the U.S. presidential system, its division of executive—legislative power, its federalism, and its two-party system. The relevance of these features for understanding local government is considerable.

Central-local government relationships in these three countries differ greatly and should be kept in mind constantly in interpreting our data. At one extreme is the Dutch system with direct national control over municipalities which is in some respects severe and quite restrictive, through central government control of local revenues and regulatory directives over expenditures. There has been a movement in recent years toward decentralization in the Netherlands which may be in the process of revising these relationships in the near future. While the Swedish central-local government relationship is also unitary, there is much less control over local revenues, and less regulation of expenditures. Direct state control of cities has decreased but indirectly the state exerts central control, in two main ways. First and most important is state regulation of mandatory duties such as the primary and secondary schools, social welfare, building, environment/health and fire. Second, and not least important, is indirect control through state grants and rules in various service areas. We will expand on these aspects of the Dutch and Swedish systems later.

The American system is obviously much more differentiated, decentralized, and unintegrated than either the Swedish or Dutch system. National control over local units of government in a formal sense does not exist;

indirect influence is varied, attenuated and minimal. Municipalities in the U.S. are essentially creatures of the fifty state governments, and under the constitutional authority of the states. The basic reality is that American cities have to raise most of their own revenues and decide autonomously on what policies, for what purposes, and with what strategies they will spend their funds. This is radically different than the Swedish, and especially the Dutch context. In addition, many U.S. cities have a "home rule" status which provides for a high degree of autonomy, despite theoretical state control. Finally, one must remember that the national multi-party system in the European systems finds its replications to a large degree in the local elections and councils, which are very partisan. In the U.S. at least 70 percent of the cities have, formally, nonpartisan systems (candidates run on ballots with no party labels). These structural features may be important systemic constraints influencing elite behavior.

The U.S. System's Development and Nature

The evolution of local government forms and the status of local units of government in the system vary considerably for these three systems. In the U.S. during the 19th century, the status of cities changed as did their types of government (Gottdiener 1987). Three developments converged. One was the emergence of a system which put more power in the hands of the elected mayor—power to appoint personnel, power to remove, supervisory power over the administration, and the veto power. A second was the rise of the "boss" and his political machine with all its consequences—electoral fraud, corruption in municipal decision-making, patronage based on rewarding the faithful rather than on merit, intimidation, lack of public accountability for leadership actions, etc. Third, this led to the Progressive Movement aimed at reforming local government in order to challenge the power of the machines and provide for more efficient government. Also, from 1875 on, state constitutions began to provide for "home rule" for cities. State legislatures were empowered (in some states required) to permit cities to write their own charters of government, in the expectation that the citizens' representatives would reform their governments. Two new forms of government were proposed and gradually came to be used after 1900: the commission form and the council-manager form. The emphasis of these systems was threefold: more citizen involvement in governmental decision-making, elimination of the role of political parties at the local level, and more professionalism in city administration (through the manager system and a merit-based civil service). It was hoped that these changes would lead to better local government and the demise of the political machines. The Progressive Movement in the U.S. had considerable impact on local government. Although it did not eliminate political machines at once, it did change local political structures and the process by which politics was conducted. Some of its reforms still influence U.S. local politics today—particularly the city-manager system and nonpartisan elections. Some research has suggested that these reforms, indeed, have had consequences, raising questions as to whether they have led to less governmental responsiveness (Lineberry and Fowler 1968).

U.S. cities, thus, went through several basic changes from 1850 to the present. Throughout these stages, they were experimenting with three basic types of local government (Figure 1.1). One was the "commission" form of government in which the heads of city departments were responsible to boards of commissions of citizens. The department heads themselves were elected and sat collectively as a city council. This form emphasized citizen involvement. Its use gradually declined. Today, fewer than ten percent of the cities use this form. The second type was the "mayor-council" form which has been the most dominant form since 1900. There are two sub-types: the strong mayor and the weak mayor form. In this system, the council and mayor are elected, the council either from districts or at-large. The mayor functions as the chief executive, having more or less power to appoint and remove departmental personnel and to veto ordinances. Large cities use this type of system almost exclusively.

The "council-manager" is the third type of local government which gradually became more attractive in the past 50 years. It now is used in 50 percent of middle sized cities and 33 percent of all cities. Under this system, the elected council is the center of power, selecting a professionally trained city manager who is responsible to the council in the last analysis. The manager directs the departments, and usually recommends the personnel to be appointed by council. This system is a product of the reform movement and emphasizes efficiency in government, while the mayor-council system presumably emphasizes political leadership. Thus, each of these three types are used, each have provoked controversy, each has its own style.

The Swedish System's Development and Nature

In Sweden, the reform of local government took place over several stages and well over 100 years. As in the rest of Europe, considerable debate over the functions, power and size of municipalities took place after the French revolution. It has been disputed to what extent the Swedish debate was influenced by the local government reform-movements in such countries as Belgium, Britain and Prussia, or was based totally on several hundreds of years of indigenous experience with local self-government. The debate was also to a high degree linked to the liberal reform of national institutions such as the replacement of the four estates with a two-chamber parliamentary system (Kaijser 1962, 11-66). The reform period ended in 1862 when the state

FIGURE 1.1   The Three Basic Forms of Local Government in the U.S.

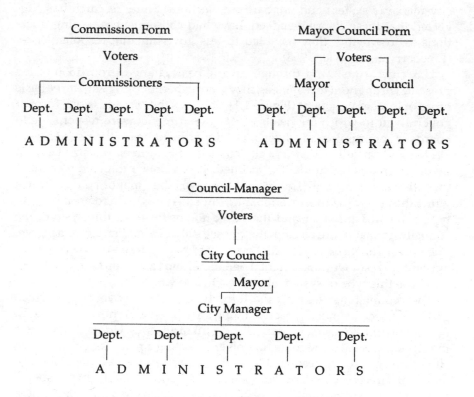

Adapted from Arthur W. Bromage, *Introduction to Municipal Government and Administration*(New York, Appleton-Century-Crofts, 2nd ed., 1957), p. 218.

defined the legal competence of the municipalities, giving them the right of taxation, providing more decision-making authority and lessening the state control. At that time there were approximately 2,500 local government units—cities, boroughs and "communes". A second wave of reform came during the first twenty years of this century when voting rights were expanded gradually to universal suffrage. During this period, the representative system was made mandatory in all communes with more than 1500 inhabitants and the proportional list-voting system was introduced. This is also the period when the main structure of the still existing mainly class-based party system was developed. However, it took a long time before party politics left its mark on the activities of the communes. This occurred gradually, beginning in the large cities (Strömberg 1974).

A third wave of reform started after the second world war. The background was the increasing responsibilities the state laid on the communes during the twenties and the thirties in building the 'welfare' state. In combination with a wavering tax base, this development led to financial difficulties for many smaller communes. Urbanization had led to depopulation of rural areas and an increase in the percentage of elderly, resulting in a weakened economic base for communes. Therefore, in 1946 the Riksdag decided on an apportionment reform in order to create communes with a population of at least 3000 inhabitants. The reform that came into effect in 1952, was confined to amalgamations of rural communes. It reduced the number from 2498 to 1037. In 1962, the Riksdag decided on a new reapportionment reform aimed at creating communes with a minimum size of 8000 inhabitants per commune, and of economic and geographic coherence around a viable center. The reform was based on gradual and voluntary participation by the communes. Despite resistance, the government in 1969 pushed through a bill that mandated the reform by January 1, 1974. The number of communes declined from 1037 in 1952 to 278 in 1974. Today, the number is 284. The median population in the new communes rose to approximately 16,300 inhabitants.

The amalgamations have produced a new type of commune. Practically all communes consist today of both urban and rural areas even if some of the larger new communes are overwhelmingly urban since they contain an old city. The basic structure of the powers and organizations of Swedish local self-government has, however, not changed. Since the reform of the 1860's, the communes have the power of taxation and do levy an income tax. They can be characterized as having "extensive powers of initiative and action" (Gustafsson 1983, 21, 33).

The competence of local government has also been increased in the last decade through several decentralization reforms in all policy fields. In 1984/85, the government presented a national program for the renewal of the public sector, which aimed at deregulation of central-local relations. There had been concern over red tape and the large control apparatus. As a part of the renewal program, the government started the so called "free commune experiment" in 1984. Nine communes (and three county councils—mainly responsible for hospitals and medical care) were given the status of "free" communes. The basic idea of the experiment is to allow these selected local governments to apply for dispensation from state laws, rules and regulation (Rose 1990; Gustafsson 1991). Furthermore, the rules for state grants have been changed and are today less detailed.[3] One should note also that in June, 1991 (after our study, however) the Swedish Parliament adopted a new communal law which gave communes more power and autonomy.

The structure of Swedish local government has changed gradually so that all communes now have a representative system of government (the

last town meetings disappeared already in the early Fifties). The organization of a Swedish commune appears in Figure 1.2. The council is the
responsible policy-making body directly elected by the citizens every third
year under a proportional list-voting system. The councils are large bodies
ranging from 31 to 100 and have in our sample on average 64 members.
From five to seven parties contest for seats in the local elections, usually the
same five parties which are represented in the Riksdag plus, in more than
half the communes, Christian Democrats and the Green party. In 1982, the
election before our study was done, the control of the councils varied
greatly: 53 percent of the councils had a Social Democratic (sometimes
supported by the small communist party) majority; 33 percent had a
conservative-center-liberal majority; 13 percent were very split with no
clear coalition in control. An executive board with usually 11 ordinary
members is appointed by the council also for three years. The executive
board has a central role in preparing all matters for the council and in
implementing its decisions. A central office is attached to the executive
board to assist in planning, budgeting and central personnel management.
The chairperson of the board, chosen from the majority party or a majority
coalition in the council, plays an important role in Swedish local politics.
Usually a man, he is often the leader of the main local organization of his
party and is without exception member of the council. However, it is not
obligatory that the members of the executive board are members of the
council, but usually half or more of these are. It is thus not correct to describe
this body as a committee of the council. The same is true for the other boards
in the Swedish system. Usually they have 7-11 members and less than half
of them are members of the council. All board members are, however,
nominated by the parties in the council and selected, as the members of the
executive board, in proportion to the number of seats each party has in the
council. There are two types of boards, optional and mandatory. The latter
have a strong independent status since they implement state regulations.
However, they are dependent on the budget decisions of the council.

The Dutch System's Development and Nature

The basic features of the Dutch system of local government were determined in the middle of the last century (Toonen 1987, 108-129; Kreukels and
Spit 1989). The constitution of 1848 and the Provincial and Municipal
government Act of 1850 and 1851 provided the original form and basis. The
647 municipalities today (compared to 1200 in 1850) operate within a
"unitary" system, with ultimate, centralized control by the national government. Dutch scholars describe a complex dual institutional framework for
decision-making. Some call this a "decentralized unitary system" although
the reality of actual decentralization of power is contested by others. Two

FIGURE 1.2   The Forms of Local Government in Sweden and the Netherlands

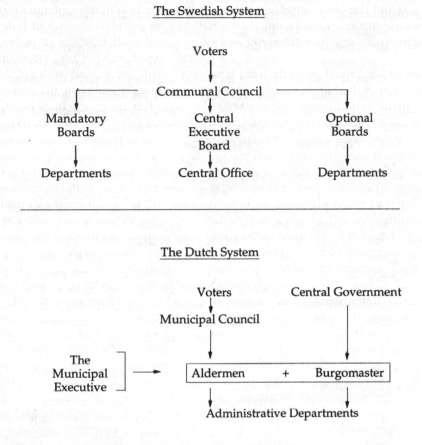

The Swedish System

Voters

Communal Council

Mandatory Boards — Central Executive Board — Optional Boards

Departments — Central Office — Departments

The Dutch System

Voters   Central Government

Municipal Council

The Municipal Executive → Aldermen + Burgomaster

Administrative Departments

Sources: Sweden: Agne Gustafsson, *Local Government in Sweden*, 1983, pp. 62-72. Netherlands: Galen Irwin, in M. Czudnowski, ed., *Elite Recruitment in Democratic Polities*, 1976, pp. 166-168.

principles are referred to: "autonomy" and "co-government." But the extent to which these principles have been actualized is widely debated. Municipalities must implement many national laws and also are responsible for their "own household" and can take limited initiatives in governing themselves. While there is ultimate hierarchical control from national level to municipality, and in conflicts over legislation national power takes precedence, it is claimed that there is no "command relationship." In practical policy-making, the power-relationship is more balanced than hierarchical. There is some leeway or ambiguity in what the municipality can do, and, thus, municipalities may enter new policy areas. Yet, the national authorities may intervene in local affairs. While there was increased centralization of tasks and control in the Sixties, recent years seem to reveal more decentralization, in two senses. First, there is more agreement about the necessity to devolve tasks to local government and to give them more discretion and financial control. Second, the power balance is presumably shifting to the local level. There is much current discussion in government circles, national and local, and in the union of Dutch municipalities over the restraints on cities and the need for more decentralized financial and expenditure responsibility and control at the municipal level. Despite certain "unitary" legalistic characteristics, therefore, Dutch cities are apparently departing from traditional centralized control and moving towards a new decentralization or a "new balance" in central-local relations.

A very extensive report analyzing the condition of Dutch cities, based on considerable research, and proposing changes in their system was submitted to the Dutch government in 1990 by the Netherlands Scientific Council for government policy.[4] The report noted that "The structure of Dutch municipalities' revenues and expenditures is unique. Nowhere else in the democratic west is the financial relationship between the tiers of government so dominated by the center." The argument is made for more decentralization" in both finance and decision-making", and in more assumption of responsibility by cities so that they can "develop and pursue active policies of their own". This is necessary to deal with "the cumulation and concentration of social problems in the cities" as well as economic problems. Dutch cities are seen in the report as in a state of decline since the 1970's because of the financial retrenchment necessary due to economic conditions. This "retrenchment at the national level made local authorities increasingly dependent on central government in both the income and expenditure sides." What little discretionary authority cities had was further diminished. The focus of the report presents proposals to strengthen the local economy and the local social structure. It recommends giving cities more responsibility, power and discretion, for raising their revenue and spending it, but retaining their accountability for performance. One of the key concepts in the report underlying these proposals is "the notion of (the city as) an urban civic and enterprise culture" in which all elements of the community take greater roles and responsibility for solving local problems.

The form of Dutch local government is basically the same for all cities, as is also the case for Sweden. (See Figure 1.2) The municipal council is the body with primary decision-making power. It varies in size from 7 to 45 members, elected on a partisan basis through a proportional representation system. The term of office is four years. The "municipal executive" consists of a mayor (burgomaster) and aldermen, who also are members of the city council. These aldermen, or commissioners, are representatives of and remain members of the council. In most municipalities the aldermen are selected from the largest parties. In the larger cities there is a growing tradition one can distinguish, then, between governing and opposition parties. In most cities the Executive functions as a daily council. The political relationships in this executive reflect those in the larger council. Formally, the executive as a whole is responsible for the administration; in practice, aldermen and burgomaster each assume responsibility for administrative departments. The mayor presides over the city council (without a vote) and also presides over the municipal executive. The burgomaster is appointed by the national government for a six year term. He or she is responsible for the police, for the maintenance of public order, and as a member of the executive for the administrative implementation of national laws. The political parties contesting for local council seats are often the local branches of the national parties. But there are also special coalitions of parties for local elections as well as "local lists" of new, small, groups or independent citizens running separately from the national party lists.

Differences and Similarities in Local Government

If we reflect on the development and contemporary character of local government in these three systems, certain similarities and differences stand out. One similarity is that the "reform history" over almost a century and half in all three countries has progressively emphasized devolution of power to the local units of government. Although Sweden and the Netherlands are unitary systems technically, in actuality they have decentralized their systems in certain respects. However, the story is not the same for each country. Sweden has given local government units more financial autonomy than the Netherlands has. In Sweden and the Netherlands, the state has used the municipalities as implementers of "welfare" state policies by giving them more and more responsibilities in such areas as housing, social welfare and schools. This process started in both countries at the turn of the century but somewhat earlier in the Netherlands than in Sweden. In the broad historical perspective, local initiative and local responsibility, thus, have been increased. Yet, at the same time the role of the central government in the formal sense has not really declined.

Ironically, in the U.S., a federal system with technically no direct authority from the central government over cities, the local authorities from time to time have become both more dependent on external sources for financial support, and constrained by state and national policies and conditions in implementing local governmental responsibilities. That is, cities in the U.S. have always had major responsibilities; they have fewer resources. Yet, American cities in the last analysis have real autonomy. The Dutch view their system as having strong national government control but also with more horizontal than hierarchical central-local relationships. The Swedish scholars speak of the "increasing interdependence between state and local authorities"(Gustafsson 1991). And, Americans since 1974 at least have been referring to federal-local relations as "The New Federalism". Historically, and today, it appears that while central-local relationships have evolved in somewhat different ways in each of these three systems, the *decentralist* theme has been clear in all three countries. and, central-local relations have perhaps become more interdependent. Municipalities over the years have been asked to do more, with less; to take more initiative, not less; to take on more responsibility, not less.

While this basic proposition about the meaning of the history of local government reform may be true, it is also quite clear that these systems differ in very significant respects as to the nature of local government structures and processes which have evolved. There are certain distinctions which are probably most important to keep in mind. One major one is, of course, the variety in municipal government structures in the U.S. system, in contrast to the standardization and homogeneity in local government structures in Sweden and the Netherlands. This is because the central government in Europe does create and prescribe and control directly and/or indirectly the type of government at the local level, while in the U.S. in the last analysis municipalities create and operate their own types of government with much more limited control from the upper authorities. If we assume that institutions influence behavior, we would then expect more variation in elite performance in the U.S. Yet, the decentralist changes in Europe may make this less likely.

The forms and practices of local government differ in these three systems. The Dutch and Swedish systems appear to be similar in some respects to the old "commission" form of government in the U.S., with boards or commissions or particular councilors having special responsibility for supervising administrative departments. The U.S. virtually gave up this system years ago and opted for mayor-council or council-manager systems. The mayor is an office today nonexistent in Sweden (although in existence before 1965). The mayor (burgomaster) is appointed by the central government in the Netherlands. In all three systems, however, the municipal council is the final decision-making authority, although in certain U.S. cities the mayor plays a dominant role and is not really very subordinate to the council.

As for the election system and the role of parties, these systems also differ significantly. Holland and Sweden have multi-party systems at the local level; a majority of American cities are nonpartisan, and only 30 percent have two party systems formally involved in local government. Parties may be very important in American city government, but if the city has a nonpartisan election system parties may operate behind the scenes or are replaced by other civic or ad hoc groups, if there is any meaningful political action at all. The election systems in our two European countries are proportional; the U.S. uses single-member districts, or multi-member districts without proportionality, and direct primaries. Voting turnouts in local elections are much higher in Europe than in the U.S.—over 60 percent in Europe (80 percent in Sweden), while the average in the U.S. is probably near 20 percent. How these differences affect elite orientations to the political process as well as their behavior and strategies for action are matters we will explore subsequently.

The Expansion of Local Government Functions and Expenditures

There can be no question that local government has assumed more responsibility in all these three countries, as the public sector has increased. By the 1980's public sector expenditure *as a percent of GNP* had grown as follows:[5]

Sweden	Netherlands	U.S.A.
1985—67%	1985—59%	1980's—35%
1965—41	1950—31.5	1941—20

The public sector increases reflect the expansion of the welfare state in post-war Sweden and Holland (although in Holland in the last decade the percentage has dropped to about 60 percent). The U.S. clearly stands out in contrast to the European countries. But, since we focus in our analysis on local government, the major question is: what have been the trends within the public sector, in the proportion of expenditures which are locally allocated? To what extent over the years has the burden of government fallen on local government?

In the U.S. the nature of the expansion of local government has been rather paradoxical, according to Anton. From 1950 on, employment in local government increased considerably and constituted 59 percent of all public sector employees in 1980 (compared to 50 percent in 1950) (Anton 1987). Yet, the actual revenue generated by local governments declined over the period. They collected 47 percent of all public sector revenues in 1929 but 15 percent or less in the 1980's (Anton 1989, 134). Local government expenditures were actually increasing during this period, however, but not in relation to total expenditures for government. And this paradox is explicable by reference to the federal and state grants-in-aid which municipalities were receiving. Federal grants amounted in constant dollars (1967=100) to $3.2 billion in 1950, increased to $19 billion in 1970, $37 billion in 1980, and dropped to $32.6 billion in 1986 (Anton 1987, 13). By 1979 a large proportion of municipal income came from the state and federal authorities: 15 percent from federal grants and 22 percent from state grants (Jones 1983, 270).

Although the federal government still collected and disbursed close to 67 percent of all revenues, local government had grown substantially as part of an overall pattern of public sector expansion and a radical restructuring of public finance relationships.

In Sweden, local government expanded rapidly from the 1920's, linked of course to the proportion of the population which lived in cities, increasing from less than 50 percent in the Twenties to 83 percent by 1980. In addition, there was a transfer of new expanded responsibilities to the communes in such areas as education, health, and welfare services. From 1965 to 1980, per capita commune expenditures increased 215 percent. Municipal and county government personnel as a percentage of the working population increased from nine percent in 1965 to 24 percent in 1982. And, thus, commune expenditures increased from 15 percent of the GNP in 1965 to 25 percent in 1980 (Gustafsson 1983, 52-57; Strömberg and Westerstähl 1984, 34-35). Communes in Sweden raised 41 percent (1981) of their revenue from the local income tax, but they also received state grants-in-aid, amounting to 25 percent of all municipal revenues (1981) (Gustafsson 1983, 109).

In the Netherlands, as we noted, the size of the public sector almost doubled from the Thirties to the Eighties. And as Toonen writes "the (new) tasks had to be implemented by the municipalities." The two key developments were: increased grants from the central government and, hence, the increased proportion of the public sector expenditure (as % of GNP) which was attributable to local government (Toonen 1987, 118-122). Of the 90 percent municipalities get from the government, one-third is so-called "free money" to be spent at the local government's discretion. The remainder is "prescribed" money. In the Netherlands, then, while there seems to be less financial autonomy at the municipal level, there is greater functional or expenditure responsibility.

A recent comparative analysis of local expenditures and revenue sources in these three countries provides the following data, as of 1985:

	U.S.	Sweden	Netherlands
A. Local Expenditures			
As a % of GDP	31.1	43.6	32.9
As % of total public expenditures	10.8	29.3	19.5
B. Revenue Sources for Local Government (% of Total 1985)			
Local taxes	42	41	2
Local fees, etc.	15	20	4
Grants from higher authorities	30	25	87
Other funds (local or non-local)	13	14	7

Based on these data Sweden ranks highest in the expenditure role of municipalities, the Netherlands next, and the U.S. lowest. However, in the responsibility for mobilizing their own revenues, the cities in the U.S. and Sweden are much more "autonomous" than is the Netherlands (Mouritzen and Nielsen 1988, 73, 103, 147).[6]

Themes in Research on Urban Politics

There has been a vast body of research on the politics of the city which provides a backdrop for our comparative study. It is a controversy-laden volume of studies - controversial in theories, in empirical evidence, and in interpretation. We can perhaps summarize the work relevant to our study of local political elites under the following rubrics. We begin with a brief review of research in the U.S. After that there is a review of Dutch and Swedish studies.

1. *The relation of social status to political power in local government.* There is still much debate over the worthwhileness and significance of data on social backgrounds of local elites. On the one hand, the "middle class ethos" of local government is emphasized, as well as the social bias in elite recruitment. For some scholars, the social unrepresentativeness of local elites has significant implications; it is irrelevant to others. The latter point to the limited role of social background factors in predicting elite ideology and behavior.

2. *The relevance of governmental structure in cities for explaining local political behavior.* The influence of the Progressive movement reformers continues and scholars still argue that the form of local government can be decisive. Most of the debate over the tenability of the "power elite" or "pluralism" models as most useful for understanding city politics has abated. But investigators are still interested in the relationship of the city manager system or nonpartisan vs. partisan election systems, and related structural variants, and elite behavior and policy outcomes. One study documented the increase in voting participation with partisan elections. Another study carefully tested the consequences of the adoption of the reform model (of the Progressives) compared to the adoption of the non-reform model - on the responsiveness of elites to class, racial, and religious cleavages. The conclusion: "the greater the reformism, the lower the responsiveness" (Lineberry and Fowler 1968). The cohesion or consensus of elites, particularly of city councils, has also been of considerable interest (Eulau and Prewitt 1973).

3. *The "City Limits,"* i.e., the constraints on cities in the funding of city services, meeting community needs, and advancing community

development. Perhaps, no subject so engrosses the attention of scholars of the city in recent years. Peterson has emphasized the resource constraints, Terry Clark and his colleagues have been involved in the study of "fiscal strain" and the innovative types of actions needed to deal with it (Peterson 1981; Clark and Ferguson 1983). Peterson posed the basic dilemma cities face. Local governments, he says, are forced to "concentrate on developmental as against redistributive objectives"—since they are forced to pursue "economic productivity... this leaves little scope for egalitarian concerns" (Peterson 1981, 69). Gottdiener engages in a long rebuttal of this position (Gottdiener 1987, 86-93).

4. *The orientations of local elites.* The comparative study of the values of local political elites in the U.S., India, Poland, and Yugoslavia directed by Jacob, referred to earlier, explored techniques for the measurement of elite values and attempted to link them to community participation and innovative outputs. The study demonstrated that linkages existed but that the relevant values differed for each country. It was concluded that the four countries were quite different in elite value orientations and different explanatory models were necessary for each country (Jacob 1971, 289-312). Other scholars have emphasized the importance of elite values (Banfield and Wilson 1963).

5. *The contextual basis for urban political research.* As Lasswell argued long ago, we again are focusing on the social and political conditions and forces which may explain city politics. This has been for long a concern of sociologists (Greer, Janowitz, Rossi, etc.). While they focused on the social cleavages and the social character of "the community", political scientists have concentrated on the political factors. We are warned of the danger of relying on "global" interpretations to the neglect of "the fundamental diversity and differentiation of cities" (Aiken and Alford 1970, 106).

There is in fact common usage these days of the concept of "urban political culture", and some attempts to describe its variations. Operational distinctions are made between "unitary" and "pluralist" cultures, "topological profiles", and "developmental profiles" (Knoke in Clark 1981; Wilson 1968). The suggestion is implicit in much of the research that political subcultures do exist in cities and that if carefully operationalized, we can utilize these cultural differences to explain city politics.

Underlying much of the writing by sociologists and political scientists in the U.S. is a basic concern. It can be expressed in one query perhaps. Given the conditions of modern democratic society how can the modern city provide good government? Our cities are open societies, non-hierarchical, largely self-regulating, very heterogeneous, and socially fragmented. They are a far cry from the smaller, consensual communities of the past. Their populations are larger, public demands are greater, there is greater freedom. The individual today has much more of a "limited liability" to the community as such and yet expects a great deal. The conflict potential is high; the community integration can be low. The self-contained community of earlier days has been replaced by a city which has become very dependent on outside political entities at the same time that it is more pluralized internally. Yet the city is a geographical collectivity with functional responsibilities. How can it perform optimally? The implication in much of the writing is that there are complex requirements if cities are to succeed: adequate financial resources, able mayors and councils, efficient bureaucrats, well structured decisional institutions, a strong associational life, a participative citizenry, and a clear set of community political norms and values, accepted by elites and the public, which center on rational, democratic, balanced community development.

While few studies explicitly assert it, and virtually none seek to test it, the necessity for able local political leadership is a major undercurrent in most of these American studies. A recent book explicitly discusses this subject, asking how important leadership is to "urban regeneration". The authors contend that "many cities have found leaders and many have turned adversity into success" (Judd and Parkinson 1990). In a sense, that is the creative assumption underlying our study. Elites are not dispensable, and good local government is difficult without able leaders. Thus, if there is one overriding purpose or significance for our study, it is to describe and seek to understand for three modern democratic systems the local political elites which have emerged, or which have been recruited and selected, to deal with "the urban problem" in each of these societies. What are the backgrounds of these elites, their perceptions and cognitions of their local politics, in what policies are they interested, what are their strategies for their work, how sanguine are they about the solution of their problems, what do they see as their responsibilities, and above all, what fundamental values do they espouse which guide their behavior? These are for us, the dominating concerns.

Swedish Research on the Communes

Before the mid-Sixties there was very little research on the communes. Historical monographs on single cities or counties and constitutional studies of local government reforms were the only scientific work in the area. Local politics and administration did not attract political or other social scientists, despite the importance of local government for the functioning of the welfare state. In 1965 this tradition was broken by the establishment of a local government research group of political scientists from all five Swedish universities. The research focus of the group was to study how local self-government and democracy would be affected by the government decision to amalgamate the then existing 1,000 communes into less than three hundred new communes.

Even with this "practical" objective the research did emphasize some of the same themes as in the U.S., addressing the same theoretical problems and using the same kinds of approaches and methods. The research group introduced a behavioristic approach and conducted large-scale empirical studies in local government. Between 1966 and 1974 the group conducted many studies, mainly using a sample of 36 communes of different sizes and levels of urbanization. Citizen participation in local politics, local electoral campaigns, organization of parties on the local level, party nominations to councils, representativeness of local councilors, decision-making processes in council and boards as well as service output in the communes were some of the themes covered in mass-data studies of voters and politicians and by participant observation of party, board and council meetings. Between 1979 and 1982 a retake of the studies was done covering the same themes and using the same methods as earlier but focusing on evaluation of the amalgamation reforms. They placed more emphasis on the local administration and the relationship between politics and administration.

Although the local government research group dominated the scene during these years, new research areas were attracting political scientists and economists in the late Seventies and the beginning of the Eighties. Local planning, state-local relations, regional development, local industrial politics and communal economy are examples of such areas, as well as studies of neighborhood councils and "self-determination" for local government employees.

While the Swedish scholars studied many of the same questions as the Americans, their accent was different. The changing conditions which Swedish communes were undergoing, on a _nation-wide basis_, has given the Swedish research a special character.[7]

Dutch Research on Municipalities

Local government research in the Netherlands centers around five questions.[8]

1. _Social backgrounds of local elites._ There are many studies on the burgomaster, there are some studies on the aldermen and there is great need for studies on the social background of councilors and administrators. In fact, up to now only the political affiliation and gender of the members of the council are known. There is virtually no knowledge

of the values, attitudes and perceptions of the local elites. The interest of political scientists in national elites has been dominant. In 1990, a new project on local elites and their values in some cities was begun to help fill this gap.

2. *Theories and research about the municipal executive.* There is a traditional and a modern way of constituting the municipal executive, excluding the selection of the burgomaster by the central government. In the traditional way the executive must be a political reflection of the council. So the largest parties were represented in the executive. Since the Sixties, especially in the larger cities, there has been a shift to a more political way of constituting the executive. This has given the political scientists the opportunity to test coalition theories. There appears to be a difference between partisan and nonpartisan municipalities in the composition of the executive. However, this difference is not very important because of the small number of nonpartisan municipalities, and because of the (very) small size of nonpartisan municipalities.

3. *Studies of participation in local politics.* People are more interested in local *problems* but, on the other hand, they are more interested in national *politics*. Because of the importance of national issues and of national laws greater interest in national politics is understandable. Yet, people know they have to go to local government for housing, social security, health, etc.; however, they realize the status of the city as implementer of national laws. The National Parliament (and the E.C.) decide major laws while local governments decide only about their "own households". National election turnout is also higher then local turnout.

4. *The meaning of size for delivering services and for political participation.* Because of a long-standing process of amalgamation of municipalities in the Netherlands there is an increasing number of studies on the meaning of size. Scientists investigated the unproven assumption that smaller municipalities have a lower administrative capacity, and concluded in some cases the opposite was true. The larger municipalities have been seen as coping with greater societal problems and therefore in certain respects they have more difficulty in fulfilling their tasks. Also, these studies suggest there is no indication for a lower place for smaller municipalities on the "democracy-scale". In smaller municipalities there is more political participation and the election turnout is higher.

5. *Central-local-relationships.* Of course, in a decentralized unitary state scientists are focused on the relationship between central and local government. Research has revealed that national laws are less compelling in governmental practice. Besides there appears to be a

power-shift to local government during the last two decades. In recent years, a new theme is occupying the study of central-local-relationships: local government in metropolitan areas. The autonomy of local government in these areas is considered too great and the steering capacity of the State and the intermediate Province appears to be failing. So local government seems to develop in a regional direction, with greater power and more responsibilities at the cost of provincial and national government. Especially as Europe moves toward integration, there will be more emphasis on a new local (regional) government for metropolitan areas, for instance for Amsterdam and Rotterdam.

Our Research Objectives

The intellectual interests which undergird our research reflect our particular theoretical aims as well as our understanding of the nature of these three, somewhat different, political societies. Further, previous scholarly work in this field has provided insights which we will also explore. The significance of the social backgrounds of elites is still an intriguing area of inquiry. The relevance of local governmental structure (for example, the role of political parties) must certainly be examined. Central-local dependency relationships, in power and financial resources and responsibility to act, as perceived by local elites is a question which we would obviously desire to explore. We intend to explore the perceived power and influence of local elites in some detail. The importance of elite values, as they converge or diverge across systems, a subject which other scholars have found to be important, is of top priority to us. And the variation in elite orientations by municipality and commune is, again, an interest which given our type of data should not be ignored.

In all of our analysis, however, a major purpose of our endeavor is to focus on elite political cultures at the local level. Are there identifiable elite cultural orientations, in terms of specific cognitions, evaluations, and values, or as a composite or "syndrome" of beliefs, which are generalizable for a political system? Do these local elite cultures differ cross-nationally, or are they similar? Does the type of society or political order in which these elites operate, and in which they were socialized, seem to be linked to the existence of a particular pattern of elite political orientations? What other factors may be important in explaining the incidence of such orientations? Are there "subcultures" among local elites - by party, by generation, by ideology, by community? These questions constitute our major intellectual focus.

Certainly, we expect to find certain uniformities across these systems, in their social status, their career backgrounds, the problems they face and the conflicts in their communities which they perceive. However, we do expect to find variance in elite orientations for these three systems. Other scholars have indicated that this is a high probability, and some of the empirical research has confirmed it. As Putnam put it: "the most persistent predictor of these politicians' (British and Italian MPS) basic attitudes has been country", or, "the tug of national tradition" (Putnam 1973, 239). And Teune: any relationship "can only be understood in the broader context of the political system of which the local political units are a part (Jacob 1971, 309). Even though local governments may appear to have a similar status today in their systems, the historical traditions, structural forms, and political contexts are very different and probably will be manifest in our data.

"Comparative Method" and Our Study

Ours is a comparative study of local governmental leaders in a representative sample of communities in three political systems. The utility of such studies is both to test theory, confirming it or denying it, and to discover or create new theory. The latter role is as important as the former. "Comparative analysis is... crucial in generating scientific theories... (and) in testing the credibility of political theories" (Almond and Powell 1978, 18). Earlier Lasswell said it this way: "the world significance of elite changes can become apparent only when the patterns within countries are treated comparatively" (Lasswell 1952, 3).

Our three systems are "western" democracies. They fall between being "most similar systems" and "most different systems" (Przeworski and Teune 1970, 31-39). While they are similar in certain respects—their democratic history and tradition, and the importance given to the role of local government—they also differ in key system characteristics. As we have noted, perhaps of most importance and relevance for our study are: the legal and financial dependency relationships of local to central government, the type of party system, the election system and voting turnout, the extent of commitment to the social welfare state ideology (and the role of municipalities in the welfare state system), and the governmental institutions for decision-making at the local level. The differences and similarities are both important to keep in mind for our discussion.

One of our comparative purposes is to describe and explain variations and uniformities in various aspects of elite political culture across these three systems. In attempting to do this, we will utilize these three levels of analysis: the individual leader, the community, and the nation. We will look at intra-systematic relationships and inter-systematic relationships. For example, we will look at the age cohorts among elites, or the type of party they belong to, and examine the relationship of age and party to elite political orientations—within systems and across systems. What we are trying to do can perhaps best be formulated in these questions:

1. Are the characteristics of political elites which we describe in one "western democratic" system (described in univariate or bi-variate terms), also found in other "western democratic" systems? If so, why? What common system conditions are responsible for this?

2. If we find that these three nations are different in elite perceptions and orientations, the question is also—why? And how can we best explain these cross-national differences? We will attempt to do it by subgroup analysis. We may find that age cohorts differ, or party affiliation groups, or politicians may differ from administrators, across systems. For example, young Swedish elites may be so much more committed to economic equality than young elites in the U.S. that this may explain why all Swedish elites are more egalitarian. If this is so, why is this? Is there some systemic explanation?

3. Further, if we do not find such extreme subgroup differences across nations by age cohorts, then age is obviously not an explanatory factor, and we have to look at other subgroup patterns. After exhausting subgroup analysis with no clear explanation we are forced to return to the assumption that culture or institutional or other systemic conditions are responsible. The question is, of course, what conditions, and how can this be demonstrated convincingly?

4. Finally, if we find within systems that cities and communes differ considerably in elite attitudes, orientations, and behavior, what contextual or "local political cultural" factors are responsible for such variations?

Przeworski and Teune proposed a much debated formulation twenty years ago:

> "If the subgroups of the population derived from different systems do not differ with regard to the dependent variable, the differences among these systems are not important . . . "

But, on the other hand:

> "... the level of analysis is shifted to systemic factors when the formulation of valid general statements is no longer possible for all of the sub-populations (Przeworski and Tuene 1970, 35).

To illustrate: if we find the age of elites is similarly linked to elite perceptions (or values, etc.) in all three systems (e.g., the young are more innovative), then a generalization across systems on the relationship of age to this dependent variable is possible. And then *presumably* system level factors and conditions are irrelevant. However, we must look at system variables if (a) age-innovation relationships are different (the young elites are innovative in country A (and older elites are not), but this finding does not hold for countries B and C; or (b) if the magnitudes of the age differences vary considerably, as:

% Pro-Innovation	Country A	Country B	Country B
Young	55	75	95
Old	45	25	5

Thus, systemic factors need to be explored in either case. The same, of course, holds true for other subgroup analyses, such as party, education, social class, elite position.

While this methodological approach may be questioned, we do indeed explore its utility in our analysis here. We wish to arrive at general theoretical knowledge about local elites. Are these democracies the same in elite behavior at the local level? In what respect? Do they produce the same basic types of elites with the same political orientations, elites who seem to function the same way despite having "learned" politics and government in their own particular system? Or are they different, and if so, how and why? Above all, we are interested in the *relevance* or *irrelevance* of the system for explaining uniform (equivalent) patterns of behavior or distinctive patterns of behavior. Thus, we are interested in system *context* as well as in *generalization across systems*.

The Research Designs

In 1984, in the U.S., we decided to replicate the study of the elites in the same 30 municipalities which were initially investigated in 1966. These cities were (in 1966) a random sample of cities in the 25,000-250,000 population groups. The aim was to return to these cities with the same basic questions for the same types of political elites (mayors, city councilors, administrators, party leaders, etc.), which were included in the design used earlier. We successfully completed interviewing in 1984 in 25 of these cities and, after matching with Swedish cities, 20 are here used as the U.S. base for this analysis.

The Swedish study, completed during the winter of 1984/85, was in all respects designed to obtain a maximum possible comparison with the American study. It followed a research project aimed at evaluating the amalgamation reform of Swedish local government. A sample of 20 of the 284 Swedish communes were selected, 15 primarily urban and five much more rural, excluding the three largest cities, Stockholm, Göteborg and

Malmö. The 15 "urban" communes were considered most comparable to the American cities and were used in this analysis. The types of local leaders selected for interviews matched or were close equivalents of the U.S. types: members of the central executive board, chair and vice-chair of the particular boards (schools, social welfare, building, health/environment, culture and recreation, etc.), key administrators (chief administrator, chief economic manager, personnel manager, and the leading administrator for each of five selected boards). Many of these leaders were leaders of their parties at the local level.

The Dutch study was completed in 1989. The twenty cities used in this analysis were part of a larger 40-city study. They ranged in population from 30,000 to 100,000 and were distributed geographically throughout the country. The respondents included mayors, aldermen, other council members and local party leaders. Chief administrators and the heads of municipal departments (such as financial, planning, education, welfare, etc.) were also included. The party affiliations of these local elites included representatives across the entire spectrum of the Dutch multi-party system, as well as some leaders affiliated only with parties peculiar to each locality.

For our comparative analysis we have randomly selected 20 U.S. municipalities, 15 Swedish communes and 20 Dutch cities. We have excluded the largest cities and the smallest, concentrating thus on the intermediate population strata in each system. Table 1.1 provides some information about the characteristics of these three sets of cities. From this, one can see that the population size and range in size is similar for all three countries. *Within* countries, the sample cities vary greatly—for example, in median family income, unemployment, and political party strength. Thus, the cities are diverse socially, politically, and in economic status, suggesting that they reflect the heterogeneity of municipalities in these systems.

In selecting the "elites" in the cities in all three countries the assumptions we made should be kept in mind. We conceptualized the elites rather narrowly, as including those in top administrative and political (elected) positions in the city, plus the local party leaders. It was a "positional elite". Initially, in the U.S. we also selected other community leaders (business, civic, etc., group leaders), but decided for comparability to exclude these in this analysis. The leaders selected are equivalent in position and role. Selection procedures were random when there were too many in a particular leadership category (for example, city councilors) than we could include in the sample. The number of leaders selected in each city varied by city and by county, depending on number of positions and response rate. The largest number per city was in Sweden, the lowest in the U.S.

A brief word should be said about the political context in which our studies were completed. Many such contextual variables might of course be considered. In the mid-Eighties when the Swedish study was done perhaps most relevant at the national level was the strong support for the "Left" as a result of the 1982 election. The Social Democrats won over 45 percent of the vote for Parliament and in municipal elections, and, together with the five percent-plus strength of the Communist party, had a majority. Registered unemployment was low (at two percent), and the welfare state was flourishing. The new system of communes, in effect for over a decade, seemed to be successful.

In the U.S., Reagan and the Republicans in 1984 (the year of our study) won a landslide election with almost 60 percent of the presidential vote and a majority of seats in the U.S. Senate (while the Democrats held a 100 seat margin in the House). The U.S. was in the grip of the "Reagan Revolution" with its emphasis on less government, decentralized government, deep cuts in social welfare, and also in taxes, high government deficits ($200 billion), low inflation, high unemployment (8.6 percent). The proportion of families below the poverty line had increased (to over 15 percent), and "the plight of the ghettos" in the cities became worse. In certain sectors this was a time of considerable decline in trust in government.

In the late Eighties, when our Dutch study was completed (1989) the Netherlands was apparently undergoing a transition. The main parties— Labor, CDA, and the Liberals—seemed to maintain their relative strength in the Parliamentary election of that year. Previously, in municipal elections in 1986, the "Left" parties had increased their strength in city councils considerably (an average of 8 percent) which resulted in the election of many new councilors, primarily young and "Left". But by 1989 the "Left" was showing signs of being fragmented due to an increase in the vote for small parties (the Greens and D '66), a trend which would continue in the municipal elections of 1990. The Christian Democrats held the prime minister position and a majority in the cabinet, a coalition with the Labor party. The welfare state was under criticism for its high costs, and some benefits were being cut back. Unemployment remained relatively high.

These national differences in the political, ideological, and economic climate may have relevance for some of our findings. We shall explore their possible meaning. But while contextually interesting, they are probably less important than what was going on politically, ideologically and economically in *each* of these cities in our study. As table 1.1 reveals, cities varied greatly on these indicators. And these are the immediate conditions which must be taken into consideration in understanding the attitudes, perceptions, and behavior of local political and administrative elites. In our study there are cities which have two percent unemployment rather than 12 percent or 23 percent, cities which are 20 percent politically "Left" rather than 60 percent, with low median family income rather than high. Obviously these contextual contrasts are critical, despite what the national averages seem to be. Local elites function after all in these varying local contexts.

TABLE 1.1   Characteristics of Cities in the Sample

	U.S.	Sweden	Netherlands
Number of Local Units	20	15	20
Median Size	65,000 (1980)	51,000 (1984)	48,000 (1989)
Range in Population	29,600—163,000	29,000—150,600	30,900—90,000
Range in Median Family Income	$15,789—42,903 (1980)	81,300—150,579 Kronor (1984)	28,260—43,520 Guilders (1989)
Range in Party Strength (% for "Left Parties)	24.7—66% (Dem.) [Last Presidential Election—1984]*	27.5—65.5% (Soc. Dem. + Communists) [Last Communal Election]	22.7—52.8% (Last Municipal Election)
% Unemployed-Range	2.4—11.6	0.7—4.2	5.0—22.7
Mean Size of City Council	10.6	64	28

	U.S.		Sweden		Netherlands	
Interviews	Number	%	Number	%	Number	%
Administrators	132	51	128	33	104	34
Politicians	128	49	261	67	201	66
Total	260		389		305	

* In the U.S. nonpartisan elections and, thus, the variability in municipal electoral data, preclude their use for comparisons of cities for this purpose.

The substantive content of the questionnaires was essentially identical in all three countries (See Appendix). Indeed, they included most of the questions initially used (tested and pretested) in the 1966 study. The sequence of the questioning dealt with the following subjects:

1. The most important problems facing their community and the perception of the seriousness of these problems (15 problems used).
2. Evaluations of the effectiveness of the action in their community in dealing with these 15 problems.
3. Personal opinions on who has (should have) the primary responsibility for dealing with these problems (i.e., what level of government).
4. Perception of the power and autonomy status of the community for acting effectively in these areas.
5. Perception of the existence of conflicts in the community, the types of cleavages, and their evaluation of the relevance of conflicts for interfering with action on problems and with community development.
6. Level of personal satisfaction with the city (nine-point scale).
7. Policy areas in which the respondent felt he or she had influence, and

the degree of influence: great, some, or none (12 areas of influence used).

8. Groups and other actors to whom leaders turn in order to secure support (17 specified).
9. Pressures on leaders by other leaders, officials, or groups (17 specified).
10. Personal values and goals. Thirty-one agree - disagree statements were used (with a four-point scale) as measures of five basic value scales.
11. Personal questions on SES and related demographic as well as political backgrounds.

There were five basic value scales used in this study: Political Participation, Conflict Avoidance (or Resolution), Change Orientation (Innovation), Economic Equality, and National-Local Commitment. These were used in the original ISVIP study in 1966, and most of the original scale items were retained here. The Swedish study added five new items. Factor analysis demonstrated that most of these international items used originally in 1966 scaled well in all three countries.

As we stated at the outset of this chapter, we need more solid descriptive knowledge about what types of leaders are making the operational decisions for local government in modern democracies. Aside from that, we need comparative—analytic knowledge which will help us explain similarities and differences in local political leadership across nations. Do Western democratic systems differ, or have they converged toward a common pattern of local political leadership? Reliable evidence on these two types of "knowledge needs" may help us understand better how democracy functions at the local level in these systems.

Notes

1. The major research effort was the study by Philip Jacob and many others in India, Poland, Yugoslavia, and the U.S. (Jacob 1971). Other attempts were by Sidney Tarrow and V. L.. Smith (a study of Italian and French mayors) and by Galen Irwin (who compares research findings on Dutch city councillors with Eulau and Prewitt's observations from their Bay area city council study).(Eulau and Czudnowski 1976).

2. Throughout this manuscript we will use the terms "city", "commune" and "municipalities" interchangeably to refer to the local units of government in our study. A particular term may be used more frequently in one country (as "commune" in Sweden), but in all countries all these terms are found in scholarly usage.

3. The initiative taken first in Sweden was followed by Denmark, Norway and later Finland. Evaluations of the first years of experiment in Sweden show that dispensations only have had marginal effects. The ministry of civil affairs which was monitoring the reform could not fight the very strong sector interest defended by ministries like the Ministry of Education and the Ministry of Social Affairs (Strömberg 1990). The same experiences have been reported in the Netherlands. (Toonen 1991).

4. See the recommendations of a new report issued by the Netherlands Scientific Council on Government Policy, *Institutions and Cities: The Dutch Experience*, published in The Hague by the Council in 1990.

5. Sources: *Sweden*—Strömberg and Westerstähl, 1984,34. *Netherlands*—Toonen, 1987, 122. *U.S.A.*—Anton, 1989,41. See also Mouritzen and Nielsen 1988, 49-50.

6. Also see, Netherlands Scientific Council for Government Policy, *Institutions and Cities*, 1990, p. 160.

7. There is no overview on Swedish local government research published in English. The Swedish Ministry of Civil Affairs published a report in Swedish 1983 (SOU 1983:15). Neither is there a summary of the results from the first local government research group. In Swedish there is a brief report with a bibliography: Bengt-Owe Birgersson 1975, Ministry of Communal Affairs. The design of the first program was presented in Jorgen Westerstähl, "The Communal Research Program in Sweden," in *The New Atlantis*, vol. 2 1971, 124-32. Three theses from the first program were summarized in articles: Lennart Brantgarde, 1971, *Scandinavian Political Studies*, vol. 6:54-86. Bengt-Owe Birgersson, and Lars Strömberg, Vincent Ostrom and Frances Pennel Bish, eds., 1977, *Urban Affairs Annual Review*, 12:243-302. The second local government research program is summarized in Lars Strömberg and Jorgen Westerstähl, 1984, Stockholm:Lerum.

8. Aside from Dutch sources cited here there is an excellent earlier bibliography of materials in English on local government in the Netherlands by Hans Daalder, 1988, *West European Politics* 12:162-185.

2

Social and Political Backgrounds

How "elitist" are Western democracies at the local level of government? This is a question we will return to at different points of this book. That question includes not only a concern about restrictions on the access to local leadership positions. It includes an interest also in the degree of congruence or "like-mindness" of elites in their perceptions, evaluations, and values; the patterns of contact within the elite fraternity; and the extent of their responsiveness in attitude and behavior to the citizens of their communities. These are the standing questions which emerged from the classical elite research of Mosca, Pareto, and Michels. These questions still interest us. It is the first of these "elitist" concerns which preoccupies us in this chapter. We look at the social and political backgrounds of local elites to discover the credentials needed for local leadership positions, which in turn will tell us who (what groups, what sectors) have power (and which ones do not), and thus, get some understanding of social bias in elite recruitment for local government. Social background analysis can tell us much about the routes to power, or to put it differently, the structure of opportunities within the system at the local level.

Our analytical interest is basically comparative. That is, we wish to learn to what extent these systems differ or are similar. Are the credentials for local leadership in these three systems much the same? Has a "homogenization" of elite recruitment taken place in these Western developed democracies? Or are there different credentialing patterns for these countries due to differing institutional, historical or social contexts? Insofar as elite backgrounds differ, what factors seem to be most relevant: different skill needs, social forces, political party strategies or cultural norms? The description and explanation of cross-national equivalence and non-equivalence, thus, is the focus of our inquiry.

Two other secondary interests engage us here. One is the "hierarchical" differences in elite social backgrounds, that is the differences in the degree of social bias, the structure of opportunities, the routes to power at the national and local levels of these systems. Are elite recruitment patterns the same at both levels, and if different, how different? Further, we hope to examine, though only partially, whether there is evidence that change is occurring in elite social backgrounds, by looking at these backgrounds by age cohorts. Are we becoming more or less "open", more or less "elitist"?

This is a controversial area of inquiry in political science. There are those who question the utility of the work on elite social backgrounds. The basic query posed, and a difficult one, is whether these findings are useful in explaining variance in elite attitudes and behavior. What is the significance of the inclusion, or (relative) exclusion of young (or old), the working class (or the upper class), the least well educated (or the highly educated), of women, or minorities, etc.? We hope to identify in our analysis the social and political background variables which may be useful in such analysis, and later to use these variables to begin to demonstrate their linkage to elite attitudes, values, and behavior. This is not, however, the only significant "so what?" question to ask. Our basic position is that it is important to know the formative backgrounds from which the elites come. And we also need to know the structure of power and influence in their communities and nations which they as elites constitute. These concerns stimulate our analysis as we present here the empirical facts about elite social and political backgrounds.

An Overview of Elite Credentials by System

If one views the large picture of the characteristics of these 1,000 local leaders in these three democracies, one might conclude rather quickly that they are very similar in social status and reveal similar patterns of social bias. (Table 2.1) While the actual percentages may vary somewhat by country, the basic tendencies seem clear. These local elites are male (over 80%), fairly well educated, with considerable class mobility, middle aged, and a fairly uniform sizeable minority (25%) with parental governmental or political experience. The types of local elites which have emerged seem, thus, to fit an "elite" pattern, an expected pattern.

In actuality, however, if we look more closely at the data, and distinguish types of elites (as politicians and bureaucrats) one discovers some important differences across nations. (Table 2.2) For example, Swedish politicians are much older and have been in public service longer than in the U.S. or the Netherlands. U.S. politicians are more likely to have university training and professional degrees. Among administrators, the Dutch are least likely to have university education. Swedish bureaucrats are much older (60% over age 50), while in the U.S. and the Netherlands 60 percent or more are relatively young. Few Swedish bureaucrats had fathers with blue collar occupations, in contrast particularly to American bureaucrats.

If one looks at the range in percentages across these systems, for politicians and administrators separately, the extent of system differences can be seen. Bureaucrats vary in their educational level; there are smaller differences for politicians. Yet, if we use the two upper level educational categories, we find a considerable range for elected officials: 75% Dutch, 66% U.S., 41% Swedish—a percentage difference of 34. The other range calculations used in Table 2.2 reveal important differences also. This suggests something about how these systems vary in elite recruitment. The least educated have had a greater opportunity for local elected office in Sweden. But the young in the American and Dutch systems have been most successful. And those with lower social class origins have a better opportunity for being selected for administrative appointments in the Netherlands and the U.S.—a differ-

TABLE 2.1 Some Crossnational Similarities in Social Status (Totals for all Local Elites)

	U.S.	Sweden	Netherlands
1. Gender			
- % women	16	18	13
2. Education			
- % university level	55	44	35
3. Social Class Origins			
- % with fathers with working class/lower class occupations	42	22	49
4. Parental Involvement in Politics or Government			
- % who had one or both parents in either a governmental or political position, or both	22	25	23

Notes: Occupational comparisons are difficult. The Swedish occupational classification system of 1958 has been coordinated here with the U.S. 1977 standard occupational classification code. The Dutch occupational code categories do not lend themselves to comparison easily.

Educational equivalents also are imprecise. By "university level" we mean (using the American definition) those who are college or university graduates (with an A.B. or comparable degree) *and* have gone on to take additional education in a graduate or professional school program. The closest Swedish and Dutch equivalents were used for this definition. The Swedish decision is probably defensible. The Dutch system is particularly difficult to translate in comparative terms. In addition to the 35% here listed as "university level" another 47% are in schools which in some respects are similar to university education.

Missing data are excluded in these calculations.

ence ranging from 56% (Netherlands) to 48% (U.S.) to 17% (Sweden)—39 percentage points. These findings suggest, therefore, some differences in the credentialing of local elites.

Although we will discuss different theories later in terms of which to understand these system differences, we should note here the contrast between the two European countries in elite social backgrounds. The Dutch elites are much more likely to have working class backgrounds than the Swedish, they are also much younger, and, for the administrators, apparently less educated at the university level. To find such differences in two systems which one might have expected to be similar requires explanations. Why is this so? Briefly stated here (expanded on in the conclusion), it is highly probable that these contrasts are linked to both long range and short term recruitment patterns and norms. A major recruitment increase of administrative personnel took place in the Netherlands in the late Seventies and early Eighties. Further, our data reveal the involvement of all parties in the Netherlands in attracting persons of lower and working class backgrounds into public service. This is not true for Sweden where only the Left

TABLE 2.2 Crossnational Differences in Elite Social Characteristics (Politicians and Bureaucrats Compared)

	Politicians			Bureaucrats			System Difference (Range)	
	U.S.	Swed.	Neth.	U.S.	Swed.	Neth.	Pol.	Bur.
1. Educational Levels								
Lower	23%	27	8	13	2	1		
Middle-Secondary	9	32	16	5	8	5		
Upper-Secondary	24	11	41	20	13	58		
University	42	30	34	63	76	36	34	11
2. Age Distributions								
Below 40	22	5	21	28	13	8		
40 - 49	35	31	37	31	26	57		
50 - 59	26	34	27	31	42	29		
60 +	17	30	15	9	20	6	22	26
3. Father's Occupation Working Class/								
Lower Class	37	25	46	48	17	56		
4. Years of Public Service								
0 - 4	41	6	17	11	4	2		
5 - 10	29	22	26	21	10	7		
11 - 20	23	44	42	32	41	32		
21 +	6	28	14	36	46	60	43	24

See notes for Table 2.1

parties engage in such "recruitment." (See Table 2.7) As for educational differences between Sweden and the Netherlands, the explanation is unclear. It may be partly due to the fact that certain types of education in the Netherlands which we have classified as "non-university" are in fact a type of specialized education leading to administrative service which is closely equivalent to Swedish and American university education. Further, it should be pointed out that there are Dutch students of municipal government who would argue that local administration is very career-oriented, as in Sweden. As one Dutch scholar put it, the Dutch have a "disguised closed system" in local administration. It appears to be an open system but higher education is obligatory and entrance is quite carefully controlled.

Church affiliation and religious activeness provide another example of how these systems differ. (Table 2.3) American elites appear much more orthodox or committed; at least their church attendance behavior suggests this. In Sweden, less than 10% attend religious services regularly (weekly), 18% in the Netherlands, but close to 50% in the United States. The percentages responding "none" when asked about denomination are very high in Sweden and the Netherlands. This development in the Netherlands parallels the decline in church attendance by the Dutch population. Weekly attendance was 75% in 1966, but only 18% in 1986 (Rochon 1987, 65; Andeweg 1982, 67-68; Irwin and Holsteyn 1989, 34-36). The local elites in the

TABLE 2.3   Religious Affiliation and Activity of Local Elites

	U.S.		Sweden		Netherlands	
	Pols.	Bur.	Pols.	Bur.	Pols.	Bur.
A. Denominational Membership						
- Protestant	48%	46%			27%	34%
- Catholic	33	45			21	24
- Jewish	6	3	*	*	—	—
- Other	8	4			2	4
- None	4	3			50	37
B. Religious Activity						
(Church attendance)						
- Attend weekly	45	60	7	1	27	25
- Attends irregularly,						
but is affiliated	51	38	46	35	21	36
- Not active or no affiliation	4	2	47	64	52	39

* Data not available.

Note: One must remember that in Sweden there is a state church (Protestant) and almost all of these leaders are probably formal members of that church, or belong to a protestant "free" church.

Netherlands are almost perfectly congruent with the national public percentage. The U.S. public percentage of weekly church attendance is estimated to be at least 50%, which also appears to closely match the percentage reported by U.S. city leaders. The relevance of the religious variable for explaining elite attitudes may, of course, be questioned; it can be tested when we investigate the relationship between religion and elite values in our subsequent analysis.

Political Party Affiliations

One interesting observation from our data is the consistency across these systems in the high proportion of local elites who support parties of the

TABLE 2.4   Political Party Affiliations of Local Elites

	Politicians	Administrators	Totals
U.S.			
Democrats	41%	46%	43%
Republicans	31	24	27
Independents	17	24	20
"Other" (including NA)	11	6	10
Netherlands			
Labor	36	45	38
D'66	8	6	7
Other "Left" (PSP, PPR, CPN, Ecology)	4	0	3
Christian Democrats	25	36	29
VVD (Liberals)	19	8	16
Other "Right" (SGP, GPV, PPF, etc.)	3	5	4
Local Party	5	1	3
Sweden			
Communists	1		
Social Democrats	47		
Centre	14	*	
Liberals	5		
Conservatives	32		
Christian Democrats	1		

Summary

	United States		Netherlands		Sweden	
	Pols.	Bur.	Pols.	Bur.	Pols.	Bur.
"Left"	41%	46%	48%	51%	48%	
Centre	17	24	25	36	14	*
"Right"	31	24	22	13	38	

* For Sweden no party affiliation data were available for administrators.

"Left". (Table 2.4) A caution is necessary here: this partisan pattern may be an artifact of the time of the study, as explained in Chapter I. Also, this uniformity is peculiar because, as we shall see later, there is actually an extreme range in party preferences of elites across the individual cities. Yet, the fact stands out: 43% in the U.S. are Democrats, 49% Dutch are "Left", 48% Swedish are "Left" (politicians only). Aside from that finding, however, the systems differ considerably. The Dutch Center party (CDA) is well represented (29%), but the Swedish Centre is not (14%). This is due to the fact that the Center Party in Sweden lost its leading position as the largest non-socialist party in many communes after the 1982 elections and thus provided fewer leaders in the sample. The Dutch and Swedish elite structures are both very pluralized, while the U.S., of course, is not. The small parties in the Dutch and Swedish systems are represented in our elite samples due to the PR list voting system and the way leaders are selected in the two countries. The other interesting point, for the U.S. and the Netherlands is that there is great similarity for the politicians and administrators in the patterns of party affiliation. One does not get theimpression (by looking at all the cities in a country together), that there is a "Left" tendency among one set of elites and a "Centre" or "Right" tendency among another set of elites. The extent of the actual partisan confrontation between politicians and administrators can be determined only by a look at individual city data, which we will do shortly.

Hierarchical Comparisons

It is interesting to note the comparisons of the data on the social characteristics of elites at the national and local levels of these systems, and also in relation to their publics. Only approximate estimates are possible because accurate and timely data are not easily available. The national elite data relied on here, came from the study of MPs and national bureaucrats in Sweden (1970-71), the Netherlands (1973), and the U.S. (1970-71).[1] Based on the best available data, elite and mass differences appear as follows:

	% working class (Based on father's occupation)			% with university education		
	U.S.	Netherlands	Sweden	U.S.	Netherlands	Sweden
National Elites (Early Seventies)	13	6	15	96	88	80
Local Elites (Mid Eighties)	42	49	26	55	35	44
Mass Level (Early Seventies)	39	48	50	26	3	5

The social status distances between the two levels of elites are considerable. (Caution is necessary here because of the difficulties in getting comparable coding.) For Sweden on education it is a difference of over 36 percentage points, for the Netherlands over 50%, for the U.S. 41%. Social class origins also are quite different. Local elites are much more likely to come from working class backgrounds, particularly in the U.S. and the Netherlands. This is true also if one looks at the data for politicians and administrators separately, for national compared to local elites. We find the following comparisons if we use the data on father's occupation:

| | *% with fathers who had working class occupations* | | | | | |
| | U.S. | | Netherlands | | Sweden | |
	Pols.	*Adms.*	*Pols.*	*Adms.*	*Pols.*	*Adms.*
National Elites	18	14	9	4	33	15
Local Elites	37	48	46	56	25	17

Local elites are therefore more "representative" of the masses in these terms (except for the politicians in Sweden). As one moves upward in the system to the national elite level there is usually an increasing "disproportion" or distance in social origins and status. If one is concerned about the "elitist" character of democracies, these data provide some reassurance. Access to local elite positions is more possible, a counterpoise in a sense to the bias in the recruitment of national elites. This point is further elaborated in the ensuing section.

Career Paths—Based on Social Class and Education

The proposition has long been accepted that: education in modern societies is the key route to achieve elite status, and in so far as social class origins constrain access to higher education, the probabilities of lower class persons being selected to elite positions are minimal. In the national elite studies of the Seventies, referred to earlier, this was found to be generally true. Not only did 96% of the *national* bureaucrats have a university education, and 80% of the MPs. But also, more importantly, only *one percent* of the national bureaucrats were persons from working class backgrounds who did not have university education. (The percentage for MPs was eight percent). This leads to the two key questions for our *local* elites: (1) Do social class and educational level coincide as credentials to the extent they do for national elites? (2) or, can those with working class origins achieve *local* elite status more frequently, without university education?

The simple answer to those questions is that the career routes for local political elites are not the same as for national elites. Those with working class backgrounds have a better opportunity to be selected even if their education is limited. But these opportunities differ for politicians and administrators, and by country. The comparable data can be summarized as follows:

	U.S.		Sweden		Netherlands	
Local Elites	Pols.	Adms.	Pols.	Adms.	Pols.	Adms.
% of the total with working class backgrounds	37	48	25	17	45	56
% with working class backgrounds and without a college degree (or equivalent)	17	11	18	1	14	4
% of the working class respondents who did not have a college degree	36	23	72	7	31	8

Clearly local elites are not required nor expected to have the same credentials as national elites. A sizeable minority can secure elective positions and, for the United States at least, administrative positions without higher education. This is not to say that university education is unimportant. It is very important, particularly for administrators (63% in the U.S. and 76% in Sweden have university education). But those with working class background and limited education are not shut out as completely as for national elites.

We describe in detail the career paths using these two factors of social class and education in Table 2.5. Several observations emerge from this. One, for politicians there is a clear relationship between social class and educational level—the higher the social class the larger the percentage with a university education. For administrators only in the Netherlands is this true. Contrary to expectations, in the U.S. and Sweden, those administrators with working class backgrounds are as well educated as those with middle or upper class backgrounds. Two, quite a few of these elites from all class backgrounds are not highly educated. One would expect this for politicians, but it is true also (although to a smaller degree) for administrators. For politicians, one notes that one fourth of U.S. leaders whose fathers held positions in middle or upper professional/managerial occupations did not themselves secure college degrees. This is more so in Sweden and less so in the Netherlands. In a sense, some of these local elites are "downward mobiles" from middle and upper class educational strata. Hence, they probably can never go beyond local elite political and administrative office. Of course, in the U.S., there is probably a higher expectation of the importance of a university education. Three, Sweden and the U.S. differ in an interesting way. Swedish local administrators are well educated, despite

TABLE 2.5   Career Paths of Local Elites, Social Class (Father's occupation) and Education

Father's Occupational Class	Percent	Respondent's Education			
		Post Graduate	College Degree	Less than College Degree	N
A. U.S.					
Politicians: Professional/Managerial	30% —>	55%	21	24=100%	33
Middle Class	34 —>	41	33	26	37
Working/Lower Class	37 —>	36	28	36	39
	100%				109
Administrators: Professional/Managerial	25 —>	68	14	18=100%	28
Middle Class	29 —>	62	28	10	32
Working/Lower Class	46 —>	65	12	23	52
	100%				112
B. Sweden					
Politicians: Professional/Managerial	14 —>	59	7	34=100%	29
Middle Class	62 —>	29	10	61	124
Working/Lower Class	25 —>	14	14	72	50
	101%				203
Administrators: Professional/Managerial	30 —>	78	18	4=100%	23
Middle Class	54 —>	75	14	11	44
Working/Lower Class	17 —>	86	7	7	14
	101%				81
C. Netherlands					
Politicians: Professional/Managerial	15 —>	61	25	14=100%	28
Middle Class	39 —>	34	45	21	74
Working/Lower Class	46 —>	27	42	31	84
	100%				186
Administrators: Professional/Managerial	13 —>	58	42	0=100%	12
Middle Class	31 —>	54	43	3	28
Working/Lower Class	56 —>	24	68	8	50
	100%				90

Note: This table should be read across, as follows: In the U.S. 37% of politicians come from the working class, *of which* 36% had graduate education, etc. Percents may not add up to 100 due to rounding.

class background, while their local political leaders tend to be middle-to-lower class persons with less education. The U.S. gives more opportunities to local administrators with lower class but these elites are well educated. The U.S. politicians are spread more evenly among social class and educational groups. The Dutch pattern is closer to the American in this respect. Almost half of the U.S. politicians come from middle or higher class backgrounds *and* have a college degree or graduate education. This is true of 43% of the Dutch and one-third of the Swedish politicians.

To get a picture of the overall distribution of politicians and all administrators separately in each country, by the two variables of social class and education level, see the nine-cell summary in Table 2.6. One notices from such data that for only a minority is there a perfect conjunction of high social class and university education—e.g., 24% for Swedish administrators, 17% for the U.S. and 8% for the Netherlands. We see then several types of local leaders using these two background variables:

Types of Local Elites	U.S. Pols.	U.S. Adms.	Sweden Pols.	Sweden Adms.	Netherlands Pols.	Netherlands Adms.
A. Well educated, professional or managerial family background.	17%	17%	8%	24%	9%	8%
B. Mixed credentials in class and educational terms (middle or higher class but less than a university education)	48	37	67	60	46	36
C. Working class background but fairly well educated (at least college degree level).	18	35	7	16	31	54
D. Working class and poorly educated.	17	11	18	0	9	2

The diversity in the social status characteristics within local elites for both systems is apparent, as well as the cross-system differences. The Swedish system is distinctive since it is skewed more toward categories B, while the Dutch and American systems are more divided between categories B and C.

The Role of Parties in Elite Social Representation

The party systems in our three countries differ greatly and the question is whether this is reflected in local elite social characteristics. Do parties of different ideological hue attract or recruit individuals from different class, educational, and age backgrounds? In the earlier study of national elites in the Seventies selective party influence was quite evident (Aberbach 1981, 59-61). Is it perhaps more true for local elites? Table 2.7 presents the relevant data.

There are some interesting anomalies in these data which partially support previous findings. The Swedish system is an excellent example of a "class-distinct" party system, with the Social Democrats being the major channel for those from the working class and with limited education. The

TABLE 2.6 Distribution of All Elites, by Position, on Two Social Status Factors (Percentages)

| | Social Class (Father's Occupation) | | | | | |
| | Politicians | | | Administrators | | |
	High	Med.	Low	High	Med.	Low
A. United States						
Education of R						
University	17	14	13	17	18	30
Middle	6	11	5	4	8	5
Low	7	10	17	4	3	11
	100%			100%		
B. Sweden						
Education of R						
University	8	18	3.5	24	41	15
Middle	1	26	3.5	5	7	1
Low	5	18	18	1	6	0
	100%			100%		
C. Netherlands						
Education of R						
University	9	13	12	8	17	13
Middle	5	13	24	6	13	40
Low	1	4	9	0	1	1
	100%			99%		

* Percents may not add up to 100 due to rounding.

Swedish Conservatives, on the other hand, recruit few from the lower class, although they do give a fairly large percent with less education a chance (provided they are not from working class backgrounds). The Dutch "Left" does well also in channelling working class aspirants but it really is not very distinctive because the other two major parties recruit also from the lower class for municipal leaderships, a striking difference from Sweden. However, at least 50% of the leaders of Dutch parties have a college degree or better. The United States is the "deviant" case in a sense. Its "Left" party, the Democrats, "recruits" fewer local elites from the working class than the Republicans (a finding identical to that for national elites!). Indeed the "nonpartisans" or independents have the largest contingent of local elites with working class backgrounds, for both types of elites. The social class data for *administrators* (not shown in Table 2.7) are as follows:

% with working class family origins	"Left" Party	"Right" Party	Center Party or Independent (for U.S.)
U.S.	44	41	57
Netherlands	50	57	61

Here the Democrats match the Republicans, but the Independents are still more likely to be from the lower class. This suggests that there is more likelihood for working class aspirants to achieve elite status in U.S. communities which are nonpartisan! In the Netherlands all parties recruit into the administration from the lower class.

As for the data on age by party, the one striking finding is the consistently large proportion of persons in the younger age cohorts of the "Left" parties in the Netherlands. This is true for both politicians and administrators— 76% to 77% under age 50. In Sweden all parties seem to either encourage older persons to be selected or to keep older people in the office longer, than in other countries. The American local elites are diversified by age cohorts for both parties and for Independents. Few, relatively, are over 60, as these comparative figures show:

Politicians (% over 60)	"Left" Party	"Right" Party	Center Party or Independent (for U.S.)
U.S.	22	13	14
Sweden	29	34	25
Netherlands	7	11	22

Thus, we have three sets of local elites: Sweden middle-aged to old irrespective of party; U.S. middle-aged to young irrespective of party; Netherlands majority of young from the "Left" parties with the "Center" and "Right" leaders more middle aged.

Generational Variations in the Social Status of Elites

We have representation of four "mini-generations" in our study:

A. The Pre-Depression Pre-War generation. Born in the mid-Twenties or before, reached age 18 by early 1940's.
    - Age at time of our study 60 or over.
    - Proportion of our samples: U.S. (13%), Sweden (27%), Netherlands (11%).
B. The immediate Post-War generation. Born just before or during the depression and reached age 18 by the end of the war or a little later (1943 to 1952).
    - Age at the time of our study 50 to 59.
    - Proportion of our samples: U.S. (29%), Sweden (37%), Netherlands (28%).
C. Post-War Reconstruction generation. Born between 1935 and 1945 and reached age 18 from the mid-Fifties to the mid-Sixties (1953-1963).

TABLE 2.7 Differential Role of Parties in Recruiting Local Elites

	United States			Sweden			Netherlands		
	Dems.	Repub.	Indep.	Social Dems.	Centre	Conserv.	Labor	CDA	VVD
A. Data for Politicians:									
1. Social Class Origins % with fathers with working class occupation	25	34	50	43	1	6	55	51	37
2. Educational Level % with graduate training	45	38	47	18	23	41	38	27	36
3. Age Distribution									
- % below 40	30	21	14	5	3	9	26	10	24
- % below 50	54	58	64	37	27	38	76	34	54
Ns	50	38	36	99	30	72	70	50	38

	United States			Sweden			Netherlands		
B. Data for Administrators:	Dems.	Repub.	Indep.	*	*	*	Labor	CDA	"Right"
1. Educational Level % with graduate training	60	69	62				44	32	14
2. Age Distribution									
- % below 40	31	16	33				8	10	0
- % below 50	65	50	56				77	52	55
Ns	60	32	40				39	31	11
Social Class Origins % working/Lower Class	44	41	57				50	61	**

* The party affiliation question could not be asked of administrators in Sweden.
** Too few cases for analysis (but it should be noted that 7 of 11 Dutch administrators of the "Right" had working class origins).

- Age at the time of our study 40 to 49.
- Proportion of our samples: U.S. (33%), Sweden (28%), Netherlands (44%).

D. The youth liberation generation. Born between the end of the war and the early Sixties and reached age 18 between 1964 and 1982.
- Age at the time of our study 21 to 39
- Proportion of our samples: U.S. (25%), Sweden (9%), Netherlands (17%).

It is interesting to look at these age cohorts of local elites, individuals with quite varied time perspectives or lifepaths, to see whether there is any discernible difference in their social characteristics. Table 2.8 presents some provocative findings. Contrasts between the recent "liberation generation" and the older "pre-war generation" appear in all systems, but they are not uniform. Thus, among politicians in the U.S. and Sweden it is clear that these systems have become more "open" in class terms, but the opposite seems true for the Netherlands. The offspring of working class fathers appear more frequently among these young elites than previously. The recent generation also appears relatively well educated, particularly in Europe. On the average, 45% of the youngest cohort have university educations compared to 33% of the oldest cohort. The young politicians tend to be "Left" in party affiliation in the U.S. and the Netherlands, but not in Sweden. Yet, there are sharp partisan splits in almost all age cohorts.

Among administrators these observations do not as clearly hold up. In class terms, the local bureaucracy is no more open to the lower classes for the more recent generation than for older generations. And educational distinctions are not as pronounced except for Dutch local administrators perhaps. The younger cohorts of Dutch administrators are significantly better educated than the older group and more supportive of "Left" parties. This finding is not as pronounced for the U.S.

There are significant differences by age cohorts among these systems. This becomes clearer if we dichotomize the age groups into those "below 50" and "over 50". We then see the following types of contrasts as illustrations:

(Politicians Only)	U.S.	Sweden	Netherlands
% with university education			
- leaders under 50	50	41	37
- leaders 50 and over	36	23	30
% supporting parties of the "Left"			
- leaders under 50	41	48	61
- leaders 50 and over	51	49	28

The Dutch politicians are different in partisan orientation from the U.S. and Sweden. The young cohort is also less educated. The implications are that the recruitment process and the credentials used in that recruitment process have much to do with these findings.

One final "social involvement" type of variable we can look at is religious affiliation and activity. And here we find for the Netherlands very high differences by generation. A comparison for the U.S. and the Netherlands reveals these contrasts by age cohort for politicians and administrators:

TABLE 2.8 Generational Differences in Social Status and Party Identification (% ages by age cohorts)

	United States				Sweden				Netherlands			
	21-39	40-49	50-59	60+	21-39	40-49	50-59	60+	21-39	40-49	50-59	60+
A. Data for Politicians:												
1. Educational Level												
% University	43	55	32	43	50	40	22	25	40	35	29	32
2. Fathers Social Class												
% with fathers from working or lower class	48	33	38	21	37	21	27	23	35	45	50	57
3. Party Affiliations												
% "Left"	53	27	42	49	42	49	49	48	67	58	27	29
% Centre (or Indep.)	9	27	11	17	5	12	16	16	12	17	40	39
% "Right"	31	32	33	25	53	39	35	36	21	21	27	18
% Local Party									0	4	6	14
B. Data for Administrators:									Under 50*			Over 50*
1. Educational Level												
% University	69	63	56	69	80	74	83	69	45			19
2. Fathers Social Class												
% with fathers from working or lower class	39	43	64	25	11	7	23	21	51			65
3. Party Affiliations												
% "Left"	53	52	31	62	**	**	**	**	61			30
% Centre (or Indep.)	27	17	28	22					28			50
% "Right"	13	27	34	16					11			17
% Local Party												3

* There were too few Dutch administrators in the youngest and oldest age cohorts to permit separate analysis.

** No data on party for Swedish administrators.

	U.S.		Netherlands	
	Age 21-39	*Age 60+*	*Age 21-39*	*Age 60+*
% of elites who say they attend church weekly				
- Politicians	44	62	17	52
- Administrators	56	69	15	46

The distance between the generations in the Netherlands clearly stands out. In Sweden the contrasts are inconsequential since only one percent of the administrators attend church weekly (7% of the politicians).

There does not appear, then, to be a consistent cross-national set of findings by generation. The younger age cohort appears to be more open or less "elitist" in class terms in the U.S. and Sweden, but not in the Netherlands. Yet, in educational terms, the differences are not suggestive of much change. But education remains significant as an avenue to political elite status in all systems.

Community Differences in Social Characteristics

Since cities differ in social structure and political party strength, one should naturally expect some variations across the cities in any country in the social and political characteristics of elites. The question is how much variability? To what extent do credentials differ by community? And is there more elite homogeneity in one political system than another? Should the U.S. because of its larger number of cities and "decentralized" system reveal more heterogeneity across cities than in Sweden and the Netherlands?

We do indeed find great diversity in the social and political backgrounds of elites for the sample of cities in each of our countries. There are cities in the U.S. where 100% of the local leaders have university education, and also cities where almost half have no college degree. The same is true for Sweden and the Netherlands. On party affiliations, there is the American city over 90% "Democratic" in contrast to one over 70% "Republican". A Dutch city whose leaders were over 80% "Left", and one 27% "Left". In Sweden there is the city over 60% Social Democratic, and the city 54% "Conservative".

Such diversity prompts us to seek to answer two questions: how great is the range across cities on specific social and political characteristics, and what is the range in elite cohesiveness within cities? Above all, how do our three systems differ in these respects. Table 2.9 presents these comparisons.

The "within country" diversity is greatest in the U.S. for all measures, with Sweden manifesting the least heterogeneity across all cities. The systems were the most similar on the educational variable, and the most dissimilar on the party affiliation variable. Nevertheless, it is quite clear that cities and communes are highly diverse, suggesting that local social and political conditions and norms concerning the credentials of elites can be quite particularistic.

A second interesting concern deals with elite homogeneity *within city*, that is the extent to which the elites exhibit unity in particular characteristics or are divided or in conflict within each city (Table 2.9). In all three countries

TABLE 2.9   Comparison of Variability by Cities in Social and Political Characteristics of Local Elites

System Ranges for Cities	U.S.	Sweden	Netherland	Differences (Range)
A. Variability Across Cities				
1. On % of elites with university education	66 (High 89, Low 23)	43 (High 71, Low 28)	54 (High 67, Low 13)	23
2. On social class origins - % with fathers who had working class occupations	63 (High 71, Low 8)	33 (High 42, Low 9)	60 (High 80, Low 20)	30
3. On age structure - % under age 40	50 (High 57, Low 7)	17 (High 17, Low 0)	44 (High 50, Low 6)	33
4. On party preferences - % of elites supporting parties of the "Left" range for cities	87 (High 94, Low 7)	33 (High 63, Low 30)	53 (High 82, Low 27)	54
- % supporting parties of the "Right"	71 (High 71, Low 0)	29 (High 54, Low 25)	42 (High 42, Low 0)	42
Means	67.4	31.0	52.0	
B. Variability in Elite Cohesion Within Cities (% of cities in which 65% or more of the elites were similar on these four characteristics)				
Means	40	38	44	

Note: The party preference data for Sweden are based only on the affiliations of politicians since party preferences of administrators could not be asked.

a majority of cities have elites which are divided on these social background variables. One is likely to find cities which are both very cohesive *and* very incohesive in these terms. Swedish cities have more cohesion on social class backgrounds of elites, the Dutch on educational level and age, and the Americans on party strength. But there is considerable *within city* lack of cohesion in all systems. One notes that in Sweden there is a city split almost evenly between elites well educated and not so well educated, as well as a city with 79% with university education. Or, in the Netherlands, one finds a city with its elites split in partisan terms—27% Left, 27% Right and 46% in the center—while also a city which is 82% Left. Thus there are examples of high and low cohesion in all countries.

Such data suggest that community "types" or "cultures" exist. In the U.S., our elite data indicate there are "working class", Democratic cities a minority of whose elites have university education. There are also cities whose elites are working class, but Republican and slightly better educated. At the other extreme, there are cities whose elites come from the "upper class" (fathers business management or professional) and who are well educated. But these cities can be either Republican or Democratic or split politically. The remaining cities have a "mix" of these characteristics.

Similarly, in the Netherlands and Sweden we find cities whose elites are "working class", with limited education, and very strong supporters of the "Left". Other cities with elites who have working class backgrounds, and are split politically. Among cities with elites with higher class backgrounds, there are cities again, which have elites with rather low education while others have elites with university-type education. Within each group of cities there are cases of cities with a predominance of "Left"-oriented elites and those supporting the Center/Right.

The "pure cases" are, of course, few. Yet, we do find the following contrasts in each country:

| | *Data For Local Elites* | | |
	% Working Class (Father's Occupation)	% Low in Education	% Supported "Left" parties
Netherlands			
- City A	62	85	75
- City B	20	53	39
U.S.			
- City C	64	57	71
- City D	38	20	27
Sweden			
- City E	33	68	60
- City F	13	32	30

While these are indeed intriguing cases, the reality is that this "pure" conjunction of characteristics is rare and more often we find cities which have elites with more "mixed" social and political backgrounds.

We have investigated to what extent community variables are linked to elite social backgrounds, by using *Pearson* correlations. The evidence reveals certain associations but they are not uniform across all three countries (Table 2.10). Population size is clearly related to educational level of elites in the Netherlands and Sweden, but not in the U.S. Elites in smaller cities in the European countries are less well educated than in the larger cities; there is no different by size in the U.S. Population size is also linked to percent of the elites who come from working class origins, in European cities, but in directly opposite ways. The only significant correlation for population size in the U.S. is the age of elites (not strongly evident in Europe). In the U.S. there is a stronger probability that the elites in smaller cities will be older.

TABLE 2.10 Correlations of Community Variables with Elite Background Characteristics by Cities

| | Social Class | | |
	Education (% Higher Level)	(% with Fathers with Working Class Occupations)	Age (% under Age 50)
A. Party Strength (% "Left")			
U.S.	.025	.257	.310*
Sweden	-.610*	.102	.170
Netherlands	.226	-.313*	.546*
B. Educational Level of Elites			
U.S.		-.208	.066
Sweden		.057	.194
Netherlands		-.368*	.315*
C. Working Class Background of Elites			
U.S.	-.208		.154
Sweden	.057		-.264
Netherlands	.368*		-.140
D. Population Size of City			
U.S.	-.084	.059	.388*
Sweden	.340	.367*	.096
Netherlands	.636	-.303*	.262

* $p = .10$ or less

Party strength is differentially related to elite social characteristics in these countries. In the U.S. it seems that Democratic cities are led by younger elites (as is true for large cities). In Sweden there is a negative correlation between "Left" party control and educational level (the more "Left" the lower the educational level) while for the Netherlands "Left" party control is related to social class origins (the more "Left" the more likely elites will *not* be from the working class). These findings make some tolerable sense if one remembers our basic data on the strikingly different party recruitment patterns in relation to social class which we presented earlier for Sweden and the Netherlands.

These correlations document again the system differences in elite selection processes for local leaders in these three countries. There is not one convincing (i.e., strong) cross national correlation which is uniform for all countries. The closest to a generalization we might come up with is that cities controlled by "Left" parties and the larger cities tend to select younger leaders. But the correlation is not strong in all systems.

Conclusions

It is obvious from these data that for local political elites social status and power are linked, but not as closely as for national elites. In certain major respects these systems are more open for elites at the local level than at the national level—to the working class and to those with limited education. They are not very open to women, however. Hence there appears to be less "social bias" relatively, in comparison to national elites, although in educational achievements this elite is considerably distanced also from the publics in these systems.

Why should the local elite structures in all systems reveal less "social bias" than national elites structures? A variety of explanations could be advanced. Local positions are less attractive to those who come from higher social class and educational status. If those with high social status take municipal positions, they seek rapid advancement or move to the private sector, unless the pay is good and the local government positions are seen as a "career", and rewarded accordingly with adequate careerist perquisites. Thus, those who come from lower and working class backgrounds see local elite positions as genuine opportunities and, indeed, are recruited by the parties who need to fill these local positions. Finally, calculations by elites as to the willingness of citizens to support leaders with different credentials at the local than at the national level may be involved here, since local leaders are from lower social class origins and less well educated. Recruitment for these positions, of course, is a complicated process. Prewitt argued long ago that it was a five-step process which he likened to the "Chinese box puzzle." And, therefore, a variety of considerations enter into the final selection of leaders. This conception of the process has been found useful in many studies, in the U.S. and in other countries (Prewitt 1970, 6-9; Strömberg 1977, 298).

Politicians and administrators are quite similar in certain respects in social status. The greatest differences are found within systems in educational level and in years of service. In social class origins they are quite similar. And also by age, and perhaps also more than one might expect in political party affiliations. The following summary reveals this:

	Politicians	Administrators	Difference
1. University education			
U.S.	42%	63%	21%
Sweden	30	76	46
Netherlands	34	36	2
Mean			23.0
2. Years of service (Over 10 years)			
U.S.	29	68	39
Sweden	72	87	15
Netherlands	24	91	35
Mean			29.7
3. Social class origins (Working class)			
U.S.	37	48	11
Sweden	25	17	8
Netherlands	46	56	4
Mean			9.7
4. Age (Below 50)			
U.S.	57	59	2
Sweden	36	39	3
Netherlands	58	65	5
Mean			3.3

Both the Dutch and Swedish systems have local elites which are more congruent (except for educational level in Sweden) than is true for the U.S.

There are certainly uniformities across these political systems. Male dominance is obviously one. The extent of parental involvement in politics and government is a second. The considerable upward economic mobility of these elites, compared to fathers, is also apparent. The career paths for administrators are similar, in the sense that education is highly credentialed (although not as highly as for national elites). If we focus on the age cohorts or "generations" of these elites we find they are fairly uniform across systems in that the youngest generation is more open to those of lower social class backgrounds than was true of the older elites (except in the Netherlands). The young are also uniformly better educated.

We find differences across these systems also. The Swedish elites are older. The U.S. elites include more, even among administrators, from the working class. American elites are much more religiously active. There are more Dutch elites who come from parties of the "Left", particularly the youngest cohort of Dutch elites. The career paths of politicians are by no means identical for these systems. For the U.S. those with working class backgrounds, of which there are 36%, are relatively well educated, at least two-thirds having a college degree. In contrast in Sweden there are fewer from the working class (25%) and the great majority of these do not have advanced education (72% do not).

Another difference is the role of parties in mobilizing and attracting persons into local elite structures. In Europe, it is the function of the parties of the "Left" (and to some extent the Center, as well as the "Right" in the Netherlands) to promote those with lower class backgrounds. While in the U.S. the Republicans and the Democrats do not attract as many from the lower class as European "Left" parties do. However, because both parties in the U.S. are involved, the net result is comparable to that of Europe, higher than Sweden, less than the Netherlands. As for opening up elite opportunities for those not well educated, there is no distinctive role for parties of the "Left", Centre, or "Right" in the U.S. and the Netherlands. In Sweden, however, the highest proportion of politicians with a university education are found among the Conservatives.

It is interesting to speculate on why systems have these differences as well as their significance. As for explanations of why, system-specific structural arrangements and political processes are of crucial importance. We should remember that in this chapter we are dealing with the results of the recruitment and appointment of local political leaders and administrators. Explanatory factors can be long-term institutional/cultural factors (such as the party system, organizational structures, and the system for recruiting administrators) and such short-term influences as election effects. These kinds of factors are especially relevant for such background characteristics as age, length of tenure, education, social class and party affiliation. Other characteristics such as religiosity among the leaders could depend more on general societal belief patterns and expectations that divide the three countries.

One of the most striking differences we discovered was that Swedish leaders are considerably older than American and Dutch leaders. Swedish politicians have longer terms of office and that of course is related to age. Dutch bureaucrats also have been in public service a long time, in contrast to U.S. bureaucrats. We therefore ought to find some structural/system factor which is common for both groups of leaders but which separate Sweden from the U.S. and the Netherlands. One such factor could be the comprehensive amalgamation reform Sweden implemented from 1965 to 1979. This reform led to a decreasing number of political posts and increased competition for the nominations in all parties. Since experience (length of term in office and thus age) is a key factor in party nominations, the immediate result was an older corps of politicians in the new amalgamated communes. As for the administrators, the same changes occurred although limited to certain job functions such as the leading administrator posts. An average of four chief administrators in four old communes competed for one such post in the new, amalgamated commune. These conditions for both politicians and administrators still existed when the Swedish study was carried out in 1984/85, but they have now disappeared.

In connection with the above analysis of age differences for politicians, the answer may lie with short-term effects in combination with structural system differences. One possible factor might be the partisan changes due to election victories. If new parties win seats, or established parties on the "Left" increase their election strength, the probability is higher for having younger politicians in the councils. However, we also know from nomination studies that in European proportional-list systems the probability of being elected is greater for older nominees because they are placed higher up in the lists than younger nominees (Westerstähl 1971). A combination of these two factors can very well explain why Dutch political leaders in our study are comparably young, much younger than in Sweden. The Dutch local election of 1986 led to considerable changes in the party composition of the councils. In that Dutch election, preceding the 1989 study, the cities in our sample showed an average increase of 8.5% for parties of the "Left" in municipal councils. In Sweden the 1982 local election was a victory for the conservative party all over the country; and conservative politicians in Sweden are slightly younger than politicians in most other parties. These contrasting electoral results may also be linked to the selection of more working class politicians in the Netherlands than in Sweden.

Another structural variable that can possibly explain the difference found in age is the variation in recruitment and career patterns. The Swedish system is merit oriented and stresses formal education and experience (years in service) more than the U.S. system, and possibly the Dutch. It is also a relatively "closed" system—Swedish administrators make their careers mainly within the local government sector (Norell 1989). This also could explain why a higher proportion of the Swedish administrators have a university degree. However, the differences should not be exaggerated. We have earlier in this chapter discussed the problems we experienced with the coding of education. Further, not all Dutch scholars feel that their local bureaucracies are less "closed", as our earlier discussion indicated.

The country differences in recruitment patterns help us also to understand the observed differences in social background for the administrators. Recruitment to university education in Sweden was—when the administrators were trained—socially biased (and still is to a high extent) despite the fact that the universities are totally financed by the state and stipends can help lower class students finance their studies. The result is that a low proportion of Swedish administrators come from the working class. The Dutch administrators are in a formal sense perhaps less university educated but more of them are trained by in-service programs which may be equivalent to the university. The higher proportion of administrators with working-class backgrounds in the Netherlands is linked to government financial support for university education for working class children, the attraction of these people to public service through the informal recruitment by parties, as well as different political credentialing norms in the Netherlands.

As has been discussed in Chapter I, party-system differences between the U.S. and the two European countries in our study are basic. The European systems, since the beginning of the century have used proportional list-voting systems. The parties in Sweden are mainly class-based, in the Netherlands class-based but also divided along religious lines. The demonstrated differences of class recruitment of politicians within the two European countries are therefore easily related to the main structural character of the party system, particularly the tendency of the "Left" parties, and to some extent the "Center" to recruit from the working-class. Dutch and Swedish parties have a much stronger control over the recruitment of local leaders than is true in the U.S.

There appears to be a set of cultural norms about elite credentials which varies from country to country. The Swedish system recruits elites with middle and upper social class origins and who are older than in other countries, but not necessarily, at least for politicians, elites who are highly educated. The Dutch also have middle levels of education, but they are young and "Left" in partisan orientation. The U.S. local elites are relatively well educated and have a sizable group with working class backgrounds, most of whom have college degrees. They are also, as the Dutch, young but not as "liberal" in party preference.

These are then, the empirically based observations about the differential character of elite credentials. The explanatory theories with most utility are those emphasizing short term election effects, party recruitment differentials, community structural variables, and elite credential norms which differ by system as well as community. And this final observation needs to be made. Community level analysis suggests that there are types of "city elite cultures" which may be more important than system-wide differences. We will explore this possibility in subsequent chapters.

Note

1. We rely here on national elite data from a comparative study of the Seventies, (Aberbach, et al. 1981, 47-55; Anton 1980; Holmberg 1974, 269). The Swedish mass level data are taken from Olof Petersson and Bo Saarlvik, analysis of the 1973 Swedish election.

3

The Problem Environments
of Cities as Perceived by Elites

To understand local elites one must know the differential socio-political contexts in which they work. The "problem environment" of the city is a major component of its culture, just as the "policy environment" is (Eulau and Prewitt 1973). Our knowledge of elites as individual leaders will be limited in the absence of contextual information, one aspect of which is the local problems they confront (or which confront them!). We, therefore, use the responses of our elite respondents in this survey in two ways, to tell us about their perceptions of their community environment, as well as about their personal reactions to and evaluations of that environment. In this way we learn about the system and about the respondent leader. It is one thing to have a leader give us his (or her) definitions of the conditions under which leaders govern in the community; it is another matter for a leader to tell us that he (or she) is sanguine or pessimistic about these conditions of government.

In trying to understand the context in which the leader works, we asked our elites a series of questions about the problems which they perceive in their city, and their degree of concern about these problems. After an introductory open-ended question, ("What do you think are the most important problems facing your city now?") there followed a list of 14 problems which we assumed had some currency in each country. We asked them to indicate for each problem whether it was "very serious," "somewhat serious," or "not serious." Subsequent questions focused on their understandings and beliefs about the resolution of these problems:

1. Who in your opinion should have (primary) responsibility (for each problem)? (National, State, Local Government or other Non-governmental agencies, or the Public?).
2. In which of these (problem areas) do you think that your local government has enough power and autonomy to act effectively?

3. Please indicate whether you think effective action(some action, or no
    action) is being taken to deal with these problems.

The same basic list of problems was used for each question with some
(minor) adaptations by question and for countries.

There are several theoretical concerns which dominate our analysis
and discussion here. The first question is how much cross national uniformity is there in elite perceptions of their problems? Do elites report the
same problems with the same frequency, rank ordered similarly, and
with the same sense of seriousness about those problems? Or, are there
important system differences in elite perceptions of problems and reactions
to these problems? This includes *reality perceptions*—what the problems
are, the resources to deal with them and the extent of effective action—
as well as *personal feeling* of obligation or responsibility to work on
the problems. Second, are there system variables which may throw some
light on why there are system differences in problem perceptions? For
example, from what we know about the economic conditions of these
societies and the structure of central-local relations are these differences in
problem perceptions, insofar as they are discovered, logical and to be
expected?

Third, within systems do we find subgroups of elites who are distinctive
in their views of their problems and their responsibility to deal with them?
Thus, do we find young elites holding different views than the older elites,
or politicians contrasted to administrators, or the politically "left" in sharp
disagreement with the "Center" and the "Right"? Or, are elites congruent
and cohesive despite subgroup differences? In short, are there significant
"subcultures" of elites in these countries who differ on these dimensions?
This includes the query also whether elite views vary by the type of
community in which they work.

Fourth, if we find subgroup differences within countries, do these hold
up across systems? That is, if age groups differ in problem perceptions in the
Netherlands, does this same pattern hold true also in the U.S. and Sweden?
If they are uniform, that is if we find the same pattern across systems, then we
may conclude that macro-level systemic factors are not relevant (but age
subgroups differences are relevant). *If not uniform*, (that is, if age groups
differ by country, for example) then we must pursue our analysis further.
Other subgroup differences must be explored. But local and national
systemic and cultural explanations must be considered as possibly the most
powerful for explanatory purposes.

Finally, what do these data tell us about local elite behavior and attitudes
in Western democracies? Are they concerned or indifferent to their problems, responsible or not responsible for problem resolution, possessed of

the power and capacity to act or powerless, and optimistic or pessimistic about the progress they are making in their community on these problems? The extent of elite engagement with their problems can tell us much about the condition of local government as well as about the state of elitism in these democracies.

It is important to keep in mind in this chapter's discussion of the problems of local government in these three countries that national-local relationships vary considerably. In Sweden and the Netherlands many policies are decided at the national level and local governments are directed to carry them out. In the Netherlands over 90 percent of local revenues come from the central government much of which is mandated for specific purposes. This is true to a lesser extent in Sweden although again many programs are directed by the national government. In the U.S. there is much more autonomy at the local government level, both as to discretion and responsibility for policy initiatives and for the generation of local revenues to finance these actions.

How Comparable Are the Problems?

A great variety of problems are mentioned by local leaders in response to the open-ended question. If we group these responses by categories of problems, the saliency of problems by country can be observed. (Table 3.1) Two findings seem immediately to emerge. There is no great concentration of concern by problem area, i.e. no strong elite congruence in perceptions of what problems are most important. This is perhaps to be expected since our study includes a wide variety of cities. And, second, there appears to be considerable cross-system agreement on the level of elite concern, with certain striking exceptions. Thus, in all countries from 20 percent to 25 percent mention the revenue and resource problems of local government, and on the other hand seven percent or fewer, surprisingly, mention social services. There is high agreement across systems, in fact, for five of the eight problem areas. But the systems differ in important respects also. The U.S. leaders are more conscious of economic development/industrialization problems, while Sweden and the Netherlands are much more concerned about "economic conditions", particularly unemployment, inflation and poverty. Urban planning and renewal do not preoccupy the Swedish elites, while in the U.S. and the Netherlands these matters are more salient. What strikes one in these response patterns is that when elites are asked what are the most important problems they don't emphasize social or human welfare needs; rather they focus at once on economic and urbanization types of problems. And governmental operations, processes and leadership also appear to be only of secondary interest.

TABLE 3.1   Saliency of Problems Identified by Local Elites (% mentioning problems)

	U.S.	Sweden	Netherlands
Problem area:			
1. Lack of resources, inadequate revenues, cost of government	21	19	21
2. Economic development, industrialization, attracting business	19	3	0
3. Urbanization - Planning, urban renewal, zoning, declining population, etc., and housing	17	8	24
4. Quality of life, concern for general welfare	11	3	6
5. Infrastructure - utilities, streets, water & sewers, etc.	11	9	11
6. Social Services - health, education, crime, recreation, etc.	5	3	7
7. Economic conditions - unemployment, inflation, poverty	4	32	20
8. Governmental administration and relationships with other levels of government; public participation; adequacy of leadership	8	15	10
9. Other	4	8	1
Ns	427	614	502

Note: Percentages are based on the total of all problems mentioned.

In order to focus our inquiry and to make sure the elites in all countries had the same frame of reference, we confronted all leaders with problems and asked them directly to indicate whether each specific problem was "very serious" or "somewhat" serious in their community. (Table 3.2) When thus pressed we get a much more complete picture of what problems they consider, on reflection, to be serious. We find that over 50 percent of American elites cite seven problems as serious, true for 9 problems in the Swedish responses and twelve problems for the Dutch. What "serious" means to each respondent is, of course, open to question. As is the term "very serious". On only three problems do sizeable American minorities see "very serious" problems, on only two problems in Sweden, whereas there are six such problems in the Netherlands.

The image at first glance which emerges here is that more European elites are aware that their problems are "serious" than in the U.S. The mean percent who view these 14 problems seriously is 47 percent in the U.S., 59 percent in Sweden, and 67 percent in the Netherlands. The following are the

TABLE 3.2 Comparison of Systems on Types of Problems Which Confront Elites

Problem Areas:	U.S.		Sweden		Netherlands		System Differences Range in % "serious"
	% see problem as "serious" ("very serious" or "somewhat serious")	% "very serious"	% see problem as "serious"	% "very serious"	% see problem as "serious"	% "very serious"	
Economic Development	70	29	77	16	74	34	7
Unemployment	69	31	97	47	83	37	28
Cost of Local Government	66	25	78	27	81	44	15
Poverty	62	7	57	5	60	13	5
Public Improvements	62	15	35	2	80	40	45
Public Safety	55	7	81	8	65	24	26
Housing	54	10	41	5	79	37	38
Education	47	9	65	7	54	11	18
Pollution	46	3	76	10	82	37	36
Social Welfare	46	5	59	5	70	16	24
Health	31	3	29	1	41	6	12
Recreation/Culture	26	4	50	4	57	16	31
Race/Ethnic Relations	23	3	32	3	59	16	36
Migration into city	19	3	44	9	48	8	29
Means	47.3	11.0	58.6	10.6	66.6	24.2	25.0

problems on which the European leaders report a higher level of concern than in the U.S.:

- Unemployment
- Public safety
- Pollution
- Social welfare
- Recreation and culture
- Race and ethnic relations
- Cost of local government

The suggestion implicit here is that American problems are less severe. Obviously, the validity of such a statement can be challenged. In actuality, these data probably mean American elites are more sanguine about their problems, perhaps resigned to them, while European elites are more pessimistic , as well as more self-conscious about their problems, for whatever reasons. A striking example is the concern in Sweden over the unemployment problem. At a time when there was no more than five percent registered unemployment in any of their cities, 97 percent of Swedish local leaders say they have a "serious" unemployment problem, and 47 percent say they have a "very serious" problem! Similarly, the level of concern over social welfare problems and over racial relations in the Netherlands (70% and 59% respectively), in contrast to the U.S. (46% and 23%), hardly seems comparatively realistic and understandable. The criteria for seriousness as well as the perspectives from which these elites view their problems obviously differ markedly.

The meaning of the word "serious" has apparently several interpretations for our respondents. The Dutch local elites may be reflecting a more general concern during a time of austerity (1989) by the national government, cutbacks in support for local programs, and a worry that adequate financing may not continue in the future. This lack of an "over-time" perspective by local elites in the U.S., plus the lack of pressure from national and state governments to deal with social welfare, racial, pollution, and other types of problems may explain the difference between the two countries in their overall level of concern. Dutch elites may have developed a different "mindset" than did the Americans. These reservations may apply also to Sweden, where the public debate on the general economic problem and the economic "crisis" facing communes was under way in 1985.

While realizing that evaluations of "seriousness" are relative, nevertheless we wish to emphasize here the similarities and differences across systems. Rank orders of problems may be useful. The leaders of all three countries indicate that unemployment and the cost of local government are among the top three problems in their communities. But after that pattern of agreement the emphasis varies by country. Note these rank orders after the top two:

U.S.	Sweden	Netherlands
1. Economic Development	Public Safety	Pollution
2. Poverty	Economic Development	Public Improvements
3. Public Improvements	Pollution	Housing
4. Public Safety	Education	Social Welfare
5. Housing	Social Welfare	Economic Development

The elite agendas overlap in some respects but also have considerable distinctiveness. Another type of evidence of system differences is in the range in the percentage of elites from one country to another who feel the problem is serious. Across all 14 problems the mean range, i.e. the extent of system differences, is 25.7 percent. Examples of significant differences are:

	High	Low	Range
Housing	Neths (79%)	SW (41%)	38
Pollution	Neths (82%)	U.S. (46%)	36
Public Safety	SW (81%)	U.S. (55%)	26
Recreation	Neths (57%)	U.S. (26%)	31
Public Improvements	Neths (80%)	SW (35%)	45

We find the greatest differences on the average (for all 14 problems) between the U.S. and the Netherlands followed by the U.S. and Sweden, with the greatest agreement between the two European countries. These are based on the percent who felt the problem was at all serious. Yet, on certain problems, such as housing and public improvements, it was the European elites who differed the most.

One final point. The extent to which the elites in each country agree in their problem perceptions is fairly impressive for large numbers of these issues. From two-thirds to ninety percent agree on the seriousness (or lack of seriousness) on seven to nine of the 14 problems. The average agreement on all issues is almost 70 percent in the European countries and 65 percent in the U.S. The California study suggested comparable levels of agreement for U.S. cities (Eulau and Prewitt 1973, 530-543). Nevertheless in our study there are problems on which elites are seriously split in their views. For example, education, public safety, housing, pollution and social welfare divide American elites (45 percent minorities on all five of these issues). In Sweden elites were divided on housing, recreation, social welfare, while in the Netherlands elites are decidedly split on education, health, recreation and race problems. The factors related to such elite differences in perception within systems will be explored in the next section.

Responsibility for Dealing with Problems

A quite different question than perception is the sense of responsibility a leader feels for the resolution of a problem by local government. The question asked (which varied somewhat when translated into Swedish and Dutch) was whether these leaders felt local government "has" or "ought to have" the *"primary responsibility"* for working on the problem. As can be seen from Table 3.3 there are significant cross system differences. Among the three countries Sweden stands out. A very high proportion of its leaders (mean 70%) reported that local government has responsibility (in the eleven problem areas), while in the U.S. only 52 percent felt they "should have" responsibility. Only 34 percent of the Dutch leaders said they had the responsibility. On only one problem (health) were Swedish leaders inclined to say that local government ought *not* have a role (this is the county's

TABLE 3.3 Elites Sense of Responsibility for Dealing with Problems

% Saying Local Government Has or Should Have Responsibility	"Should Have Responsibility"		"Has Responsibility"
	U.S.	Sweden	Netherlands*
A. Prima Facie "Local" Problems			
1. Housing	50	90	70
2. Public Improvements	89	92	61
3. Education	56	77	16
4. Public Safety	87	51	39
5. Recreation/Culture	75	80	71
6. Race/Ethnic Relations	48	67	51
Means	67.5	76.2	51.3
B. Possibly "Local" Problems			
7. Economic Development	63	75	13
8. Pollution	36	83	19
9. Health	30	33	14
10. Unemployment	18	58	8
11. Poverty	21	65	8
Means	33.6	62.8	12.4
Means (all 11)	52.1	70.1	33.6*

Note: These percentages for the U.S. and Sweden refer to all those who say local government should have responsibility. The Dutch data are not strictly comparable because of the wording of the question, the coding, and different possible interpretations of the question.

problem). Even though police is not primarily a local problem in Sweden, 51 percent still say they should have responsibility for public safety. In the U.S. on four problems a minority of respondents wanted to assume responsibility. The discrepancy between Sweden and the other two countries is greatest for five problems (listed at the bottom of Table 3.3), such as economic development, pollution, unemployment, etc.,—a thirty percentage point difference between Sweden and the U.S. One should note also that for the most part Swedish leaders were cohesive in their assumption of responsibility (except for public safety and health), while in the U.S. leaders are more inclined to be split or negative.[1]

These findings are puzzling and require, indeed provoke, some clarification as well as interpretation. The first point is that the Dutch study used different language—asking whether local government "has" responsibility, while in the U.S. and Sweden the language was "should have" responsibility. Second, the temporal frame of reference is not clear in the U.S. and Swedish questions. "Should have" could mean "should have now" should have in the future" (but does not have now, *or* does have now)! Third, an inspection of the pattern of responses adds to the confusion. The Dutch leaders seem to be denying responsibility in problem areas in which they clearly under national directives do have responsibility (such as health, and possibly economic development and racial relations, etc.). The findings in Table 3.3 are difficult to understand in this context. Perhaps the Dutch are actually responding to the question in "should have" terms! The Swedish responses are also not completely clear because they reject responsibility for health, for example, and that may be a reaction to the status quo—i.e., who "has" responsibility rather than who "should have" (or both!). Further, responsibility for "health" in Sweden is divided—hospital care is assigned to the counties, while other types of "health" are the responsibility of the communes. Hence, only if we assume a common frame of reference for the U.S. and Sweden (using the language "should have" to mean should have in a general or future sense) can we conclude that the sizable system differences between the U.S. and Sweden are valid. Comparison with the Netherlands then seems out of the question.

This question of responsibility could be related to elite views about their power. We asked for all these problems individually whether the leader felt local government had enough power (and authority) to act. It is useful to look at elite perceptions of power in relation to their sense of responsibility. Analysis of these two sets of responses will indicate system differences and similarities in elite perceptions of capability to act and willingness to act.

The analysis of power perceptions could conceivably also be complicated by the way in which "power" is understood. It could mean "power to initiate" new actions, or "power to implement" policies mandated by the national government, or power in the sense of adequate resources, etc. We assume that its meaning as used here is understood to be the power to take action in a policy or problem area, i.e., to engage in a particular municipal function. We find that on the average for the eleven policy areas we are dealing with the Swedish leaders have a perception of greater power to act: 66 percent, compared to 55 percent for the Americans, and 44 percent for the Dutch. It is difficult to understand why the Dutch and Americans are so low. Except for individual policy areas such as education (and perhaps health in the Netherlands and public safety in Sweden), there is no reason to assume that more services are mandated by one of these European welfare state systems than the other. The reluctance of American elites to accept power is equally obscure. One notes that for some of these problem areas elites are split 50-50 or 60-40, indicating confusion as to what their power prerogatives are under their own systems. One may want to argue that poverty and unemployment are problems which are more properly the province of Swedish local elites than Dutch or American elites, but it would be difficult to support that logically in systemic terms. But it certainly is a major difference in terms of elite perceptions!

A careful comparison of power and responsibility responses, keeping in mind language variations in the questions, leads to some clear conclusions. One, the Dutch are a clear case of either misconceiving their current power and responsibilities or rejecting them, or both. Even when they have power, they are very likely to deny responsibility. Two, the Americans are not eager to admit power or responsibility but they do so at a higher level than the Dutch, and they are consistent. If they say they have power, they are inclined to say they should have responsibility. Not so the Dutch. Three, the Swedish elites *want* more responsibility, even if they do not think they have the power. Only for health is there a major discrepancy between their power perceptions and their desire for responsibility. If we take five very current problems in these five systems—economic development, pollution, housing, race relations, unemployment—and look at the elite differentials we find the following average comparisons:

	U.S.	Sweden	Netherlands
Have Power	45%	62	40
Have or Should Have Responsibility	43	75	32

The Dutch are the most negative, the Americans the most consistent, the Swedish most responsible! One cannot escape the conclusions that (1) Swedish leaders are more willing to admit they have the power to act, (2) are more willing to say they ought to have the responsibility to act, and (3) are more ready to accept responsibility to act when they do not think they have the power to act!

There is one final observation to make here. The question can be posed whether these systems differ also in elite perceptions of *national* government responsibilities. If local elites in Sweden are willing so frequently to assume responsibility for local government to act, do they less frequently assert that the national government should have a role? Conversely, do American elites *shift* responsibility to the national government? In fact, neither of these conclusions emerge from our data. The following summary reveals the reverse of that expectation:

% for all elites (Average for 11 policy areas)	*National government is responsible*	*Local government is responsible*	*Non-Governmental agencies or the "People" should be responsible*
Sweden	54.9	70.1	21.0
U.S.	39.0	52.1	20.7

Elites Beliefs that:

Elites in Sweden are obviously more inclined to insist that both national *and* local government have a responsibility than is true for the U.S. Since the responsibility question in the Netherlands asked whether these levels of government "have" responsibility, the findings are not directly comparable. The Dutch percentage for the national level is 47 percent (exceeding the U.S.), and very low (6.5%) for non-governmental agencies or the people.

What one can interpret these findings to mean then is that in the decentralized U.S. system local leaders take three positions: (1) they are split on whatever they should have the responsibility to act; (2) two-fifths feel the national (and state) governments have a basic responsibility; (3) a sizable minority want to pass these problems off to nongovernmental groups. The major difference with Sweden is that local leaders feel that *both* national and local leaders have responsibility. Americans are more ambivalent and uncertain about their responsibility as local leaders, and feel that national and state governments are failing them because of inadequate support. Under the Swedish unitary system the central-state relationship is different. The national government develops programs under their welfare state system working with local government authorities. The national government provides directives informing local leaders of their responsibilities, and regularly provides 30 percent of their funds necessary at the local level to meet expenditures. Cities are told to raise the balance of revenue needed by local taxes and fees. The system is standardized, more homogeneous, and relations and responsibilities are not ambivalent, but rather are clearly specified. This appears to be much more a system of mutual understanding, and acceptance, of responsibility linked to strong central-local financial and administrative mutual support relationships. As a result Swedish leaders understand their obligations with more clarity, and accept them. Note these illustrations:

% of local elites who say they should be responsible for:	U.S.	Sweden
Housing	50	90
Pollution	36	83
Race/Ethnic relations	48	67
Poverty	21	65

This appears to be in part an abdication of responsibility by local leadership in the U.S. system, and to a certain extent it is. It is also in part a product of defeatism, and isolation, and deflection of responsibility to higher government. The Swedish system of national government—local government "partnership" stands in sharp contrast.

We must now relate the above findings to the question we began with—which problems are "serious". That is, do local leaders feel more responsibility (actual or desirable) to solve problems they identify as the serious ones? Do the differences in the sense of responsibility for these three countries disappear when we control for the seriousness of problems as perceived by these elites? (See Table 3.4 for a full set of data on all these questions). It is not true that Swedish leaders are more inclined to see problems as serious than Americans or Dutch leaders. In fact, Dutch leaders are more likely to see problems as "serious" or "very serious". If we divide these problems into two groups based on whether the problem is perceived to be serious and whether there is power to act, we can see the linkage with the sense of responsibility which leaders feel. The comparative data are as follows:

	U.S.	Sweden	Netherlands
1. Mean % who see problems			
- as very serious	11.0	9.8	24.6
- as serious or very serious	49.5	58.2	66.7
2. Mean % who feel a sense of responsibility:			
A. For the five most serious problems for which a majority say they have power to act	67.6	71.2	53.8
B. For the remaining problems, which are either not serious or for which a majority say there is *no* power to act	38.0	69.6	13.0

What one concludes from this is that there is a relationship between perceived seriousness of problems and a sense of responsibility to act, for the U.S. and the Netherlands. But virtually no relationship for Sweden. Swedish leaders have a sense of responsibility, (or a desire to have responsibility) for all problems whether they feel they have the authority to act or not. For the U.S. and the Netherlands there are important instances where this is not true. For the U.S. there is the example of housing—considered serious, but only 50 percent see a responsibility to act. For the Netherlands, examples are economic development and education—considered serious, but elites express minimal responsibility. In short, the Swedish leaders are concerned about problems, and feel they ought to have responsible; the Dutch are very concerned and say they do not have responsibility; the Americans are less concerned and on some problems have no sense that they ought to have responsibility.

The final, somewhat puzzling, point to be made here is that the Swedish leaders are also the most cynical about the extent of effective action on these problems. Their expectations for action seem to be higher than in the other countries. One might have expected in all these countries that these leaders would have evaluated the work of their own community governments more positively. But the averages who feel there is effective action are: U.S. 26.5 percent, Netherlands 26.0 percent, and Sweden 12.5 percent. And these averages don't change much if we restrict the calculations to those problems considered serious. But if we consider only those problems on which the leaders feel they have the power to act we see some change in the U.S. and Dutch percentages: 39 percent see effective action, compared to 32 percent for the Netherlands, while the Swedish percentage remains low at 11.0 percent. Thus, the Swedish leaders are consistently pessimistic about action. Yet in all three countries the percentages are low. We should add that a higher percent (40 percent on the average) in each country felt "some action" was being taken on these problems. Nevertheless the great majority would not label this action as "effective".

Explanation of Differences Across Systems

While we have noticed some uniformities for these three countries the major differences are apparent and an attempt should be made to explain them. Our comparative findings are clear: (1) Both sets of European elites fairly consistently are more likely to see their problems as serious than are American elites; (2) The Swedish elites feel that local government should have responsibility to deal with these problems more than the Americans do; (3) The Swedish elites are also more ready to say they have the power to act than the Dutch and Americans; (4) Swedish elites are more ready to accept responsibility to act in those areas where they see their power to act is limited. How do we explain these nonequivalencies in these three

TABLE 3.4 Combined Analysis of Problems, Responsibility, Power, and Action (% of all elites)

Problem Area:	U.S.				Sweden				Netherlands			
	Problem is serious (1)	Have power to act (2)	Have responsibility (3)	Effective action (4)	Problem is serious (1)	Have power to act (2)	Have responsibility (3)	Effective action (4)	Problem is serious (1)	Have power to act (2)	Have responsibility (3)	Effective action (4)
Economic Development	70	58	66	33	77	50	75	14	74	36	13	40
Public Improvements	62	82	88	43	35	90	92	15	80	59	61	36
Public Safety	55	81	89	42	81	56	51	6	65	42	39	21
Housing	54	59	53	32	41	76	90	15	79	52	70	52
Education	47	55	52	40	65	44	77	20	54	28	16	21
Pollution	46	37	36	29	76	54	83	10	82	32	19	32
Health	31	53	35	.5	29	70	33	9	41	42	14	11
Recreation	26	86	77	44	50	90	80	14	57	87	71	24
Race/Ethnic Relations	23	56	52	27	32	81	67	9	59	64	51	14
Poverty	62	23	19	.5	57	71	65	6	60	20	8	8
Unemployment	69	15	18	.5	97	47	58	20	83	18	8	27
Means	49.5	55.0	53.2	26.5	58.2	66.3	70.1	12.5	66.7	43.6	33.6	26.0

Note: The variations in language for the responsibility question should be kept in mind. See the discussion in the text.

Western democracies? We shall approach this by looking at elite subgroups to see whether their patterns are different, *within* and *across* systems. Three subgroups will be used: party, age, and position (whether politician or administrator). After such analysis macro- or system level interpretations can be attempted.

The probability that the types of parties in these three countries may be related to the differences in elite attitudes toward problems and their resolution is high and, therefore, a good place to start. Sweden and the Netherlands have multi-party systems with strong social democratic parties on the "Left" and strong bourgeois 'conservative' parties on the "Right", while the U.S. has a two-party system which is theoretically less "class-distinct" and less noted for ideological distance between the Democratic and Republican parties. The basic data on the four key measures suggests that party differences *across systems* are indeed considerable (Table 3.5). For the parties of the "Left" the system differences range from 16 percentage points (on the seriousness of problems) to 23 percentage points (on the power to deal with problems). For parties of the "Right" the differences are from 12 to 26 percentage points.

Conservative party elites in all countries are more inclined to feel that local government has the power to deal with its problems. But no such generalization is possible on the other three measures. Not all "Left" parties are equally "Left" and many elites in "Right" parties in one country take positions which are quite different from their partisan counterparts in other countries. The cross-system differences are greater than the within system difference, by party, a significant comparative finding.

The major question for us, however, is: Do party differences across systems help us explain the differences in elite perspectives, perceptions, and evaluations? We can illustrate how this may be (or may not be) the case by using elite responses to the question of how "serious" local government problems are. Here is a summary of the findings:

	% Saying Local Government Problems Are Serious			
	U.S.	Sweden	Netherlands	Differences
Initial Finding for all Elites	50	58	67	17
Parties Analysis				
"Left"	55	61	71	16
"Center"	48	64	70	22
"Right"	48	52	61	13
Left-Right Differences	7	9	10	

What is clear from this is that *within systems* the elites of the different parties are fairly homogeneous and like-minded, but *across systems* there is

TABLE 3.5 The Relevance of Party for Elite Attitudes Toward Political Problems

Elite views on (Average % for all problems):	United States			Sweden			Netherlands			System Differences (Range)	
	Dems.	Indep.	Social Reps.	Social Dems.	Centre	Conser-vatives	Labor	CDA	VVD	Left	Right
1. See problems as serious	55	48	48	61	64	52	71	70	61	16	13
2. Say local government should have or has responsibility for dealing with the problem	51	54	54	73	68	65	37	34	36	22	12*
3. Agree that local government has the power to act on the problem	53	55	63	65	63	74	42	43	58	23	13
4. Claim that effective action is being taken on problem	28	32	36	11	15	8	27	32	26	17	26
N's	112	52	71	100	29	83	127	79	45		
Average within system difference Left vs. Right	7.0			9.5			7.0				

Note: The Swedish Liberals (11 cases) have been combined here with the Centre. The D'66 in the Netherlands (20 cases) has been combined with the Labor party.

* On responsibility (Item 2), the proper comparison is between Sweden and the U.S. because of the way the question was worded.

more variance. Further, the *proportions* of different party elites in our samples cannot be considered the factor which is responsible for the difference. These are the sample proportions:

	% of Elites From Each Party		
	U.S.	Sweden	Netherlands
"Left"	48	47	51
"Center"	22	19	31
"Right"	30	34	18

These differences in proportions (for Center and Right) cannot be an explanation of the basic finding, for an increase in the U.S. or the Netherlands of *any* party group in these samples would not make any difference in the finding. It is *the substantive direction* of elite attitudes toward the question of responsibility which is the real factor, not *the proportionate size* of the elite subgroups. All Dutch parties have local leaders who are just much more ready to say that problems are serious than U.S. or Swedish parties. There appears here to be, then, a consistent and pervasive elite orientation or "mindset" towards the seriousness of problems in the Netherlands which cuts across all the parties. This is not as clearly or strongly evident in the other countries. We have found two system differences then: (1) in the greater readiness of local Dutch elites to say they have problems which are serious, and (2) in the greater pervasiveness of this readiness across all Dutch parties than across all Swedish and American parties. If Swedish and American "Left" parties were concerned at the 71 percent level (as the Dutch leaders were), we could have discovered a crosscultural uniformity. But this we did not find (true also for Center and Right parties). Why are Dutch elites more concerned in all parties about their problems, why this system difference? This is a question still to be probed.

If we pursued this same type of analysis with other elite subgroups— age cohorts and a comparison of administrators and politicians—we arrive at the same general observation. (See Tables 3.6 and 3.7.) If we use again the seriousness of problems question as the example, and note the percentages for politicians and administrators, here is the summary of our findings:

	% Saying Local Government Problems Are Serious		
	U.S.	Sweden	Netherlands
Initial Finding for all Elites	50	58	67
For Politicians	58	47	70
For Administrators	52	53	67
Difference:	6	6	3

TABLE 3.6   The Relevance of Elite Position in Problem Perceptions

	United States		Sweden		Netherlands		System Differences (Range)	
	Pols.	Adms.	Pols.	Adms.	Pols.	Adms.	Pols.	Adms.
A. Seriousness of problems: Average % seeing problems as serious	47.4	52.9	58.0	51.5	70.1	66.9	23	15
B. Responsibility for local government to act: Average % seeing local government as having a responsibility (or should have)	55.1	50.5	68.8	68.4	35.7	35.7	14	18
C. Power to act: Average % saying local government has power	55.4	54.9	66.8	62.7	46.1	44.5	21	18
D. Effective action: Average % saying effective action is being taken on these problems	31.3	31.0	11.3	10.7	27.5	29.0	20	22
N's	128	132	272	117	196	99		

Difference Between
Politicians and Administrators:

A.	5.4	A.	6.5	A.	3.2
B.	4.6	B.	.4	B.	0.0
C.	.5	C.	4.1	C.	1.6
D.	.3	D.	.6	D.	1.5

Note: These calculations are confined to the same eleven problems used for each country for each type of question.

Again, we find that there is no significant difference for political leaders *by position* within these three countries. There are the same basic cross system differences irrespective of leader's type of position. The same pattern is basically true for elite perceptions of the power to act, and their evaluations of the extent of effective action (see Table 3.6). Hence, the same conclusion must be arrived at as for the party variable: these three systems differ in the extent to which politicians and administrators perceive local problems and their resolution. Elite subgroups are quite homogeneous within systems, but are not uniform across systems.

The same basic finding is true, with slight modifications, for elite age cohorts. Note these summary findings:

	U.S.	Sweden	Netherlands	System Differences (Range)
			% Saying Local Government Problems Are Serious	
Initial Finding for all Elites	50	58	67	17
Age Subgroups:				
Elites under 50	52	60	68	16
Elites 50 and older	47	54	69	22
Proportions in the Samples:				
Elites under 50	58	37	59	
Elites 50 and older	42	63	41	

Elite consensus by age groups within systems is high, but cross-system differences reveal less agreement by age groups. Thus, age cohort analysis reconfirms the existence of a basic system difference on the assumption of elite perceptions of the seriousness of local problems: whether old or young, whether "Left", "Centre", or "Right", whether politicians or administrators—Dutch local elites are consistently much more likely to perceive their problems as serious.

This observation is also true for elite perceptions that local government has the power *to act* on their problems. The following summary of our findings documents that conclusion:

	U.S.	Sweden	Netherlands	System Differences (Range)
			Average % of Local Elites Who Feel They Have Power to Act on Local Problems	
Basic Initial Finding for all Elites	55	66	44	22
Subgroups analysis:				
A. Party groups				
"Left"	53	65	42	23
"Center"	55	66	43	23
"Right"	63	71	58	13
B. By position				
Politicians	55	67	46	21
Administrators	55	63	45	18
C. By age groups				
Under 50	55	70	45	25
50 and over	55	63	47	16

The major finding here is that elites in conservative parties are more likely to assert their power to act, in all countries. This would reduce the differential between Sweden and the other two countries if the conservative

TABLE 3.7 The Relevance of Age for Elite Problem Perceptions (Four Age Cohorts)

	United States				Sweden				Netherlands			
	21-39	40-49	50-59	60+	21-39	40-49	50-59	60+	21-39	40-49	50-59	60+
A. Seriousness of Problems: Average % seeing problems as serious	56.0	48.4	47.5	48.3	51.4	62.6	54.9	54.0	63.6	69.5	68.2	72.3
B. Responsibility for Local Government to act: Average % seeing local government having a responsibility (or should have)	52.2	47.3	54.3	62.0	62.3	70.2	72.2	63.3	34.3	35.5	37.5	36.0
C. Power to Act: Average % saying local government has the power	58.7	53.6	56.2	53.2	72.1	69.6	63.6	63.2	49.1	43.1	44.9	51.4
D. Effective Action: Average % saying effective action is being taken on problem	36.8	36.4	31.1	30.5	11.5	10.6	12.5	10.3	18.8	27.2	30.4	40.8
N's	64	84	72	34	23	91	110	82	48	124	84	35

Difference within countries:
Young vs. Old

	United States	Sweden	Netherlands
A	+ 8	- 3	- 9
B	- 10	- 1	- 2
C	+ 5.5	+ 9	- 2
D	+ 6	+ 1	- 22

party elite *proportions were increased* in the U.S. and the Netherlands. But the initial cross system difference would still stand. As would the basic observation that Swedish elites from all parties are consistently more conscious of their power to act, just as they are consistently more conscious of their responsibility to act.

The Explanation of Cross-System Differences

What theory or theories can possibly comprehend such system differences? One approach might be called "the institutional theory of elite differences". That is, systems may differ in their historic, constitutional patterns of local-national power and dependency relationships. One might argue that there has developed over time a stronger tradition in Sweden that local units of government have power and the obligation to solve more problems than is true for the U.S. and the Netherlands. From our comparative survey of the state of central-local relationships, however, this does not seem to be the case. The U.S. cities operate in a decentralized context and the Dutch refer to their system as a "decentralized unitary system". It is interesting that a review of all eleven of the problems reveals a degree of consistency in the tendency of Swedish elites to assert their power and responsibility which belies this interpretation. For example, on the question of the "power to act" the Swedish elites surpass the Dutch elites on all eleven problems, and the American on eight of the eleven. Further, there is no theory of central-state relations based on institutional differences which can explain why on problems like unemployment, poverty, race and ethnic relations, pollution, etc., Swedish elites are more pro-power than Dutch elites or more pro-responsibility than American or Dutch elites. A possible variant of this theory is that in the contemporary period, at the time of our study, central-local government relationships may have been stronger in Sweden (1985) than at the time of fiscal austerity in the Netherlands (in 1989). This conceivably could have led to more anxiety for Dutch local leaders about their problems and their capacities to deal with them. This explanation does not fit the set of American findings, however, and is not convincing in the light of the pervasiveness and consistency of the Dutch findings.

A second theory one might advance related to the first theory, is the "political culture theory". That is, simply, local elite orientations towards political action differ in political systems. Local leaders in every system acquire through the recruitment process, their education and training, and their role socialization in their positions a certain set of perspectives toward their elite positions. They learn how to view themselves as actors within their system. They develop certain orientations about their system of local government, how it works, and the tasks and roles of local leaders in that system. Special cultural orientations such as we have discussed here seem to be diffused throughout the elite levels of the system, transmitted through generations, and shared by politicians and administrators alike. These orientations are components of basic elite conceptions of how the democratic state should function, as well as reflecting personal value preferences acquired by elites during their career life paths. There is not complete homogenization in a system, for "Left" positions may differ somewhat from the "Right", and the old somewhat from the young. But particular orientations exist, grounded in a fundamental concept of government and the deviation from it is not great. This theoretical position may seem to accord more with our facts than the "institutional differences theory". But before accepting this position completely, one must explore elite subcultures and the contexts in which they work further, which is the task of the ensuing section.

Variations in Elite Problem Orientations for the Cities

Much as we might want to generalize for the entire polity, one must recognize community differences and try to develop a theory to comprehend those differences. To establish that communities vary greatly in elite problem perceptions in all three systems is not difficult (Table 3.8). The range in average elite scores for cities is considerable in all countries, particularly in their assessment of the seriousness of the problems, in their feelings about their power to act, and their evaluations of the effectiveness of action. The highest average range is in the U.S., the lowest in Sweden. Examples of extreme inter-community differences are:

Comparison of Cities High and Low on the Dimension:
(% of Elites in Each "High" and "Low" City Who Hold a Position)

	U.S.		Sweden		Netherlands	
	High	Low	High	Low	High	Low
1. Seriousness of pollution problem	85	6	97	18	100	27
- Of housing problem	100	15	78	12	100	38
2. Responsibility for dealing with						
the housing problem	80	27	100	81	93	60
- For pollution problem	45	8	96	67	46	0
3. Power to act on housing Problem	92	23	95	49	83	27
- On pollution	70	7	68	40	63	10

Clearly there is great diversity *across cities* in their beliefs in the need for action and the possibility of action. The extent of elite cohesion or elite dissent by cities varies also with systems and across systems. Generally (that is, in aggregate terms) there appears to be a 50 percent (U.S.) to 67 percent (Netherlands) agreement among elites, for example, as to whether

TABLE 3.8   Community Differences in Elite Problem Perceptions

The measure used is the average % of elites in each city giving a response	United States	Sweden	Netherlands	System Differences (Range)
A. Elites awareness that problems are serious: Range Among Cities				
High	80	75	89	
Low	31	53	49	
Difference	49	22	40	37.0
B. Elites belief that local government has the responsibility to deal with problems (or should have): Range Among Cities				
High	63	80	46	
Low	46	60	30	
Difference	17	20	16	17.7
C. Elites perception that they at the local level have the power to act on those problems: Range Among Cities				
High	68	73	60	
Low	37	55	33	
Difference	31	18	27	25.3
D. Elites evaluation that effective action is being taken on the problems: Range Among Cities				
High	57	23	36	
Low	18	6	19	
Difference	39	17	17	24.3

their problems are serious. But cities differ in the number of problems on which there is "significant elite dissent" (defined as 35 percent to 49 percent minority on a particular problem). We find as follows for elite perceptions of the seriousness of problems, by city:

	U.S.	Sweden	Netherlands
1. Range among cities in number of problems on which in the city there was a significant elite minority	1 to 8	3 to 7	2 to 11
2. Percent of cities with a significant dissent on 4 or more (out of 14) problems	50%	27	45

Individual city analysis thus suggests there is a considerable variation in elite agreement by city, and also by problem area. To cite a few examples— on health, 14 Dutch cities report significant disagreement, three Swedish cities, and five of the American cities. On pollution, Dutch city leaders are very much in agreement (all but one city reporting strong agreement that it is a problem). The same was true in Sweden. In the U.S., however, in half the cities there was a large majority concerned about the pollution problem while in the other half there was strong disagreement, a 55 percent to 45 percent split. In other problem areas such as education, recreation and social welfare, half of the cities had a dominant and consensual elite, and half revealed strong dissensus.

This is evidence again of particularistic patterns of urban, elite behavior, and perhaps of less elite cohesion at the local level (at least in many cities) than at the national level in these systems (Eulau and Prewitt 1973, 483-488). These findings on inter-community variations suggest that *context* or *locale* may be very important. Perhaps more important than the macro-level systemic "culture"? If elites in City A overwhelmingly (80 to 90%) claim they have the power to act on housing, for example, and elites in City B deny this (only one-fourth feel they have such power), then the local context assumes a critical role in explaining differences in elite beliefs and in their interpretations of how the system works.

Variations In the Problem Environments of Cities

Years ago in urban research, it was suggested that each city has a "policy environment" which is a "composite variable" by which we can character- ize a city—the cumulative set of policies which have been adopted to deal with problems.[2] In a similar sense, each city has a "problem environment", the result of policies adopted and not adopted in objective as well as subjective, perceived, terms. Our elite interviews tell us what problems have been satisfactorily addressed by the city's governors (as they see it) and which ones remain, some more serious than others. There are indeed considerable differences *across systems* and *within systems* in the perceived "problem environments" of cities. Cities vary in two basic ways: (1) in the degree and extent of concern elites have about their problems—some cities have very sanguine leaders, others actually alarmist; (2) in the types of problem areas which are the focus of their problem perceptions. If we use the same criterion for determining the *level* of high concern (65 percent of elites or more saying that a problem area is serious) it is clear that these systems differ considerably. There are *no* Swedish cities in which elites are sanguine, only *one* in the Netherlands, and 8 (or 40%) in the U.S.! On the other hand, in European cities we find more frequently extreme concern over these problems (i.e., elites concerned about all or almost all problems at the 65 percent level). Using this measure we find 70 percent of Dutch *cities* whose elites are very concerned, 53 percent of Swedish cities, and only 25 percent of American cities.

The patterns of concerns vary considerably also. If we contrast cities where the elites are sanguine with those where there is considerable concern, we find only economic development is a concern of "sanguine cities". But in "very concerned" cities there is variation on which problems are considered serious. One of the most striking findings perhaps is the high concern of elites for economic welfare of citizens, in most cities in all three countries.

What is clear above all in this analysis is that each city has its agenda of problems, a very extensive list in some and a relatively short list in others. And this variation is true in all countries. The policy problem context within which these leaders work varies greatly, therefore, in content and intensity.

Having established the existence of such sizeable community differences in elite problem perceptions, what approaches can be used to bring some enlightenment to this set of findings? Population size of city is obviously one condition which might be related to the incidence of problems as reported to us by elites. The larger the community, the more likely the existence of problems of the type we have investigated here. And we indeed find some evidence of this relationship. It is a stronger relationship for the U.S. than for the European democracies. And it does not hold true for all problems. In the U.S., for example, poverty, unemployment and pollution are problems perceived by elites as critical in small cities as in the larger cities at the time of this study. In Sweden and the Netherlands, health, housing, social welfare and unemployment were cited as frequently as serious in small cities as in larger cities. In the Netherlands this was also true for pollution. There is some connection, then, of size to problem perceptions but it is not an overwhelmingly important factor, nor consistently linked.

The actual correlations of population size with elite perceptions of the seriousness of problems document these findings and reveal the differences by systems:

Correlations of Population Size of Cities and Elite Perceptions of the Seriousness of Problems (The Most Significant Findings)

	U.S.	Sweden	Netherlands
For all 14 problems	.438	.401	.094
Education	.529	.511	.241
Safety	.649	.503	.217
Health	.557	—	−.633
Poverty	—	.488	—
Welfare	.365	—	—
Housing	.325	—	−.360
Race (or Immigration)	—	.684	.297
Pollution	—	.471	—

Clearly, population size is less relevant in the Netherlands (at least among the cities included in this study). For the U.S. and Sweden there are some very strong relationships, however.

Secondly, as one might have expected, particular economic or social conditions in cities are linked to certain problems. If we group cities by their level of unemployment we find, particularly for the U.S., a much higher likelihood that elites will report the need for jobs as a serious problem when unemployment is high: 91 percent in the cities highest in unemployment, 42 percent in the cities with less unemployment. This is not as true for the European cities. Similarly, in U.S. cities with the highest proportions of blacks 61 percent see race relations as a serious problem, compared to only 7 percent in cities with a small black population.

It is clear that in general the economic climate of a city is linked to elite perceptions. The *Pearson* correlations for some of these community variables reveal the variance across system:

	Correlations With Percent of Elites, By Cities, Seeing All 14 Problems As Serious		
	U.S.	Sweden	Netherlands
Median family income	−.287	−.322	−.536
Unemployment rate	.509	−.220	.500
Poverty level	.699	—	—

The anomaly is Sweden (for unemployment level). One explanation of this for Sweden is that the variation in unemployment rate there is small. Otherwise, the picture is quite consistent. See Table 3.9 for further illustrations of these relationships.

A third approach is to group cities by their partisan character to see if cities with a "Left" (Democratic or Social Democratic or Labor) party dominance have elites with different problem perceptions than cities where conservative or centre/right forces are dominant. The *Pearson* correlation coefficients by city for the relationship of "Left" party strength to overall perception of the seriousness of problems (for all 14 problems) were: U.S. .232, Sweden .045, Netherlands .242. There is apparently no relationship in Sweden and modest relationship for the U.S. and the Netherlands.

We present illustrations in Table 3.10. In the U.S. the Democratic cities have elites who are more inclined to see certain problems as serious (such as race, housing, pollution, social welfare) than do the elites in strong Republican cities. This is also true for elite perceptions of the existence of unemployment and poverty problems, but much less so for such problems as safety, education, and health. One might argue that such a finding is to be expected because the "Democratic cities" are those with the most severe economic conditions. But in reality this is not entirely true, as the following reveals:

	Poverty level (Means)	Unemployment Level (Means)
The 10 strongest Democratic cities	8.28	9.30
The 10 strongest Republican cities	8.24	6.73

The range in unemployment rate for "Democratic" cities was 2.4 to 20.5; for "Republican" cities it was 2.6 to 11.6. For percentage of population below

TABLE 3.9 The Linkage of Objective Community Data to Elite Perceptions of Problems (Average % of elites who see the problem as serious)

Classification of Cities	U.S.	Sweden	Netherlands
1. The Unemployment Problem			
- Cities with the highest unemployment rate	91	100	99
- Cities with the lowest unemployment rate	42	94	76
2. The Education Problems			
- Cities with highest educational levels	42	61	
- Cities with lowest educational levels	52	65	
3. The Problem of Race Relations (U.S. only)			
- Cities with high % of the population black (12-71%)	61		
- Cities with small % of the population black (2-8%)	26		
- Cities with virtually no black in the population (.05-1.0%)	7		

Note: The categories of cities were as follows:

	U.S. (1980)	Sweden (1984)	Netherlands (1989)
1. On unemployment rate:			
- Upper group	7.4-20.5%	2.9 - 4.2%	12.2-27.7%
- Lower group	2.4-5.6%	.7 - 2.7%	5.0-11.6%
2. On educational levels of population (% of population 25 years and over with a high school education or equivalent)			
- Upper group	65.8-91.3%	55.0-68.0%	
- Lower group	56.2-65.6%	46.0-52.0%	

the poverty level, the ranges were: "Democratic" cities 2.5 to 16.9; for "Republican" cities 2.2 to 12.8. Thus, elite perceptions of problems in "Democratic" cities, higher than in "Republican" cities, is not clearly and primarily a function of the economic conditions of these cities.

In Sweden and the Netherlands, we do not find such consistent and significant evidence supporting the American argument. In fact the Swedish findings are contrary somewhat to the American findings, if they are significant at all. It is the Swedish elites in cities which the conservatives control who are more likely to emphasize the existence of problems such as social welfare, immigration or housing. On problems such as pollution, safety, education there are no differences by cities based on the partisan strength variable. For the Netherlands there is some evidence that this variable may be of some explanatory value for certain problems, particu-

TABLE 3.10 The Partisan Character of the Community as a Condition Relevant to Elite Perceptions of Selected Problems as Serious (Percentages)

Division of Cities Based on Partisan Dominance Patterns in Elections	United States				Sweden			
	Housing	Pollution	Race	Welfare	Housing	Pollution	Race	Welfare
"Left" (or Socialist) Parties Dominant	56	50	31	52	32	75	29	48
Centre/Right (or Bourgeois) Parties Dominant	49	37	16	37	48	74	34	67

	Netherlands			
	Housing	Pollution	Race	Welfare
"Left" Parties Dominant	81	83	71	76
Centre/Right Parties Dominant	82	85	49	66

Note: The categories of cities were as follows: (based on election data)

	U.S	Sweden[*]	Netherlands
"Left" Dominance	45 to 70% Dem.	53 to 66% Left	41 to 45% Left
Centre/Right Dominance	23 to 40% Dem.	27 to 52% Left	17 to 40% Left

[*] Swedish election data are actually based on the percentage of party seats held in the communal council.

larly for social welfare and immigration (or race). On these two types of problems, the Dutch resemble the Americans. Thus, this approach to the analysis of community differences seems to be somewhat more useful in the U.S. than in these European systems.

A fourth approach is what might be called "the dominant elite" theory. The hypothesis is that the elite which constitutes the majority (or strong plurality) in a community will influence other elites to support the dominant elite position. Thus, for example, Democrats in Republican dominated cities will be more likely to support "the Republican position" than would Democrats in other communities where Republicans are not dominant. Similarly, Republicans would move toward an acceptance of Democratic positions in cities where Democrats are in control. In a sense this is an application of the early "clustering effect" thesis of Herbert Tingsten (1937), or the "breakage effect" of Berelson, Lazarsfeld and McPhee (1954). Tingsten showed how the working class vote was heavier for socialist parties in areas where they (the working class) were more numerous (Tingsten, 177-180). And Berelson and his colleagues described the tendency of the social forces in a community to pull others in the direction of the general community, i.e., the dominant political climate (Berelson et al. 1954). Other scholars have reflected on and analyzed this phenomenon in different ways. Eulau and Prewitt classified city councils on their "collegiality" (Eulau and Prewitt 1973, 127-137). Verba and Nie on the "concurrence" of local leaders with the policy views of the community activists (Verba and Nie 1972, 302-308). A Dutch scholar, Toonen, advances a similar theory as ours:

> "The political preferences and preferred strategies of a Social Democratic alderman in a predominantly Christian Democratic city... may differ from the preferences of his colleagues from a big city... where Social Democrats are the dominant party" (Toonen 1987, 119).

This is the basic proposition we are now advancing as a major explanation for what happens also to local community elites. They tend to "join the bandwagon", to gravitate to the dominant elite position as a result of what Lindblom calls "mutual adjustment tendencies", interaction, discussion, as well as the influence by dominant leaders over others. In a sense, this means that they may desert the position of their partisan colleagues in other communities.

There are three possible hypotheses which one could advance here. These are:

1. A dominant party's leaders influence the positions of opposition leaders in a city. If the dominant party is positive or negative, the opposition parties tend to follow the lead of that party.

2. When no party is dominant and political control in the city is split, competition induces most leaders to take the same position, either positive or negative.
3. A contrary hypothesis: The political status of a party in a city, whether dominant or oppositional, is irrelevant; the party has a basic perceptual, attitudinal, or value position which it adheres to in all cities irrespective of the political control situation.

What do our data indicate? We test these propositions with the responses of elites to the responsibility question—whether local government has (or should have) the (primary) responsibility to deal with these specific problems.

There is strong evidence in our date for the first proposition (Table 3.11). In all three countries, if the dominant party takes a positive position on the responsibility of local government, the other leaders seem to accept the leadership of the dominant party and "climb on the bandwagon." When the dominant party opposes local government responsibility there is a striking "fall off" for the opposition party leaders' acceptance of responsibility. The differentials are as follows:

	Change In a Feeling Responsibility By the Opposition Parties
U.S.	37%
Sweden	17%
Netherlands	29%

Many examples could be cited. On housing policy in the U.S., for example, when either major party is dominant in a city *and* feels local government has the responsibility, 68 percent of the opposition leaders agree. But when the dominant party is negative or split on whether housing is or should be a local responsibility only 39 percent of the other leaders are positive. An example for the Netherlands is on the policy of public improvements. If the dominant Dutch party in the city (Labor, CDA, or VVD) is positive on the local responsibility question, 66 percent of the other parties agree; if the dominant party is negative only 49 percent agree. (Sweden examples are difficult to come by since in so many cities there is such a strong consensus on responsibility.)

Before completely accepting this "dominant elite majority" thesis, however, one should note that when no party is dominant in these cities and the parties are very competitive, there is a fairly high proportion of elites who have a sense of responsibility for local initiative. The proportions are not as high as when there is a dominant party which favors responsibility, but still relatively favorable to the idea of local government responsibility. Table

3.11 documents this. It appears that party *competition* as well as party *dominance* can be functionally conducive to the assumption of responsibility by local elites. These findings suggest that the political subculture of the city is very relevant for explaining elite orientations. Political forces socialize elites, pressure elites and constrain elites to adopt particular positions related to policy action and particularly increase responsibility.

Conclusions

We have found important uniformities and many nonequivalencies in the ways local elites perceive and evaluate their problems. We also have found that factors such as age, position, and party operate differently across these cultures. "Left" partisans as well as "Centre" and "Right" partisans are not uniform across systems in their problem orientations. Elite subgroups differ in the three countries. But elites within systems *seem* to be homogeneous. This suggests that one should jump to the conclusion that nationally local

TABLE 3.11 The Influence of Party Dominance or Party Division in Cities on Elite Orientations Toward Responsibility

	Summary of Basic Findings		
% of elites who say	*In cities where one party is dominant*		*In cities where there*
local government has or should have responsibility for action (average on 11 issues)	*and the leaders of this party tend to be positive on responsibility*	*and the leaders of this party tend to be negative on responsibility*	*is no dominant party % of leaders of all parties who favor local responsibility*
United States			
1. % of leaders of dominant party favoring responsibility	81	28	
2. % of leaders of other parties favoring responsibility	75	38	55
Sweden			
1. % of leaders of dominant party favoring responsibility	80	33	
2. % of leaders of other parties favoring responsibility	76	59	74
Netherlands			
1. % of leaders of dominant party favoring responsibility	76	33	
2. % of leaders of other parties favoring responsibility	71	42	59

Note: A combination of data from local elections, seats on councils, and the party affiliation of elites in our samples was used to classify the cities in each system.

elite cultures are somewhat distinctive, in the aggregate and for certain elite subgroups. The special institutions and elite cultural traditions of a country *seem* to be determinative. These elites seem to be not only specially socialized to certain perceptions and evaluations, they also seem to be responding to the special conditions, needs, and expectations of their societies. What complicates the task of generalization greatly is that we also find that the individual community is also very important. Elite views seem to be often largely fashioned by and responsive to the particular economic conditions and political governance of the particular city in which these leaders have grown up. Our comparative theory must be built on that kind of empirical understanding. Nation-to-nation variance in local elite perspectives if at all true, certainly needs to be qualified by community-to-community variance, which is equally (perhaps more) true.

This analysis of elite perceptions of, and responses to, their problems can evoke considerable bewilderment as well as concern. What seems to be the state of local "elitism" in these Western democracies? We have referred to several "puzzles" which emerge from the data. One is that on some issues, elite expressions of concern may not jibe with objective reality (such as the perceived unemployment in Sweden). One wonders to what extent these elites are realists. Of course, if the goal is employment for everyone, the perception of any unemployment may be "serious." Swedish socialists have always seen any unemployment as a problem. A second "puzzle" concerns the disagreements among elites in the same country as to whether they have the power to act (on housing, for example, there is a 50 to 60 percentage point differential by city on the question of authority to act). One wonders whether these elites understand their power and institutional contexts. A third puzzle is to what extent local elites believe they have or should have the responsibility to act. If they do have the power, why should they say they should be given the responsibility? The Swedish responses seem particularly confusing on this point. The explanation may lie in the intense decentralization debate on this question which began already in the Seventies and continued at the time of our study in 1984-1985. The question at that time was whether even more responsibility for making policy decisions should be given to local government, especially for health and care for the elderly. And this may explain the confusion apparent in our Swedish responses. As we shall see in the analysis of values later, over 90 percent of these Swedish leaders favored more commune autonomy.

A fourth puzzle is, of course, the low proportion of elites in all systems who say that effective action is being taken to deal with their problems. This raises all sorts of questions (including the meaning of "effective" and "action"). It does seem to suggest that local elites may indeed be realists in their evaluations, a realism which leads them to a sort of "self-demeaning" or "local government demeaning" cynicism. It is difficult to see any cross-system rationale for these patterns. The tendencies noted here hold for welfare-state systems in Europe as well as for the U.S. Ironically, perhaps the only difference is that there are more U.S. cities in our sample with elites sanguine about their problems than in the welfare state systems in Europe!

There are several other disturbing or provocative types of findings which should be pointed to in a summing up. When local elites confront their problems, the level of their concern for certain modern problems is not high. In the U.S. there is low recognition that race, health, pollution, for example, are serious local problems; in Sweden it is health and immigration; in the Netherlands, despite the high average level of concerns for all problems, on health and education the proportions expressing concern are relatively low.

Yet, it is not the question of level of concern which is most disturbing. Rather it is, a sense of limited responsibility (Netherlands) or of needing more responsibility, or perhaps abdication of responsibility at the level of local government. This is more so for the Netherlands whose elites are very likely to say that they have more power than responsibility in most of those policy areas. But even in the U.S. (except for public improvements, economic development, recreation, and public safety) 50 percent or more of the local leaders imply that they do not have responsibility and should have more (on race, health, housing, pollution, etc.).

Finally, what is most disturbing in these data is the disjunction between *power* and *action*. On the eleven problems, here is the basic data on that disjunction:

	U.S.	Sweden	Netherlands
Elite Average			
Have the power	55.0%	66.0	43.6
Say that effective action is taken	26.5	12.5	26.0

Even in problem areas considered serious, this striking disjunction persists, although the discrepancy is less in the Netherlands, primarily because of the lower perception of the power to act. If we take the five most serious problems in each country (excluding unemployment and poverty since they are in two of these countries least likely to be seen as the province of local government), we find this disjunction:

	U.S.	Sweden	Netherlands
% saying the problems are serious	57	70	76
% admit that they have power to act	63	63	45
% reporting effective action	36	14	36

Elites in effect say that they and their colleagues do not act or have not acted, when they could. And this is true in welfare states in Europe as well as in the U.S. This is a major puzzle to unravel. Is there some intervening factor to explain this? Lack of financial resources? If so, it must be argued differently for the three countries. In the Netherlands which secures 90 percent of its income from the Central government, one might try to attribute this action or ineffective action to the decisions at "the top." In the U.S., it must be explained in a different way, since in the Eighties municipalities had to (and could) generate their resources locally. In Sweden, in between these two systems, the argument can only partially approximate that of the Dutch. But this explanation is not really satisfactory. Certainly effective action is possible despite the alleged inadequacy of, and attrition in, resources. The key finding is that while macro-level or national level percentages of elites' reports of effective action are abysmally low, the individual city reports reveal that effective action is being taken, by certain cities on certain problems in each system. The inter-city variations in elite reports of policy action are crucial in this regard. We have reported on this in general in the preceding analysis. Here are the significant data by policy area:

	% of Elites By City Reporting Effective Action					
	U.S.		Sweden		Netherlands	
	High City	Low City	High City	Low City	High City	Low City
Policy Area:						
Housing	92	19	39	0	65	9
Recreation	60	0	53	0	89	14
Pollution	75	7	27	0	75	0
Economic Development	70	7	27	3	75	0
Social Welfare	46	0	29	4	61	6
Public Improvements	62	17	46	4	80	0
Health	50	0	23	0	67	0
Education	69	0	54	10	71	8
Race or Immigrant Relations	46	0	28	0	72	0
Average Differences:	57		34		69	

Clearly neither central-state relationships, nor financial resources limits, nor a welfare state ideology have placed the leadership of all these cities in a straitjacket of policy inaction. In some cities in all three countries, these leaders report much action is being taken, despite the alleged systemic restrains. And that may be the most important message emerging from our analysis. Leadership in some cities claims they can act, and claims they have acted, on some very difficult policy problems. In other cities there is operational stagnation.

Notes

1. In a study of public attitudes Sidney Verba and his associates conducted with the NORC in 1967 they found a low level of *public* support in the U.S. for the responsibility of local government to solve problems. For instance, only 29% felt that local government had a major responsibility to provide adequate housing. Verba and Nie 1972, 372-373.

2. A similar analysis was done in the 1965 California study of 82 cities, finding that 60 percent of the city councils had majority agreement on broad problem areas. See Eulau and Prewitt 1973, 530-43.

4

Elite Perceptions of
Conflicts in Their Communities

Politics has much to do with societal divisions and conflict, reflecting antagonisms among social interests. The leadership of any community must cope with such tensions, some of which are more basic and enduring than others. The role of politics is not always clear in dealing with conflicts, and it varies over time and by community. Whether politics has the role of "resolution" of conflicts, or their "management," or their "containment," or even their exacerbation can long be argued. Knowledge of the cleavage and conflict *context* within which leaders must function is critical for understanding their performance. Ideally we need a detailed mapping of the conflicts in each community. But in a comparative study of many cities as this such detailed and precise data for each community are difficult to secure. We use here the reports from our local elites about the "differences which divide people in your community." These perceptions plus their evaluations of the relevance of such divisions for effective action, and for the development of the community, constitute the type of raw material we have available for analysis. We also ask their value positions on political conflict, and the link of these values to their perceptions and evaluations will be explored.

The scholarly approach to the study of conflict has been diverse and controversial. The argument over many years has addressed a variety of issues: the importance of conflict and its desirability; the functions which the expression and representation of conflict serve—political change or stability; the durability or transitory character of community conflicts; the sources of conflict—economic, sociological, political, or psychological; and the relevance or impact of conflict, and of elite conflict perceptions, for political attitudes and political action (Eldersveld and Siemienska 1989, 309-329). Dahrendorf has argued the importance of conflict and its value for social change: "by conflict alone the multitude and incompatibility of human interests and desires find adequate expression in a world of notorious uncertainty." Conflict is linked not only to system effectiveness and system stability. Dahl takes the same position, decrying "the stability fetish" among certain scholars and stating that "conflict and change" are necessary, and not threatening, for democracy.

In describing and analyzing elite perceptions of conflicts in their cities we are interested in three questions which other scholars have dealt with. One is the variation across cities and nations in the extent and types of conflict. How indigenous or how generalizable are they? Are conflicts locale-specific, or nation-specific, or uniform across democracies? Are the conditions of American, Dutch and Swedish social, economic and political life such as to reveal their populations as divided differently or similarly? Second, what are the sources of these conflict patterns? Since we are asking elites to give us their perceptions and evaluations, are their responses a reflection of their own values or predispositions about conflict with some elites more sensitive and perceptive than others? Or are elites influenced by their position, by their party, or other socializing agencies? Or are their perceptions a product of their close proximity to the realities of life in their particular community, or of their exposure to a particular political culture? Third, what is the relevance of elite conflict perceptions for other elite attitudes and behavioral inclinations? Which model is more valid?

Only limited research is available on these matters. Studies of national elites document significant differences by nation in the proportions who perceived conflict as typical or dominant (Putnam 1973, 101; Eldersveld and Siemienska 1989, 313). These studies have explored the role of position (whether elected politician or bureaucrat), of party and ideology, as well as social class origins as determinants of elite views on conflict. They conclude that all of these factors may have explanatory utility. This poses a basic query for us—are elite conflict orientations a product of early socialization to politics, or the result of exposure to party and group politics, or explicable in terms of the community context in which they are leaders? Putnam argued: "Perspectives on social conflict...seem to be laid down fairly early in life, (to be) relatively immune from the impact of later, more overtly political experience" (Putnam 1973, 136). How can we square this with contextual theory?

Elite conflict orientations are seen by several scholars as linked to other attitudes and even community activeness. They influence a leader's role perceptions as well as his or her approach to specific problems and their resolution. They also are related to a leader's support for pluralist politics, particularly the participatory role of citizens in the system (Putnam 1973, 118-121; Aberbach 1981, 170-208; Eldersveld 1981, 121-124). In the early "Values Project", the four country study of elite values and community activeness, it was found that for the U.S. where political leaders in cities held a pro-conflict value orientation there was more likely to be community activeness and participation, whereas in cities where leaders took negative views on political conflict there was less community activeness (Jacob 1971, 309). For other countries in this study (Poland, India, Yugoslavia) the reverse finding emerged: elite conflict was not conducive to community activeness. Such findings from previous research, although time-bound and place-specific, provide a backdrop for our research.

We asked three questions of our local leaders in the present study:

1. "Are there some major conflicts which interfere with getting things done in your community?" (Yes or No). If Yes, would you please name one or two?
2. "To what extent do these conflicts come in the way of the development of your community?" (Very much, Some).
3. "To what extent do differences such as the following tend to divide people in your community?" (Very much, Somewhat, Not at all). (Eight types of differences are listed).

In addition there were seven agree-disagree items presented to the respondent which were used to build a value scale called the "conflict resolution scale" (See Chapter Seven). With minor language changes these were used in all three countries.

Our theoretical concerns are basically the same here as in our discussion of problem perceptions in the previous chapter. We look first at the extent of cross national uniformity in the findings. Then we seek to explain system differences by an analysis of elite subgroup patterns within and across systems. We then report in detail on the differences by community, in an effort to see to what extent conflict perceptions are explicable contextually. Finally, we seek to link conflict perceptions to values and other attitudinal and behavioral variables. In all this we keep the focus on the major question: Are elite attitudes and perceptions about conflict trans-national or are there local elite political cultures which are distinguishable nationally, or locally?

How Comparable Are the Conflict Perceptions of Elites Across Countries?

We asked all respondents to indicate one or two major conflicts which interfere with getting things done in their community. Hopefully what emerged from this open question is a set of priority or salient concerns over conflicts. It is perhaps noteworthy that the first system difference which appeared is that over 70 percent of the Swedish elites mentioned no major conflicts, compared to 45 percent of the Dutch and 30 percent of the Americans. For those who had such priority concerns there were, again, differences by country. The breakdown of responses is as follows, using all the types of conflicts which were mentioned:

	Most Salient Concerns		
	U.S.	Sweden	Netherlands
1. Conflicts about the performance or conduct of leaders in the government or their relationship to each other.	31%	23%	24%
2. Conflicts over policy matters or issue positions.	19	43	5
3. Political or social group conflicts or rivalries.	25	20	33
4. Conflicts in intergovernmental relations with other units of government.	20	0	38
5. Miscellaneous conflicts.	5	14	0

The Swedish leaders are much more conscious of conflicts which have a policy focus while the Dutch more frequently mention conflicts with other units of government or other cities. The Dutch also tend to emphasize political or social group conflicts more. Yet there is little saliency in all three countries of social class conflict. The Americans are somewhat more inclined to report conflicts which focus on governmental leadership relationships and performance. While there seem to be national differences in types of conflict which are salient, leaders' responses are also linked to the locality. Hence they can be interpreted as probably relevant at both the macro and micro level of politics.

In order to structure the analysis of comparability we asked all elites in each country a series of identical questions about conflicts ("differences" which "divide people") in their communities. A methodological point should be made here in the use of these data. The phrasing of the question assumes that we can tap important disagreements and antagonisms ("conflicts") by presenting respondents with eight possible "divisions" between types of city residents. We ask them to respond "very much," "somewhat," or "not at all." This phraseology can be considered as more subdued than using the word "conflicts." Nevertheless, we do ask them directly whether there is evidence of considerable division or disagreement in a variety of potential cleavage areas: employer-employee relations, religious beliefs, income levels, educational levels, views about social change, age group differences, and central city versus suburbanites, and in political views. We assume that we are therefore securing from these leaders, as expert informants about their communities, reliable insights on what types of conflicts are very evident and which ones are only of moderate importance, and which are unimportant. We think this is a fair assumption.

The results are presented in Table 4.1. For these eight types of conflicts there are considerable differences. Swedish and American elites see much more conflict than do the Dutch—on average a differential of about 30%. On social status or class differences (income, education, and worker-manager conflicts) the system contrasts are at the 40% level. But one should note that in both the U.S. and Sweden there is a considerable awareness of social class differences. Religious conflicts are relatively minimal and more similar by

TABLE 4.1   Elite Perceptions of the Existence of Specific Conflicts in Their Communities

	U.S.		Sweden		Netherlands		
	Very Much	Total % Seeing Conflict	Very Much	Total % Seeing Conflict	Very Much	Total % Seeing Conflict	Range for 3 systems (very much/ somewhat)
To what extent do differences such as the following divide people in your community?							
1. Differences in education	10	74	27	89	2	34	40
2. Differences in income	21	84	32	91	6	52	39
3. Differences in religious beliefs	6	43	9	46	4	25	21
4. Differences in political views	20	77	19	70	6	50	27
5. Differences between city residents and suburbanites	19	50	12	69	5	42	27
6. Differences between manager an employees	8	63	10	71	1	32	39
7. Differences between those desiring social change and those opposing it	17	76	16	71	5	56	20
8. Differences between the young and old	5	60	10	73	5	56	17
Means	13.3	65.9	17.0	72.6	4.1	43.1	29.5

system. Why the Dutch elites should be comparatively so much more unaware of, or reluctant to report, group and class conflicts, given the history of social segmentation and polarization in Holland, is difficult to explain easily. Perhaps the gradual disappearance of those sharp divisions in Dutch society (the "Zuilen") and the appearance of cooperative associations as well as the actual merging of political, trade union, and other groups has led to elite perceptions which now correctly deemphasize group and class conflict. In any event, whatever the explanation (and it is surely both more complex and subtle than we have indicated), the Dutch persistently differ from the U.S. and Swedish elites. It is true that the rank orders of types of conflicts are quite similar for the three countries if one uses the proportion who see "very much" conflict, as the following summary reveals:

		Most Important Conflicts Rank Orders for Elite Perceptions	
Conflicts:	U.S.	Sweden	Netherlands
Over Income Differences	1	1	1-2
Over Political Views	2	3	1-2
Over the Need for Social Change	4	4	4

In the U.S. city, suburban relations rank 3rd, in Sweden educational differences rank second, while in the Netherlands young versus old differences rank high also. Despite such patterns of similarity, however, the great differences in elite recognition of conflicts remain. Dutch elites are strikingly dissimilar, in that few Dutch local leaders say there is "very much" of *any* conflict in their communities.

These system differences in elite perceptions of conflict become more interesting, as well as puzzling, when evaluative responses are analyzed. (Table 4.2). While Swedish elites report the highest awareness of the existence of conflict, they are the least concerned about the impact of conflict. While the Dutch elites reveal the lowest awareness of the existence of conflicts they are much more concerned about their interference with effective action, and also high (with American elites) in their concern for the relevance of conflicts for community development. Here is a simple summary:

	U.S.	Sweden	Netherlands
Average % seeing conflict (very much or somewhat)	66	73	43
% seeing conflict as interfering with action	64	24	53
% seeing conflict as interfering with development	67	24	51

TABLE 4.2   Country Differences in Elite Conflict Perceptions: Summary of Findings

	U.S.	Sweden	Netherlands	System Differences (Range)
A. Awareness of Conflicts				
Average % who say 8 types of				
"divisions" exist in their community.				
- Very much	13	17	4	
- Somewhat	53	56	39	30
- Not at all	30	26	52	
	96	99	95	
B. Evaluation of Impact of Conflicts				
1. Are there conflicts which				
interfere with effective action to				
meet community problems?				
- Yes	64	24	53	40
- No	36	76	47	
2. To what extent do these conflicts				
come in the way of the development				
of your community?				
- Very much	27	9	19	18
- Somewhat	40	15	34	25
- No conflicts interfere				
(or no response)	33	76	47	43
N	260	389	305	

(1) The eight types of conflict are: in education, income, religious beliefs, political views, between city residents and suburbanites, between manager and employees, between those favoring social change and those opposing it, between young and old.
(2) The missing data are excluded from B1 calculations. The B2 question as used in Sweden and the Netherlands screened out all those respondents replying *No* to the B1 question.

The Dutch are consistently concerned, the Swedish consistently sanguine, the Americans most concerned in their evaluations of the effect of conflict.

Explanations of System Differences: Variations by Elite Subgroups

A large number of local elites operate with a "conflict perception model" of local government. They are not inclined to be alarmists about the presence of conflict, however, since no more than one-fifth to one-fourth take extreme positions (say there is "very much" conflict) in either reporting the *existence* of conflict or in *evaluating* the impact of conflict on local development. Nevertheless, while not extremists, a large percentage is conscious of some kind of conflict. Two-thirds or more of the American and Swedish elites reveal such awareness, while over 40% of the Dutch do. And while the Swedes downplay conflict's negative effects, 50% or more of the Dutch and Americans feel conflict may be dysfunctional. Thus, in one sense or another social and political conflict is a concern of 40% to 70% of these local leaders.

This pattern of findings in some respects appears to be remarkably similar overall to the findings from the cross national study of national political and administrative elites in the Seventies (Aberbach 1981, 144-147). That study was done in the U.S. and six European countries. Approximately one-half of the MP's and bureaucrats at the national level felt that conflict was typical in their systems, that conflicting interests were clearly discernible in the policy process, and that inter-party differences were prominent. Particularly, social class and socioeconomic group differences were important to perhaps half of these national leaders.

Although this was the general pattern for national elites, if one looks more carefully at the differences by particular systems the findings reveal contrasts for national elites. As for *awareness* of the existence of conflicts, Dutch politicians were high (78% reported important conflicts) while the Swedes were low (45%). The Americans were also high (68%). As for *concern* about conflict, that is, their reconcilability, the Dutch national politicians were also high (58%) while both the American and Swedish MP's were low (16% and 24%, respectively) (Eldersveld 1981, 236-240).

The findings from our study of local elites, although conducted a decade later, can be compared with these national elite findings. We focus on the elected politicians here for whom we have complete data. While on the average we find about the same level of *awareness* of conflict (61%) there is somewhat higher *concern* about the implications of conflict at the local level (48% of the local politicians are concerned compared to one-third of the national MP's).[1] Of more importance, however, are the *system differences*. Significant disjunctions occur between the conflict perceptions of national and local elites, and they vary by country. A summary of these data highlights both these disjunctions and congruences:

	U.S.	Sweden	Netherlands
% aware of conflict			
National MP's	68	45	78
Local Politicians	65	71	46
% concerned about conflict			
resolution or impact			
National MP's	16	24	58
Local Politicians	65	25	55

Swedish and Dutch politicians disagree (comparing national and local leaders) on *how much* conflict there is while American leaders show high congruence. But Swedish and Dutch politicians (national compared to local) are remarkably in agreement on whether conflict is harmful or reconcilable—the Dutch high, the Swedish low. American national and local leaders are in striking disagreement, however, on whether conflict is resolvable or harmful to the achievement of development goals.

If we keep in mind the time difference between the national studies (early Seventies) and the more recent local studies these data suggest both changes and continuities in elite perceptions. The Swedish elites appear *more* aware of conflicts now, the Dutch *less*, the Americans *no change*. It seems that the Dutch have left their segmental conflicts behind and now reflect more shared and consensual perceptions.

One way to picture the way these systems differ in the comparison of national and local politicians' view is shown in the accompanying diagram:

Elites Concern about Impact of Conflict (% Concerned)

		National Leaders	
		High Level of Concern	Low Level of Concern
Local Leaders	High Level of Concern	Netherlands	U.S.
	Low Level of Concern		Sweden

On the dimension of elite conflict orientations obviously systems differ greatly as to the level of concern among national elites and local elites. Our focus in the analysis here is on the extent of cross-system differences among local elites. And the question is, how can we best explain these differences? The magnitude of these differences can be summarized as follows:

All Local Elites	U.S.	Sweden	Netherlands	Range across 3 Systems
1. % who see conflicts dividing people (averages on 8 types of conflicts)	66	73	43	30
2. % who evaluate conflicts negatively as interfering with development	67	24	53	43

To attempt a first explanation we look at the responses of the politicians and administrators separately (Table 4.3). What one finds is remarkable similarity in the views of local leaders *irrespective of position*, and a persistence, therefore, of these system differences. Take, for example, the contrast between the local leaders of Sweden and the U.S. on the question of whether conflicts interfere with development. The Americans, we found, tend to say "yes" (67%), the Swedes "no" (only 24% "yes"). But administrators and politicians do not differ radically on this question in these two countries. If we had found that bureaucrats were much more negative in their responses than the politicians, we would have had a cross-national finding of interest, and one which might have thrown some light on our general observation of system differences. However, this we do not find. Politicians in two of the countries (Sweden and the Netherlands) are more concerned than bureaucrats. But the important observations are: (1) high congruence *within* each country for politicians and administrators, and (2) in Sweden politicians *and* administrators are much more sanguine, take quite a different view of conflict, than in the other two countries.

"Subgroup analysis", hence, establishes clearly that cross-system differences are most relevant, *not* within system differences by position.

Similarly, on the existence of conflicts, the Dutch elites, both administrators and politicians, consistently play down conflict in their responses, even where one might have expected otherwise. Here are a few examples:

	Administrators			Politicians		
	U.S.	Sweden	Neth.	U.S.	Sweden	Neth.
% saying there is conflict on:						
1. Religion	42	51	20	41	41	30
2. Education	77	92	35	73	86	35
3. Political Views	9	69	46	76	73	57
4. Worker-manager Relations	68	69	30	60	68	36
Means	66.5	70.3	32.8	62.5	67.0	39.5

There appears to be an elite conflict orientation norm which is internalized in, and perpetuated by, their individual systems, and whether these leaders are bureaucrats or politicians makes no real difference.

A second subgroup analysis involves the party system. Putnam has argued that political leaders of the "Left" persuasion are more inclined to "stress conflict" while "rightists stress harmony", yet his data show the far Right is also quite conflict oriented (Putnam 1973, 106, 129). The seven-nation study of national leaders did indeed demonstrate that Left partisans are more likely to operate with a conflict model of politics (Eldersveld 1981, 240). But there were important system differences. For the countries in our present study, the differences for national MP's were:

	% seeing little or no conflict		% feeling conflict is not reconcilable	
	Left	Centre/Right	Left	Centre/Right
U.S.	35	33	11	6
Sweden	20	84	27	5
Netherlands	5	44	50	19

"Left" MP's were much more aware of conflict (than MP's of the Centre/ Right) in Sweden and the Netherlands, but there was no real difference for U.S. Democratic or Republican Congressmen. Dutch MP's of the "Left" were also much more concerned about the resolvability of conflicts and the American Congressmen not very concerned at all, whether Democrats or

TABLE 4.3 Subgroup Analysis for Elite Conflict Perceptions: Politicians and Administrators

	U.S		Sweden		Netherlands		System Differences	
	Pol.	Adm.	Pol.	Adm.	Pol.	Adm.	Pol.	Adm.
A. Eight specific conflicts at mass level:								
1. Average % seeing "very much" conflict	13	14	16	16	5	4		
2. Average % seeing "very much" or "some" conflict	65	67	71	73	47	43	25	33
B. Evaluation of extent conflicts come in the way of community development:								
1. Very much	27	27	12	6	21	16		
2. Somewhat	38	40	13	6	34	33		
	65	67	25	12	55	49	40	55
Difference Between Politicians and Administrators:								
A. (2)	2		2		4		8	
B. (Total)	2		13		6		15	
N	128	132	272	117	196	99		

Republicans. Except for the U.S., then, we find fairly sharp differences by party at the national level: "Leftists" indeed do see more conflict and are more concerned about its effects; Centre/Right politicians are more sanguine.

Turning to our local elite data by party, we find much less evidence of the left-right differences which were noted among national elites, either in the awareness of the existence of conflict or in evaluations of the consequences of conflict (Table 4.4). The largest difference is the twenty points which separate the Democrats and the Republicans in the U.S. on the evaluation of conflicts. Partisans of the "Left" do tend to be more conscious of conflict, but the within-country party differences are small. It appears that at the local government level partisan differences, in the aggregate by country, do not make as much difference as one might have expected. Cross-system differences are, again, more prominent. That is, local Dutch leaders are much less conscious of conflict *irrespective of party* than in the U.S. or Sweden. And in Sweden there is very low concern about the impact of conflict on development *irrespective of party*. Put another way, the differences across systems in local elites views on conflict are reinforced by findings about left-right partisan orientations. The following summary documents this conclusion:

	U.S.	Sweden	Netherlands	System Difference
Original finding for all local elites on % who see conflict as dysfunctional to development	67%	23	51	44
Partisan Groups:				
Left partisans	74%	25	50	49
Centre partisans	70	30	48	40
Right partisans	54	21	50	33

The system differences remain for party groups. That is, Swedish Social Democrats do not share the views of American Democrats or Dutch Labor partisans at all. Nor are the views of Swedish conservatives similar to those of American and Dutch Conservatives. Rather, there is a within-country elite norm on conflict which is pervasive in all partisan groupings within a country. System level norms are more determinative than cross-national norms by partisan orientation.

Similarly, the same conclusion emerges from our data on elite awareness of the *existence* of conflicts. The responses on whether specific conflicts exist reveal system differences, particularly between the Dutch and Swedish "Left" and "Right" partisans, as this summary indicates:

TABLE 4.4 Subgroup Analysis for Elite Conflict Perceptions: Party Affiliations

	United States			Sweden			Netherlands			System Differences		
	Dems	Reps	Indeps	Social Dems	Centre	Conser-vatives	Labor	CDA	VVD	Left	Centre	Right
Eight specific conflicts at mass level												
- Average % seeing "very much" conflict	17	10	13	21	16	9	5	3	3			
- Average % seeing "very much" or "some" conflict	69	66	68	73	77	66	50	42	38	24	35	29
Evaluation of extent conflicts come in the way of community development												
- Very much	33	18	33	10	20	11	19	18	16	49	40	33
- Somewhat	41	36	37	15	10	10	31	30	34			
	74	54	70	25	30	21	50	48	50			
Differences between Left and Right Parties												
A. (2)		3			7			12				
B. (Total)		20			4			0				
N	112	71	52	100	29	72	105	79	44			

For the U.S. "Independents" are treated in this analysis as the "Centre."
Abbreviations: (Netherlands) CDA - Christian Democratic Appeal (Centre) VVD - People's Party for Freedom and Democracy (Conservative)

% who say there is	U.S.		Sweden		Netherlands			Dutch Compared to Swedish % Difference	
conflict on the following differences:	D	R	Social Dems.	Cons.	Labor	CDA	VVD	Left	Right
1. Education	72	80	91	77	43	29	30	48	47
2. Income	86	84	98	86	53	49	50	45	36
3. Religion	39	50	38	46	30	24	18	8	28
4. Worker-manager Relations	70	60	82	76	40	31	17	42	59
5. Political Views	86	76	66	89	56	50	48	10	41
Average Right-Left differences for each country		8		13		12		Average System Differences 31	42

The within-system party differences in conflict awareness are relatively small, but the cross system differences are large. That is, we note again that Swedish Social Democrats do not resemble Dutch Labor Party leaders (they look more like American Democrats!), and Swedish conservatives do not resemble Dutch conservatives at all (the Swedes look more like American Republicans!). Hence it must be that the political culture of the system is determinative, not cross-national partisan orientations toward conflict.

A final comment on the non-congruence of national and local elite conflict orientations by party. One must remember that a decade separated the national and local studies and that this may have a bearing on these findings. If we accept this comparison as useful, however, two observations emerge from a look at the data from both levels: (1) Local leaders reveal much more congruence than national leaders, that is, "Left" - "Right" party differences are less pronounced for local leaders; (2) cross system differences by party are greater for national leaders than for local. The following summary demonstrates this:

	National MP's 3 Countries		Local Politicians 3 Countries	
	Left	Right	Left	Right
Average % seeing onflict	80	45	64	59
System differences (Range)	30	51	23	31

What is most significant, as stated earlier, is that within systems local elites are relatively in agreement despite their party affiliations, which is contrary to what we found for national elites except for the U.S.

Our subgroup analysis by age cohorts produced essentially the same basic finding: whether old or young, local elites do not diverge very much from the basic elite norm for the system. The following simple summary makes this clear.

	Average % of Elites Who Perceive Conflict in Their Communities		
	U.S.	Sweden	Netherlands
Overall Finding—			
All Local Elites	66	71	43
Age Subgroups of Elites			
- Under 50	69	72	48
- 50 and older	64	70	42

Younger leaders are slightly more inclined to see conflict, but the contrasts between Dutch age cohorts at all age levels and the American and Swedish age groups are striking and consistent. As for the evaluation of conflict we note the same uniformity within systems, generally, despite age cohorts, although the young American local elites are more concerned about the effect of conflict on community development than are the older elites—a distinction not evident for the other countries. To summarize the findings:

	% Who Feel Conflict Interferes With Development		
	U.S.	Sweden	Netherlands
Elites under 50	75	25	56
Elites 50 and older	56	19	47

Young elites generally are more concerned, but the proportion and difference is small and is very low in Sweden. Above all, age differences within systems are, except for the U.S., negligible. These findings, then, reinforce the basic argument we have made here. Subgroup analysis reveals that the initial differences by system which we found in elite conflict orientations must be understood as part of a pervasive elite culture, distinct from system to system, and not varying much by elite position, party affiliation or age of elites.

Community Differences in Elite Conflict Orientations

The previous discussion focused on the macro-level, the larger political system. It is important to remember, however, that these elites operate in particular communities and that the patterns of conflicts as well as the patterns of elite perceptions, therefore, will vary by community. We established in the previous chapter, in our discussion of elite views about their city's problems, that this was true, both in their perceptions of the seriousness of problems and in their acceptance of or desire for responsibility and power to act on these problems. We now ask the same question about conflicts—to what extent do elite views vary by community?

That the elites in cities in all three countries vary considerably in their conflict perceptions is immediately apparent in our data (Table 4.5). The range in high and low percentages vary by type of conflict and by country. The highest variance in elite perceptions concerns urban/suburban or rural conflicts, followed by their views on the existence of religious conflicts. In contrast, we found much more agreement as to the incidence of age group conflicts. The Swedish elites show the lowest variance across cities while the Dutch average is the highest. This attests again to the relative homogeneity among Swedish local elites, as we found also in the analysis of elite problem orientations. Thus, we find that cities differ, but systems also differ in the extent that cities differ! There are cities in each of these countries a high percentage of whose leaders report conflict over religious views (53% to 92%), but also cities with apparently minimal or no such conflict (0 to 18%). There are cities in all three systems which report considerable "class conflict", such as worker-manager differences (60% to 89%), but also cities apparently with minimal class conflict (7% to 33%). There are cities a high percentage of whose elites report conflict over political opinions (85% to 100%), but also cities where political controversy is less salient. One is struck in examining these data by the different conflict contexts which apparently exist in these cities based on elite reports to us. One should note also the agreement level among elites by city which exists, a cohesion which varies also for the three countries. The measure of elite cohesion used here is the percentage of all cities with a majority of 65% or more of the elites agreeing on whether each of these eight types of conflict exist in their cities (i.e. agree that conflict does or does not exist).

The comparative findings are:

	Levels of Elite Cohesion on Conflict Perceptions		
	U.S.	Sweden	Netherlands
Average % of cities where 65% or more of elites agreed on existence of conflicts (Means for 8 types of conflict)	74	78	51
Average % of cities where elites were split	26	22	49

TABLE 4.5 Variations by Cities in the Existence of Conflicts at the Mass Level (Based on Elite Perceptions)

The measure used is the average % of elites in each city giving a particular response		U.S.	Sweden	Netherland	Average Variation for Three Countries	Range in Differences (Comparing Systems)
1. In Education	High	94	96	82		
	Low	27	73	15		
	Diff.	67	23	67	52	44
2. In Income	High	100	97	82		
	Low	55	82	0		
	Diff.	45	15	82	47	67
3. In Religious	High	92	73	53		
Beliefs	Low	18	15	0		
	Diff.	74	58	53	62	21
4. In Political Views	High	100	89	85		
	Low	47	53	31		
	Diff.	53	36	54	48	18
5. Between Urban	High	100	93	87		
Residents and	Low	0	11	7		
Suburbanites	Diff.	100	82	80	87	20
6. Between Managers	High	86	89	60		
and Workers	Low	33	30	7		
	Diff.	53	59	53	55	6
7. Between Those Desiring Social	High	88	92	90		
Change and Those	Low	55	49	33		
Opposing It	Diff.	33	43	57	44	24
8. Between the	High	75	92	83		
Young and	Low	42	54	31		
the Old	Diff.	33	38	52	41	19
Mean Difference or Range		57.3	44.3	62.3		

Thus the Dutch elites were distinctive in two respects. They reported less conflict, but their elites were much more likely to be in disagreement as to whether conflict did or did not exist. U.S. cities had 90% of its cities with a high majority agreement on certain types of conflict (e.g. on the existence of conflict over political views), the Swedes had 100% of its cities where elites agreed on the existence of conflict (e.g. over education and income), but in the Netherlands we found that usually 50% or fewer of its cities had elites who had high majorities agreeing on the presence of conflict. Thus there was much greater elite congruence within cities in the U.S. and Sweden than in the Netherlands.

Elites' evaluations of the effects of conflicts (whether they interfere with development) also vary greatly by city in each country. We can summarize the ranges in elite opinions by city as follows:

	% who feel conflicts interfere		
	U.S.	Sweden	Netherlands
High city	91	62	91
Low city	35	8	20
Difference	56	54	71

One interesting question is whether there is a relationship by city between perceived levels of conflict and elites' evaluations of conflict. That is, are cities with the largest amount of perceived conflict also the cities where elites are inclined to be negative toward conflict? We do find a modest relationship in the U.S. and Sweden, but the expected relationship does not emerge at all from the Dutch data. The results are as follows:

	Average % of elites seeing conflicts as interfering with development		
	U.S.	Sweden	Netherlands
Types of Cities:			
A. Cities highest in perceived conflict	74.8	29.0	51.0
B. Cities perceived as having a moderate level of conflict	65.9	24.0	53.6
C. Cities perceived as low in conflict	58.0	19.0	55.6

Except for the Dutch finding (the reverse of expectations) the proposition holds up. But in all categories of cities, even in the U.S., there are large percentages of elites who are positive about the possibility of development despite the level of conflict perceived by elites.

An Attempt to Identify Factors
Relevant for Explaining City Differences

The explanation of these striking differences in cities in elite conflict perceptions requires a complex type of analysis, for not all of which do we have the necessary data. Any theoretical approach obviously must begin with the economic and social conditions of the population in each community. In cities where the population suffers the greatest socioeconomic distress presumably more conflict should exist and would be more salient to elites. Such awareness is probably accentuated if there is a competitive party system or other political group intermediate structure linking the public to elites. Where groups are active and competitive, elite cognizance of public needs, demands and conflicts is presumably more likely. Yet, a leader's awareness of conflict is also no doubt related to his or her own political interaction networks—who the leader goes to for advice and support and what pressures from outside the leader is subjected to. Frequent contacts with community groups may be linked to an awareness of conflicts. Finally, of course, other elite attitudes and value orientations might play a role, although the direction of the relationship is not clear. The leader who is attentive to conflict, accepts it as a necessary part of the democratic governance process, who feels it is functional to progress, is more likely to be sensitive to conflicts in the community than a leader who has negative value orientations toward conflict. However, one must be cautious in one's expectations here, because those with negative value positions may see just as much conflict as those tolerant of conflict (possibly even more!), but tend to condemn conflict as having serious consequences for city government and development.

Our model looks like this:

Factors Explaining Conflict Orientations of City Elites

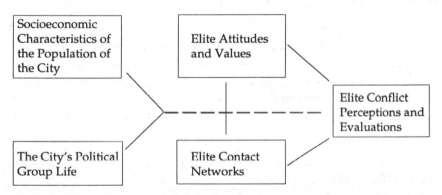

Population size of a city might well be our starting point in this analysis. One would expect that elites might well observe and report more conflicts in large cities. And indeed we find this to be true in all countries (although the differences are not great in the Netherlands). Here is a summary of the differences:

	Average % of elites who see "very much" conflict on 8 types of conflict		
	U.S.	Sweden	Netherlands
Population Size of Cities (Dichotomized):			
Largest Cities	16.3	18.4	4.9
Smllest Cities	10.8	15.4	3.7
Pearson's Correlation:	.413	.389	.097

City size appears to be somewhat associated with conflict perceptions.

Another possible explanation concerns the relevance of community social and economic conditions for elite conflict perceptions. Using census type data we can demonstrate that there is indeed an association of elite perceptions and the median family income of a community, in all three countries. In more affluent communities elites report less conflicts. (Table 4.6). But another community variable, unemployment level, does not correlate as well in Europe, although the correlation is high (.518) for the U.S. Nor do these variables relate consistently to elite values concerning the harmful effects of conflicts on development. While useful for the U.S., they are less relevant in Europe.

As for the relevance of party strength in these cities, in the U.S. we find evidence of a fairly consistent pattern (Table 4.7). Communities in the U.S. with a strong Democratic vote and dominated by Democratic leaders are more likely to be aware of conflict. Some of these are also cities with high poverty and unemployment levels, but not all of them. There is no perfect overlap in that sense. This finding of the linkage of party control in cities to elite conflict perceptions is also evident for European cities in our study, but the correlations in Sweden are not as strong.

Elite Contact Networks as a Factor

One theory with some promise is that the pattern of elite associations in their communities with other elites, with interest groups, and with the public, is linked to their views about politics. We will explain these contacts in detail in Chapter VI. The question here posed is whether such patterns are linked

TABLE 4.6   The Relation of Community Variables and Elite Conflict Perception (Pearson Correlations, by Cities)

	U.S.	Sweden	Netherlands
A. Awareness of Conflict*			
1. Median Family Income	− .203	− .232	− .337
2. Unemployment Rate	.518	− .012	.182
3. Poverty Level (U.S. only)	.679		
B. Evaluation of Conflict as Harmful to Development of Community**			
1. Median Family Income	− .187	.292	− .343
2. Unemployment Rate	.436	− .158	.468
3. Poverty Level (U.S. only)	.409		

* Average % of elites perceiving "very much" conflict on the 8 types of possible community divisions.
** Average % of elites who saw conflicts as interfering "very much" with community development.

to conflict perceptions. Presumably a leader with wide contacts will be more alert to conflicts in the community. Since we asked our respondents to tell us whether they initiated contact or were approached by any of 17 types of leaders and groups in the community, we can test this proposition. We did find a wide variation in such elite networks. Not only did individuals vary in the number and types of contacts, but cities also varied in the extent to which their elites were active in developing group support strategies.

The relation of elite contact patterns to conflict orientations can be demonstrated to some extent. Table 4.8 presents the basic results for the cities of all three countries. It is important to state first that cities do vary in the frequency of elite efforts to contact other elites and interest groups in the community. The range for U.S. cities for elite contacts with five of more community groups is 73% in City A and 9% in City B. In Sweden the contrast is between 11% and 40%; in the Netherlands zero percent and 33%. Thus, with such variance by cities the interesting question is whether there is an association between frequency of contacts initiated by elites and conflict perceptions. The answer is apparently yes for the U.S. and Sweden—elites in cities with a large number of contacts are more aware of conflict. (The correlations are .441 for the U.S. and .391 for Sweden.) Elites who go to

TABLE 4.7   The Partisan Character of the Community as a Condition Related to Elite Perceptions of Conflict

	United States		Sweden		Netherlands	
	Average % - "very much" conflict	*Average % - conflict interferes with development "very much"*	*Average % - "very much" conflict*	*Average % - conflict interferes with development "very much"*	*Average % - "very much" conflict*	*Average % - conflict interferes with development "very much"*
Partisan Character of Cities (Based on distribution of elites in our study)						
1. "Left" party elites dominant	18	41	19	10	6	25
2. Elites split	12	26	16	9.5	4	15
3. "Right" party elites dominant	10	15	16	7	3	18
Pearson Correlations:	.431	.397	−.233	−.024	−.488	.311

The correlations and percentages are based on the party affiliation of elites in our sample, by city.

community groups in the U.S. and Sweden, for the purposes of getting support for their policies, do this in the context of conflict awareness and/ or as a result of such contact become more aware of community cleavages. This is not true for the Netherlands (a correlation of -.149!)

We find also that if we look at the amount of pressures on elites initiated by interest groups and other actors, there is also a positive relationship to awareness of conflict. (See Table 4.8 also for this). There is a consistent difference for the U.S. and Sweden—those cities with more pressure group activity have elites with more conflict awareness. The correlations are .298 and .585, respectively. But the finding does not hold for the Dutch (a correlation of .025). In fact this set of findings may be even more convincing that contacts may have an impact on elite perceptions. However, as we noted earlier other factors can be relevant also (e.g., city size).

These are important relationships, even though not uniform for all three countries. The major point to keep in mind, however, is that elite contacts vary by city and, hence, the variations by city in conflicts may be a consequence, in part, of the extensiveness of elite involvement with community life.

Elite Attitudes and Values as Explainers of City Variance

In attempting to explain city variations in elite conflict perceptions certain basic elite attitudes could conceivably be helpful. We have already suggested that elite problem perceptions are linked to conflict perceptions, and we now find some support for this proposition when we examine carefully the relationship of these two elite orientations by city (Table 4.9). Cities vary considerably by both types of elite attitudes. And our data reveal how close the linkage is between these attitudes and their views on conflict. In all three countries where elites are more perceptive of serious problems, in those cities also elites perceive more conflicts. It is a simple uniform relationship for all these countries. However, values operate differently in the three countries. Cities differ in each country in the percentage of their elites who are pro-conflict on our value scale (explained in Chapter VII). There are cities where barely 50% of the leadership is pro-conflict and other cities where over 80% are pro-conflict. The link between their value position and their conflict perceptions is interesting. In the U.S. and Sweden in cities where elites are presumably pro-conflict they are more likely to downplay the negative impact of conflict, while in the Netherlands this does not hold. Indeed, in the Netherlands cities where elites are more pro-conflict in their value position elites tend to be more, not less, concerned about the dysfunctional effects of conflict. Value orientations do not predict as well across systems, therefore, as do elite problem perceptions.

From the foregoing analysis of relationships one can conclude that there

TABLE 4.8 The Relevance of Elite Contact Networks in Their Communities for Elite Perceptions of Community Conflict

	United States		Sweden		Netherlands	
	Cities with High Contact	Cities with Lower Contact	Cities with High Contact	Cities with Lower Contact	Cities with High Contact	Cities with Lower Contact
A. Contacts Initiated by Elites with Community Groups						
1. Mean % of elites who see "very much" conflict (on eight types of conflict)	18	10	18	15	5	3
2. The highest average % of conflict reported by elites on any of eight types of conflict in each city	49	27	36	32	15	12
3. Mean % of elites feeling that conflict interferes with city development	36	20	11	8	21	18
B. Pressures on Elites by Community Groups and Other Actors						
1. Mean % of elites who see "very much" conflict (on eight types of conflict)	16	11	19	15	5	4
2. The highest average % of conflict reported by elites on any of eight types of conflict	43	33	36	31	15	12

Cities were ranked on the basis of the % of elites who reported contacts with five or more community groups.

are certain factors which seem to be associated with elite conflict "aware-ness" in all countries: population size, affluence (median family income), party strength (proportion of elites with "Left" partisan affiliations), and problem perceptions. Other variables may be significant in only a particular country (as the rate of unemployment in the U.S.). Elite contact patterns

TABLE 4.9   Elite Problem Perceptions and Values Orientations: Do They Explain City Variations in Conflict Perceptions and Evaluations?

	Average % of elites who see very much conflict		
	U.S.	Sweden	Netherlands
A. The Linkage of Problems and Conflict Perceptions			
1. Cities with highest % of elites seeing problems as serious	22	18	5.2
2. Cities with lowest % of elites seeing problems as serious	10	13	3.4

	Average % of elites who felt that community conflicts interfered with community development		
	U.S.	Sweden	Netherlands
B. The Linkage of Elite Values and Conflict Perceptions			
1. Cities with highest % of elites who were personally pro-conflict in value position	58	19	59
2. Cities with lowest % of elites who were pro-conflict in value position	74	29	53

seem relevant for the U.S. and Sweden, but not for the Netherlands. If we change the dependent variable from elite "awareness of conflict" to elite "perceptions that conflict is harmful (or not)," it is difficult to find factors which are equally important for all countries. Cities in the U.S. and the Netherlands with a high unemployment rate have a higher proportion of elites concerned about conflict; this not true in Sweden, however. Dutch and American cities where the elites are primarily affiliated with parties of the Left are more likely to have elites worried about conflict; again, this is not true for Sweden. Thus, the conditions linked to elite evaluations of the consequences of conflict vary by system to a considerable extent.

Profiles of Two U.S. Cities:
Contrasts in Contexts and Elite Orientations

The importance of the community context must not be ignored in understanding elite attitudes and behavior. We have attempted to analyze the relevance of urban contexts in a variety of ways thus far. We can demonstrate that very strikingly by comparing the profiles of two American cities in our study, cities "A" and "H". The contrasting profiles for these two cities are presented in Table 4.10. City "A" has a set of structural conditions which clearly reveal its economic profile—high (20%) unemployment, 17% of its families below the poverty level, a median family income in 1980 below $20,000. Seventy percent of the population is black. In contrast, city "H" had only two percent unemployment, a very high family income, virtually no blacks, and minimal poverty. The labor force in "A" is 46% "blue collar", in "H" 5%. The type and intensity of the problems which elites in these two different communities face are obviously not the same. The average percent of elites in city "A" who say they have serious problems is 80%, in city "H" 41%. Both sets of elites say they have housing needs and economic development concerns, but in city "A" health and unemployment, and social problems are also dominant—but not in city "H". The following composite quotation from city "A" officials reveals their concerns:

"Our problems are many but perhaps poverty, crime, and unemployment head the list. The drying up of outside funds makes it impossible to address these problems. Industry has declined. The city has a bad image. There is inter-racial conflict as well as conflict among blacks, and severe political dissension between state, county, and city leaders, as well as among leaders within the city. Crime is rampant and police cannot (or will not) solve it. Above all, there is a lack of coordinated policy on decent housing, employment, and the environment."

Community "H" is described by its leaders in quite different terms:

"Because (H) is well to do, we have great difficulty in attracting young people. They cannot generally afford the necessary mortgage payment. We are greying. Property taxes are too high for some of us. But we have a new and vital economic development package including downtown shopping and retail development. These changes have caused considerable trauma (to some), but hopefully such wounds are being healed as the good results become evident."

Thus, the types of problems are different and the level of confidence is dramatically different also. In city "A" there is abject pessimism, in city "H" the leaders see considerable hope and progress.

The elites which have emerged in these two cities have contrasting profiles. In "A" they are much more from lower social class origins, are younger, over 50% black, over 90% Democratic. In city "H" the leaders are middle and upper middle class, older, all white, and are split 40% Democratic, 35% Republican, 25% Independent.

The elites reflect these situational conditions not only in their personal characteristics, but also in their attitudes and beliefs. As noted, their problem perceptions are radically different. Their perceptions of conflict in

TABLE 4.10 Profiles of Two U.S. Cities

	City "A"	City "H"
A. Population (1980)		
- Size (in 000's)	152	31
- Median Family Income (in ooo's)	20	43
- Unemployment Rate (%)	16	2
- Poverty Level (%)	17	3
- Proportion Blacks	71	1.7
- Labor Force - % Blue Collar	46	5
- Education Level - % HS Grads	69	90
- Voting Behavior - % Democratic	80	50
B. Elite Perceptions and Evaluations		
1. Seriousness of problems (% saying serious)		
- Average 14 problems	80	41
- Specific problems:		
- Health	75	10
- Housing	65	60
- Jobs	94	30
- Racial	77	40
- Economic Development	94	70
2. Effectiveness of action		
- Average % saying effective action is being taken on these problems	18	48
3. Conflict perceptions		
- Average % saying "very much" conflict on one or more of eight types of conflict	35	12
- Specific types of conflicts		
- Political views	82	7
- % feeling conflicts interfere with community development	65	14
4. Power to act on problems		
- Average % feeling they have power	37	56
- Power to act on specific problems:		
- Education	12	50
- Housing	41	60
- Safety	53	80
- Pollution	29	70
- Economic Development	24	70
5. Value Orientation of Elites		
- % favoring economic equality	40	18

their communities also diverge. In "A" every leader reports serious conflict, while in "H" only 50% do. The contrasts in some of the perceptions of specific community conflicts are significant:

% of city leaders who see very much conflict over:	"A"	"H"
- Political Views	82	7
- Educational Status	24	0
- City and Suburbs	77	7
- Religion	0	36

In addition to the existence of basically diverse conflicts in their communities, elites also differ in whether these conflicts interfere with community development—65% yes in "A" but only 14% in "H". And this is linked, in turn, to the elites differential perceptions of effective action in the serious problems they face—48% positive in "H", but only 18% positive in "A". One should note also that the elites in "A" are more committed to economic equality, much more so than in "H".

To sum up then, we have here clear evidence of two types of cities, whose elites came to power in different community contexts, and who were recruited from populations which differed in social class, racial, and political characteristics. These elites face quite different sets of problems. They also reveal different political orientations. They differ basically on (1) whether they have the power and resources to solve these problems, (2) whether the social and political cleavages are great enough to permit a solution to these problems, and, therefore, (3) whether effective leadership action has been taken and can be take to achieve progress in community development. The community context produces elites socialized by local social and political conditions which induce different attitudes and patterns of behavior. It is the locale, the local culture, which counts.

Profiles of European Cities: Major Contrasts

Contrasting profiles for cities emerge from the Swedish and Dutch data also (Table 4.11). There is a consistency in pattern which holds for many, not all, of the variables. Cities with relatively low median family income, high unemployment rate, and strong support for "left" parties reveal certain distinctive elite perceptions and evaluations. The differences are usually more striking in the Netherlands, but apparent also in Sweden. The more affluent and politically conservative community seems to produce elites who are:

1. less of the opinion that their problems are serious on the average, and this is particularly true for certain key problem areas.
2. less likely to be aware of conflicts in the community but not necessarily less concerned about the dysfunctional consequences of conflict.

3. more of the opinion that they have the power to act, particularly on key problems facing their communities.
4. less committed to the value of economic equality.

On all of these dimensions, except on the impact of conflicts, these findings parallel those in the U.S. A configuration of elite political perceptions and values, linked to certain community characteristics, is found in these profiles to have considerable cross-system validation in these three democracies.

Conclusions

We have looked in this chapter at community conflicts in the cities of our three democracies, as perceived by their local leaders. We inquired into the nature of these conflicts and whether elites saw them as harmful. Our comparative analysis focused on cross-system differences and within-system differences in the incidence of conflict-differences in elite conflict perceptions by elite position, party affiliations, and age. We presented a detailed analysis of variations in conflicts by cities. Our major queries were: Do systems and communities differ in conflicts as perceived by their elites, and how can we explain these variations? Certain generalizations have emerged from this theoretical and empirical exercise which we will sum up here.

Most of these local leaders do operate with a conflict model of social and political life, if we combine the responses to our open and closed questions about conflict. The Dutch are, perhaps surprisingly, most consensual, the Swedes most conflictual, the Americans close to the Swedes, if one uses our data about the existence of conflict in their cities. But the concern of these leaders is not extreme, less than one-fifth in all countries say there is "very much" conflict. Socio-class (income) differences as well as differences in political questions rank highest in all countries, but there are also distinctive types of conflict reported by the leaders in all three countries: age group differences in the Netherlands, educational differences in Sweden, city-suburb differences in the U.S. The depth of the concern of elites about the consequences of conflict varies—very low concern in Sweden, very high in the U.S. Thus, across all three democracies there is considerable lack of uniformity in the character of conflict and its perceived impact.

We explored in our subgroup analysis across systems the importance of elite position (whether administrator or politician), of party affiliation, and of age. We found that position was really irrelevant as a discriminating variable—at the local level the two types are almost identical in their perceptions in each system. Politicians and administrators in the Netherlands both are different than in the U.S. and Sweden; yet, in each country there is high congruence of perceptions and opinions by elite position.

TABLE 4.11 Contrasting City Profiles for Elites in Sweden and the Netherlands

	Sweden			Netherlands	
	City X	City Z		City B	City S
Community Characteristics					
- Median family income	low	high		low	high
- Unemployment rate	2.4	0.7		14.4	6.6
- Partisan character:					
% "Left" in local election	59	28		58	43
Elite Perceptions and Evaluations					
1. Problems - How Serious?					
- Average % seeing problems					
as serious (14 problems)	75	56		89	58
- Specific problems:					
Education	82	56		89	71
Jobs	96	72		100	35
Immigration	62	25		94	24
Economic Development	96	64		94	53
2. Conflict Perceptions					
- Average % saying "very					
much" conflict	22	15		57	35
- Average % saying conflicts					
interfere with development	19	28		56	57
3. Power to Act on Problems					
- Average % say "Yes" on					
11 problems	67	73		40	46
- On specific problems:					
Jobs	49	68	Health	33	56
Pollution	41	60	Housing	50	60
Immigration	69	93	Public Improvement	33	56
Economic Development	37	68	Econ. Development	33	47
4. Effectiveness of Action					
- Average % saying effective					
action is being taken	13	6		29	31
- On specific problems:					
Housing	15	7	Housing	35	71
Health	10	0	Recreation	18	60
Jobs	36	14	Cost of Government	24	60
5. Value Position on Economic					
Equality Scale					
- Average % favor economic					
equality	62	44		50	36

Similarly, elites irrespective of party are also quite congruent within systems, and thus noncongruent across systems. Thus "Left" partisans do not necessarily stress the existence or dysfunctionality of conflict more than

"Right" partisans do. Rather, the partisans in each country adhere to the overall country norm. Our analysis of age differences reveals the same pattern. So that in summary we find in these analyses that within-system differences are minimal and cross-system differences considerable, as follows.

	Elite Conflict Perceptions	
	Within System Differences	*Cross System Differences*
Subgroup Analysis	*(averages for three countries)*	
1. By Position	2.8%	28.9
2. By Party	7.5	29.3
3. By Age	4.3	27.0

Clearly the uniformity we discovered is intra-systemic, not cross-systemic.

In our analysis of city-by-city findings we were able to demonstrate great variations in conflicts as perceived by local leaders. Sweden was the most homogeneous, the Netherlands most heterogeneous. And we also found relatively high elite cohesion by city in the U.S. and Sweden. There was considerable difference of opinion among elites in Dutch cities. We used a simple model to try to explain these city variations, testing for the utility of community populational and structural factors, the role of the local party dominance pattern, for the part which elite contacts might play, and for the linkage of elite attitudes and values to conflict perceptions. We found strong evidence that in the U.S. social and economic conditions of cities were significantly related to conflict perceptions, but not such clear evidence for the Netherlands and Sweden. The role of the party system was clearly relevant for the U.S., where cities in which the Democrats were more dominant tended to have elites more aware of conflict and more concerned about it, than in cities with other partisan/nonpartisan orientations. In European cities "Left" party dominance revealed no such linkage. Elite contact patterns were definitely linked to conflict perceptions for the U.S. and Sweden but not as clearly for the Netherlands. And finally, we find a clear association between elite problem perceptions and their views about the conflicts in their communities. But elite value orientations while also associated with conflict perceptions, operate differently in these countries—in the U.S. and Sweden the more pro-conflict elites are in value preferences, the less they are concerned about conflict, while the reverse is true in the Netherlands (although the difference is small).

Thus, the model works differently in these three systems. All four components of the model are useful in the U.S., while in the European analysis party is more central as well as other elite attitudinal orientations.

The diversity of the conflict contexts in these three countries is what emerges in the large from this analysis. Diversity in types of conflicts, diversity in elite perceptions of conflict, diversity in elite evaluations of the functionality and value of conflict, diversity in elite views in the cities in each system. Not all elites are conflict-oriented nor conflict-tolerant. Indeed, a large minority of 30% to 50% are not aware nor concerned about conflict nor value conflict. The implications of this for the governance of the cities in these democracies are considerable.

One senses that the way in which local elites respond to conflicts differs by city and suggests a basis for typologizing cities. On the one hand there are communities where elites deny the existence of much conflict and ignore those conflicts they see. This is the "Consensual City Polity", presumed or actual. Again, one senses there are cities where elites press ahead with their programs while recognizing the existence of much community conflict and opposition but accepting it as inevitable. This is the "Progress Despite Conflict Polity." And there is the community where elites perceive conflict, consider it harmful, and seek to proceed with those programs which are possible while avoiding conflict. Perhaps this is the "Harmony at the Cost of Progress Polity." Other variations of these constructs are of course possible. And the presence of these types varies probably by country. Clearly diversity in types of city polities exists within each country. National norms for elites also appear to exist when one looks at these data in the aggregate. These appear however to be epiphenomena, while the reality lies in the social and political life of each community.

Note

1. A cautionary note: "concern" in the national study refers to whether conflicts could be reconciled; "concern" in the local study refers to whether conflicts would interfere with community development.

5

Elite Influence Perceptions:
Differential Patterns and Structures*

Political influence is a very controversial subject. It has evoked many different approaches at conceptualization and measurement. As Lasswell said, echoing the belief of many that influence is at the core of political science, "The study of politics is the study of influence and the influential." But he quickly added, "different results may be obtained by different criteria of influence" (Lasswell 1936, 233).

Early theorists had a unitary conception of elite influence. For Mosca there was a minority elite, the ruling class, and the rest of society which "merely submit to it." Although this is somewhat misleading, since Mosca saw also the contest for influence between rival elites, essentially he presents a dichotomous perspective (Meisel 1965, 2). In more recent scholarship the controversy was between the community power theorists emphasizing a dominant "power elite" (Hunter 1953; Mills 1956) and elite pluralist or elite coalition theorists, following the intellectual line of Dahl. For him "political power is pluralistic in the sense that there exist many different sets of leaders" (Dahl 1967, 188). In his earlier study of New Haven, his chapter on "the ambiguity of leadership" discusses the problems in discovering who has influence and "who governs" and demonstrates empirically the heterogeneity and independence of the 50 main leaders in terms of their differential influence in three policy areas. His emphasis is that those who govern are not a closed group, but a diverse, specialized, often conflicted set of actors, and influence is not concentrated in a single elite group which acts as one (Dahl 1961, 89-103). Aside from these two polar conceptions of political elite influence, the classical unitary and the more recent pluralist models, there have been many other theoretical proposals and modifications. The controversy continues. Yet, in democratic societies

---

*Tom Watts was responsible for beginning the analysis of this chapter before he died.

today scholars are more likely to accept the assumption that power and influence is probably diffuse and shared by a large number of actors than oligarchic and narrowly concentrated in the hands of a few. In a study of local political elites we at least begin with that assumption for the U.S., Sweden, and the Netherlands.

As for the measurement of influence, progress has been slow and the approaches used are usually considered inadequate and produce argument (Page 1985, 132). The "community power" studies of the 1950s exemplify the bitter controversies which occur. There are many problems in discovering who has influence, direct and indirect, actual and potential, reputational or demonstrable. As Dahl noted, there is no universally satisfactory way. He was particularly concerned with discovering those who really had power, aware that "the distinction between the rituals of power and realities of power is frequently obscure" (Dahl 1961, 89). And he actually utilizes six different ways to determine whether people have influence on decisions (Dahl 1961, 330-331). Whatever measurement technique is used seems contingent on the objectives of the research, the conception of influence involved (influence over whom or what), the availability of data, and the predispositions of the investigator. What is needed is a measurement technique which is comparatively useful and conceptually valid. In the absence of anything better, we are inclined to study "positional elites" (like the mayors, councilpersons, administrators and party leaders in our study) and to attempt to determine the relative influence of these positional elites on policy decisions. To do that exhaustively (as Dahl did in New Haven) for many cities in different countries requires great resources, extensive data and intensive interviewing. As a result of resource constraints we use here a simple measurement approach which we found is comparatively feasible.

Our focus is limited to leaders' influence over policy in local government, and the analysis rests on elites' perceptions of their influence over a variety of policies in *their cities or communes*. That is our emphasis—the intra-city patterns of elite influence. The question we asked was "How much influence do you feel you have on what is accomplished in your city in the following (policy) areas", followed by a list of 12 policy areas. The response categories were: "much," "some," "no influence." This is obviously a very subjective basis for measurement, and assumes accurate perceptions and a capacity for discriminating judgments on the amount of own influence. Implicit in this question are associated questions: What issue areas are important to you? What is your policy agenda as a city leader? On what aspects of city government do you spend most of your time, and on which of these do you have an impact? Thus, although a fairly simple forthright question, there are not-so-hidden meanings which individuals may put on the question. Nevertheless, it is the type of simple, direct question which presumably can and must be asked of leaders everywhere and which hopefully will produce truthful and valid responses which are comparatively useful. That must be our assumption.

The responses to this question permit an inquiry into a series of theoretical matters about elites which have preoccupied scholars for some time, and which concern us. In the type of democracies we study local leaders are not automatons of regional, provincial, state and national governments, but do indeed have influence over policy. The first question is how much, and what is the variance across systems and within systems, by city, in the proportion of city leaders who have (say they have) policy influence? Related is the second question, in which policy areas do elites report the greatest influence and how does that vary by elites and systems? We concentrated our attention here actually on ten policy areas, ranging from "traditional" concerns such as revenue policy and public improvements to more "social welfare" types of issues as health and housing policy. A third interest, close to this, is the extent of specialization by elites in policy agendas. Do local elites select one or two policies to become expert on or do they seek to have influence over a broad spectrum of six or seven policy areas, or more?

Much research, particularly on "community power" leads to a fourth area of interest. As the literature reveals, the "influence distribution pattern" for communities, and for the system generally, is of considerable interest. That is, do elites by their responses reveal a hierarchic and centralized pattern of influence (a few leaders with much influence), a decentralized or dispersed pattern (many leaders with much influence), or a balanced pattern with rather equal proportions of elites with "much," "some," or "no" influence, and a wide diversity in the number of policy areas in which they work? Once these patterns have been sorted out, the fifth question obviously is who are the most influential leaders, what are their characteristics, backgrounds, and orientations toward politics? And, finally, the inquiry would not be complete without attempting to identify the factors and conditions which help explain the differential elite influence patterns by system and city, including a look at environmental, social, and institutional constraints and factors.

These six types of concerns constitute the outline for this chapter. We see elite influence perceptions as part of the political culture and seek to enlighten the extent to which systems differ in this respect, and, if possible, why? Cultural differences, if they exist, need explanations; they are not just unexplained or unexplainable givens (Thompson, Ellis, Wildavsky 1990, 218). The amount of local leaders' influence (i.e. the number of policy areas over which they can have much influence), the centralization or pluralization of that influence, the specialization patterns, and the social basis or credentials for influence are the critical theoretical concerns we address here. They have been the subject of much speculation by many scholars. But few have looked at the empirical realities for local government leaders in a comparative research context.

The Breadth of Influence

The first question is to what extent do local elites feel they have influence over local policy decisions, and the comprehensiveness of that influence in terms of the range of policy areas. Elites, we say, are those who have influence over the decisions of government, or as Lasswell put it, those who feel they and their views and preferences are "taken into consideration" in policy-making. Accepting this, one would expect few leaders to say they have no influence. Unless they were retiring, or ill, or excluded from the caucus, or at the very beginning of their local government careers. Even then they might claim influence. It is also of course possible that local leaders may sense constraints on them from the higher authorities leading to denials of the possibility of influence in certain policy areas. How much of this do we see in our data?

At first glance (Table 5.1) there appears a remarkable similarity across systems in the proportions of elites who say they have "much" influence *in their own cities or communities*. The first measure is based on an "Influence Distribution Index" (scoring each respondent for type of response for 10 policy areas). By this index, 31% of the U.S. leaders score high,, 24% of the Swedish and 29% of the Dutch. Similarly for the second measure (which averages the percentages who replied "much", "some" or "no" influence), the finding for "much" influence is very similar. The range in cross national percentages is very small (seven or five percent). Further, the extent of specialization among elites by country is also very similar. The "general-ists", those who claim influence in three to ten policy areas, are a minority similar in size in the three countries—from 23% to 30%.

The differences among the three countries emerge when one takes all the information into account, probes with other measures, and differentiates by policy areas. The U.S. has fewer leaders who feel they are powerless or not very influential. This is a considerable difference using the "Influence Distribution Index." While 44% of the Swedish leaders are admittedly low in influence, only one half of this proportion, 22%, are low in influence in the U.S. (34% in the Netherlands.) The other measures consistently support this finding. Thus, while almost 40% of the European leaders say there are no areas in which they have "much" influence, only 24% of the U.S. leaders do.

Another striking difference emerges when we classify these policy areas, as to whether they deal with the "traditional" functions of government (for want of a better label), or the "social" policy areas such as health, housing, culture and recreation, and social welfare. Among those who have influence the contrasts between the U.S. and the two European countries is great: 40% of U.S. leaders are influential in "social" policy areas, while 71% and 82% of

TABLE 5.1   Elite Influence: Major Cross-National Differences
(Summary Measures)

Average %, All Cities	U.S. N = 260	Sweden N = 389	Netherlands N = 305	System Differences (Range)
1) Influence Distribution Index (% of all elites in each index category)				
Very High (Score 14 - 20)	9	6	8	3
High (Score 11 - 13)	22	18	21	4
Medium (Score 7 - 10)	47	32	37	15
Low (Score 4 - 6)	15	26	20	11
Very Low (Score 0 - 3)	7	18	14	11
Mean Score:	9.0	7.4	8.1	1.6
2) Perceived Influence in Ten Policy Areas				
Have "much" influence	20	15	16	5
Have "some" influence	52	46	49	6
Have "no" influence	28	39	35	11
3) Extent of Specialization by Policy Areas (% who have "much" influence in:)				
5 or more areas	9	7	7	2
3 or 4 areas	21	16	19	5
1 or 2 areas	47	38	36	11
0 areas	24	39	38	15
4) Types of Policy Areas in Which Leaders Have "Much" Influence (Average % for each category of policy area; based only on those who have influence)				
"Traditional" areas only	60	18	29	42
"Social" areas only	5	15	22	17
Both areas	35	67	49	32
Total % in "social" areas	40	82	71	42
N =	198	233	186	

1. See Table 5.2 for the policy areas.

2. "Traditional" policy areas used here were: Public Improvements, Education, Revenues, Public Order, Labor Relations, Economic Development. "Social" policy areas were: Housing, Health, Culture, Recreation and Social Welfare.

3. The Influence Distribution Index (described in Appendix) scored each respondent in each of 10 policy areas as follows: Much influence (2), Some influence (1), No influence (0). Total maximum score is 20. This index was adapted from John A. Williams (1976).

European leaders are active in these areas (See Table 5.2 for the data on each policy area).

The reasons for these findings are not entirely clear. The greater autonomy of local government in the U.S. and hence fewer constraints "from above" on local leaders would lead to an expectation that U.S. leaders, particularly mayors and councilors, would more likely assert that they have influence. This, however, would vary by the structure of local government in the U.S. and also, of course, may vary over time. Why American leaders should claim that they have more influential roles than European leaders do is more difficult to explain. One is tempted to attribute it to more central government control in Europe. Although that is not irrelevant, more probably it is a consequence of how local government is organized in Europe. In Sweden (and probably also in the Netherlands) there is a greater specialization by policy function, or by department, than in the U.S. This is called the "sectorization" of local government, particularly for the bureaucracy. Stromberg and Westerstahl describe the Swedish context as follows:

> Politicians and local administrators with central positions, who have been assigned the role of coordinators and guardians of more general interests, are in opposition to those who advocate special, sectorial interests. Loyalty toward one's own organization is, thus, characteristic for both politicians and local government officers... The sectorization... falls back on the way in which communal activity is organized (and) reflects the "segmentation" which characterizes the entire society...

Yet, they also observe that administrators are more than narrow specialists, since "they have a number of channels through which to influence communal activity in addition to the influence they can exercise within their own fields" (Stromberg and Westerstahl 1984, 61-63). There appear to be opportunities for wide influence but less exploitation of these opportunities (Wallin, Back, and Tabor 1981).

Given the demands on local government in Europe to deal with "social policy" requirements (specified to a great extent by national government) one might well expect a greater interest in and influence over housing, welfare, and health policy concerns than in the U.S. And this is indeed what we find in our data. Thus, two elements or patterns of perceptions differentiate local political elite culture on the two sides of the Atlantic. The agenda and interest, of American local elites is focused on social policy much less than in Europe. But American local leaders feel they have more influential roles than do their European counterparts. The Americans, however, expend their influence more on public improvements and resource problems and public safety. The Europeans more on social needs.

TABLE 5.2   Perceived Influence of Local Leaders: By Policy Areas
(% of leaders who say they have influence in each area) (Summary measures)

Policy Area:	Influence Level	U.S. N = 260	Sweden N = 389	Netherlands N = 305	System Differences (Range)
Economic Development	Much	15	12	7	8
	Some	67	47	58	20
	None	19	42	35	23
Housing	Much	9	19	22	13
	Some	60	52	53	8
	None	30	29	34	5
Public Improvements	Much	36	14	21	22
	Some	51	50	54	3
	None	14	37	25	23
Health	Much	10	5	7	5
	Some	52	27	38	25
	None	39	68	55	29
Culture, Recreation, and Sports	Much	20	23	25	5
	Some	58	51	52	7
	None	22	27	23	5
Education	Much	18	14	12	6
	Some	37	46	46	9
	None	45	40	42	5
Public Revenue/Tax	Much	42	36	27	15
	Some	40	55	50	15
	None	18	9	23	12
Public Order/Safety	Much	28	4	11	24
	Some	49	28	42	21
	None	24	69	47	45
Social Services/Welfare	Much	7	18	20	13
	Some	55	48	52	7
	None	38	34	28	10
Employment and Labor Relations	Much	11	10	6	5
	Some	57	55	55	2
	None	33	35	39	6

How much specialization and how much cumulation of influence is there? The pluralism model would suggest there should be considerably specialization. And, indeed there is, in all three countries. While the proportion who say they have much influence in only one or two areas seems larger (Table 5.1) for the U.S. than in Europe, actually the proportions who specialize *among those who have influence* are almost the same. The proportions reporting influence in one or two policy areas are: 61% (U.S.), 62% (Sweden), 58% (the Netherlands).

If we look at the aggregate data for each country for all elites, we can isolate four types of local leaders, estimated proportionately as follows:

	U.S.	Sweden	Netherlands
Those with little or no influence	22	39	34
Those with specialized influence in one of two policy areas	47	38	36
Those with high influence in multiple policy areas	22	18	21
Those with very high influence in many policy areas	9	6	8

These data could be interpreted to indicate that the influence patterns in these countries are partially hierarchic, with a cumulation of policy influence in a relatively small minority at the top, but with also considerable diffusion of influence and specialization at the base of the pyramid. However, there is a larger than expected proportion of non-influentials, those withdrawn or excluded from influence by their own admission, particularly among elites in European cities. As we further explore these data, the extent to which these patterns are varied *within systems* can be analyzed, particularly when we distinguish the patterns for bureaucrats and politicians.

Linkage of Influence Perceptions to Power and Responsibility

How do power perceptions relate to influence perceptions? One might hypothesize that the reason such a relatively large proportion of local leaders say they do not have much influence is because they have a sense of powerlessness to act on their problems. One must keep in mind that we base our analysis here on two different questions: (1) "Do you think your *local government* has enough power and autonomy to act effectively?" (2) "How much influence do you feel you have on what is accomplished in your city?" The first question deals with inter-governmental power relations, the second with personal influence within the community. Despite these different intellectual contexts, the question posed is, are those leaders who operate in a perceived environment of limited power for local government more likely to say they have limited influence than those leaders who operate in a perceived environment of considerable power? The data do not support this expectation (Table 5.3). On the average two-thirds of the U.S. and Swedish elites feel they have the power to deal with their problems, and half of the Dutch do too. But the disjunction between power and influence is high, i.e. many more leaders say the city has the power to act than say that they, as decision makers, have "much" influence. The same is true for the responsibility to act. There are several possible interpretations of this disjunction. One is that perceptions of a city's power status and a leader's influence status are not comparable and cannot be juxtaposed. To some degree this may be true, as the data seem to suggest. On the other hand, our

TABLE 5.3 Comparative Perceptions of Power, Responsibility and Influence (Average % of all elites who say they have power, responsibility, or "much" influence in a given policy area)

Policy Area:	United States			Sweden			Netherlands		
	Power	Resp.	Infl.	Power	Resp.	Infl.	Power	Resp.	Infl.
Economic Development	58	66	15	50	75	12	36	13	7
Public Oder/Safety	81	89	28	56	51	4	42	39	11
Public Improvements	82	88	36	90	92	14	59	61	21
Education	55	52	18	44	77	14	28	16	12
Housing	59	53	9	76	90	19	52	70	22
Health	53	35	10	70	33	5	42	14	7
Culture/Recreation	86	77	20	90	80	23	87	71	25
Averages:	68	66	19	68	71	13	49	41	15
Disjunction:									
Power—Influence		−49			−55			−34	
Responsibility— Influence		−47			−58			−26	

Note: If those who say they have "some" influence are added to this analysis the proportions are as follows:

	United States	Sweden	Netherlands
Average % who feel they have some or much influence	72	56	64
Disjunction:			
Power-Influence	+4	−12	+15

Note: One must remember that the responsibility question was worded differently in the Netherlands. The question was whether local leaders *had* responsibility; in the U.S. and Sweden the question was whether they *should have* responsibility.

findings suggest a lack of "influence efficacy", or a lack of trying to have influence despite a recognition that they could be and should be, influential. This may be a misleading explanation, however. Rather, these data comparisons of power and influence may primarily be a further documentation of the specialization and diffusion of influence in local government: leaders select one or two areas in which to try to be effective, areas in which they know local government can act, while leaving the other areas to the expertise of their colleagues. As an illustration, culture and recreation ranks highest in the percentage who say they have the power to act. But whereas over 80% feel the city has the power, only 20-25% say they have much influence. The implication is obvious—despite the possibility of exerting influence in the culture and recreation area, only one fourth at the most put this on their influence agenda.

It is true that the analysis of the rank orders by country reveals that as power perceptions decline, influence perceptions decline. There is a 10 to 15 percent differential in proportions of elites with strong influence perceptions for policy areas with high and low power perception percentages. Yet the disjunction is great for all policy areas. And even in the Netherlands where less than 50% feel they have the power to act, the disjunction exists for all policy areas. It seems clear that a leader's desire to be influential in a policy area, and his or her feeling of influence efficacy, is not closely related to whether they perceive the city to have the power to act in these policy areas.

The Analysis of Subgroups:
Do They Explain System Uniformities and Differences?

At the system level of analysis we have found these three western democracies similar or equivalent in certain respects in the influence patterns of their local elites. We have also found them considerably different in certain respects. A quick summary of these major finding is necessary in order to highlight our next analysis. The summary is:

	U.S.	Sweden	Netherlands
Uniform Findings:			
1. % with high influence	31	24	29
2. % of elites specializing (among those with influence)	61	62	58
Different Findings:			
1. % with little or no influence	22	44	34
2. % influential in "social" policy areas (among those with influence)	40	82	71

How can we explain these findings? Our comments already about the differences in these systems in national-local governmental relationships and in the welfare-state orientations of their national systems are useful and relevant. In addition, we now turn to the analysis of subgroups across systems to see if these data will shed additional light on these systemic uniformities and differences.

Comparing the influence patterns of politicians and administrators reveals some important differences in all three countries (Table 5.4). As expected, the politicians report a much higher level of influence. If we take the two highest categories on our "Influence Index" the contrasts by role for each system are:

	Politicians	*Administrators*	*Within System Difference*
United States	43	20	23
Sweden	31	10	21
Netherlands	35	16	19

Here then is a uniform finding across all systems and confirms the earlier finding. Second, we find that administrators are more likely than politicians to be specializers in policy areas (having influence in one or two policy areas). And these proportions are also greatly dissimilar for all three countries.

Third, when we look at the bottom strata of the influence pyramid, however, we find big system differences. There are many more elites (both politicians and administrators) with very little influence in the European countries. And this is particularly true of European administrators. Here is the quick summary for administrators:

% Low Influence (0-6 scores)	
United States	33
Sweden	65
Netherlands	46

In fact the pattern in Europe is "hierarchic" for both politicians and administrators: a small percent at the top with influence and a large percent at the bottom. In the U.S. the influence pattern is much more diffused or balanced. (Again, there may be a difference among the countries in organizational structure of systems, although we sought to select top political elites of similar types in all systems.)

A fourth observation is that when we dichotomize policy areas into "traditional" and "social" policy, we see the cross system differences remain for both politicians and administrators. The latter in Europe are

TABLE 5.4 Elite Perceived Influence by Role

	U.S.		Sweden		Netherlands		System Difference (Range)	
	Pols. N= 128	Adms. N= 132	Pols. N= 270	Adms. N= 114	Pols. N= 200	Adms. N= 102		
Average % of Leaders							Pols.	Adms.
A. Number of policy areas in which they claim "much" influence								
No policy areas	25	23	36	47	41	34	16	24
1–2 areas	35	58	34	46	27	50	8	12
3–4 areas	29	14	21	6	23	13	8	8
5–6 areas	9	4	8	1	6	3	3	3
7–10 areas	2	2	1	0	3	0	2	2
Within System Difference								
No areas of influence	2		11		7			
3 or more areas of influence	20		23		16			
B. Type of areas in which respondents say they have "much" influence (For those who say they do have "much" influence)								
"Traditional" only	55	65	23	34	23	39	32	31
"Social" only	1	8	20	27	23	20	22	19
Both types	44	27	57	39	54	41	13	14
N	96	102	177	62	119	67		
% in "social" areas (Policy areas 2 and 3)	45	77	77	66	77	61	32	31
Within System Difference	10		11		16			
C. Power Distribution Index Scores								
Very high (14–20)	17	1	6	5	10	3		
High (11–13)	26	19	25	5	25	13		
Medium (7–10)	47	48	36	24	37	37		
Low (4–6)	7	23	20	38	14	33		
Very low (0–3)	4	10	13	27	14	13		

Note: See Table 5.1 for the specific policy areas included here under "Traditional" and "Social."

somewhat less involved in "social" policy but still much more than in the U.S.: 66% in Sweden, 61% in Netherlands, but only 35% in the U.S. Thus, the uniformities and differences which we saw earlier for type of policy area are confirmed when we break these data by role.

While the above generalizations can be made, one must realize that there is a complex array of variations by country, by role, and by policy area. We can use three types of policy areas to demonstrate this:

| | % of elites who have "much influence" | | |
Policy Area:	U.S.	Sweden	Netherlands
1. Public Improvements			
Politicians	40	16	21
Administrators	32	8	21
2. Recreation			
Politicians	27	26	29
Administrators	14	16	16
3. Housing			
Politicians	7	23	25
Administrators	12	10	16

The greater role for elected officials is consistent in all three areas except for the U.S. on the housing issue. U.S. elites reveal greater influence in the first policy area but not in the other two. On housing, particularly, European politicians exert more influence in their localities. Cumulating the evidence into generalizations for all policy areas is important but the selection of particular areas for analysis could modify these observations considerably.

The Nature of Party Differences in Local Elite Influence

We have made the analysis by party only for the elected politicians since Swedish data on party were not available for administrators. Since we have found that politicians claim more influence than administrators, and are more likely to be policy "generalists" than "specialists", it is important to ask whether these generalizations hold up for different sets of elite partisans.

The first set of findings concerns the "Left". In Europe, there is evidence of more alleged policy influence for at least one Left party, the Dutch Labor party, than for the Swedish Social Democrats and the Democrats in the U.S. (Table 5.5). Thus, on our "influence distribution index" 50% of the Dutch score high, compared to 32% for the U.S. (37% for Sweden). Further, fewer of the Dutch "Left" say there are no policy areas in which they have "much" influence. The Dutch "Left" is thus quite distinctive.

The parties of the "Right" also differ. The Swedish Conservatives appear

TABLE 5.5   Elite Perceived Influence By Party (Politicians only*)

Average % of Leaders	U.S.			Sweden			Netherlands			System Difference (Range)		
	Dems. N=52	Inds. N=21	Reps. N=39	S.Dem. N=124	Cent. N=37	Cons. N=86	Labor N=70	CDA N=50	VVD N=38	Left	Center	Right
A. Number of policy areas in which they claim "much" influence												
No policy areas	35	5	26	30	39	41	23	34	53	12	27	
1–2 areas	36	24	41	36	21	39	34	38	13			
3–4 areas	23	38	23	24	31	10	33	22	18			
5+ areas	6	34	11	10	10	10	10	6	16	4	6	
Left - Right difference (No policy areas)		9			11			30				
B. Type of areas in which elites have "much" influence (% in "Social" areas)												
All elites	31	48	26	50	51	45	64	48	35	33	3	19
Elites with influence	47	50	34	66	83	76	83	73	73	36	33	42
Within System Difference: Left vs. Right:		5			5			29				
		13			10			10				
C. Power Distribution Index Scores												
Very low (0–3)	6	0	5	9	10	19	10	16	21			
Low (4–6)	8	4	10	16	21	25	9	10	13			
Medium (7–10)	54	35	49	38	30	35	31	39	29			
High (11–13)	26	30	23	27	26	16	39	25	19			
Very high (14–20)	6	30	13	10	13	5	11	10	19			

* Since administrators in Sweden could not be asked their party affiliation, we use politicians only here for purposes of comparison.

to be the deviant case, with a relatively small proportion scoring high on the influence index—21% compared to 36% and 38% for the U.S. Republicans and Dutch VVD, respectively. However, the Dutch conservatives have a high percentage who assert they have limited influence (53% say there is no policy area in which they have "much" influence). Hence the U.S. Republicans are decidedly the conservative party with probably the most influence in local party actions. Here again then is a cross-system difference by party.

As for the "Center" parties one finds the European parties with fairly similar levels of elite influence on our index, but their status in their own systems differs: in Sweden the Center elites are virtually equal to the Left in policy influence, while in the Netherlands the CDA is less influential than Labor. The U.S. Independents are a special case, indeed! They score very high on influence, and very few say they have no influence. Given the fact that there are quite a few nonpartisan city governments as well as independents, this assessment of their influence, though strikingly high, is probably tenable and significant in the U.S. setting. Independents do seem to have a major role in the political influence structure of American local governments.

On two other findings we find no great differences from earlier reports. That is, the degree of specialization (i.e. the response of having influence in only one or two areas) seems quite similar for the parties (with the possible exception of the U.S. Independents, the Swedish Center, and the Dutch VVD parties, which are low). The reported influence in "social" policy areas is high in European parties as might be expected. The contrasts are great for the Left parties: 47% four U.S. Democrats, but 66% for Swedish Social Democrats, and 83% for the Dutch Labor party. The cross-system difference is bolstered, then, by these findings by party.

The final question concerns the degree of hierarchic relationships in influence within parties. Upon analysis this turns out to be interesting because the individual parties differ so greatly. (Table 5.6) Different methods could be used to calculate the degree of hierarchy. We based our deductions on the relative size of the proportions for each party's elites which scored high and low in influence (ignoring the middle influence category for this purpose.)

The degree of hierarchy differs by particular party, by ideological direction, and also by system. We do find the Swedish conservatives the most hierarchic and the Dutch Labor party (along with the U.S. independents) the least hierarchic. The differences between these extremes are great, ranging from very hierarchic (-23) to very democratic (+56). It is interesting that as we move from "Right" to "Left" we move from much hierarchy to little hierarchy. The only deviation from this is for the U.S. Republicans.

TABLE 5.6 Patterns of Hierarchy in Elite Influence for Specific Partisan Sets (Based on the Influence Distribution Index)

	U.S.	Sweden	Netherlands
"Left" Parties			
% High (11 +)	32	37	50
% low (0 - 6)	14	25	19
Ratio Differential of High : Low	+18	+12	+31
"Right" Parties			
% High (11 +)	36	21	38
% low (0 - 6)	15	44	34
Ratio Differential of High : Low	+21	−23	+4
"Center" Parties			
% High (11 +)	60	39	35
% low (0 - 6)	4	31	26
Ratio Differential of High : Low	+56	+8	+9

Rank Order on Hierarchy Scale		Differential
Most Hierarchic	Swedish "Right"	−23
	Netherlands "Right"	+4
	Swedish "Center"	+8
	Netherlands "Center"	+9
	Swedish "Left"	+12
	U.S. "Left"	+18
	U.S. "Right"	+21
	Netherlands "Left"	+31
Least Hierarchic	U.S. Independents	+56

Note: The scores on the "Influence Distribution Index" were used to calculate these differentials. A percentage difference was arrived at by subtracting the proportion scoring in the lowest strata of influence from the proportion scoring in the highest strata of influence. A plus sign means there was a higher percentage of those with high percentage than low; a minus sign means the reverse (or a more hierarchic tendency).

These data by party, then, must change one's image of the overall hierarchic pattern of influence. We can illustrate this as follows:

	Influence Index Differentials		
	U.S.	Sweden	Netherlands
All politicians	+32	−2	+7
Left Parties	+18	+12	+31
Right Parties	+21	−23	+4
Center Parties	+56	+8	+9

The deviation from the country mean for politicians is considerable in all three countries when the party data are used alone. Further, the parties contribute differently to the explanation of the country means: the independents to the U.S. mean, the "Right" to the negative Swedish mean, and the Dutch "Left" to it's country's positive mean. Finally, note that Right and center parties have elite influence patterns which can be quite different, although the parties of the "Left" are uniformly non-hierarchic. No doubt the exigencies of current politics in these cities and countries, as well as the differential patterns of control within parties, had much to do with these divergent patterns of partisan influence.

How Relevant Are Age and Length of Tenure for Influence Perceptions?

One might develop two types of hypotheses about age and tenure in this context. From an attitudinal viewpoint one might expect the young and those most recently in local elite positions to be the most optimistic about their influence while the older (and wiser) leaders are more skeptical as a result of their experience. Or, we might expect the older leaders to report to us that they actually have acquired more influence in local politics while the newcomers and younger elites would report they had not yet achieved a position where they were exerting much influence. The actual findings reveal great differences by systems and seem to reflect quite different statuses in these systems for the young and the newcomers compared to the middle-aged, older and more experienced leaders. (See Tables 5.7 and 5.8.)

If we look at age cohort differences first we see that the youngest cohort (age 21-39) particularly among politicians, is more likely to feel they have influence in the U.S. than in Europe. There is a larger proportion in the U.S. who are involved in several policy areas, and their overall influence score is much higher. The older U.S. politicians are inclined to report less influence and to limit the number of policy areas in which they exert influence, that is to be more policy specialists. These summary data document this:

	% Scoring High on Influence Index (Score 11+)		
Age cohorts (Politicians only)	*U.S.*	*Sweden*	*Netherlands*
21-39	50	33	31
Over 50	32	33	40

The differential favors the young cohorts of politicians in the U.S., but age is irrelevant in Sweden, and the Dutch picture is the reverse of that in the

U.S., since the older Dutch cohorts report the most influence. This system difference is not true for administrators, however. (Table 5.8)

Another finding concerns the attention to "social" policy areas (Housing, Social Welfare, Health, etc.) by the young politicians in all systems. In the U.S. whose local leaders are comparatively low in these concerns, 61% of the young elites report influence in these areas, higher than any other age cohort for the U.S. This is still considerably below the high proportions of young cohorts in Europe, however.

The extent of "hierarchy" or pluralism as manifested by influence scores is dramatically different, by country, by age group, and by type of elite

TABLE 5.7   Age Cohort Differences in Influence Perceptions: Politicians

		U.S.	Sweden	Netherlands
A. Breadth of Influence % who say they have "much" influence in 3 or more policy areas Age Cohorts:		N	N	N
21–39		53 (28)	36 (30)	28 (42)
40–49		41 (44)	29 (77)	27 (74)
50–59		32 (31)	32 (96)	42 (55)
60+		32 (25)	24 (68)	24 (29)
B. Involvement in Social Policy Areas % who say they have "much" influence in social policy areas (of those with influence in at least one area) Age Cohorts:				
21–39		61	83	90
40–49		38	65	71
50–59		32	80	79
60+		57	82	76
C. Influence Distribution Index Scores % high influence (Score 11+) % low influence (Score 0–6) Age Cohorts:				
21–39	High	50 +36	33 +6	31 –17
	Low	14	27	48
40–49	High	44 +37	26 –11	33 +4
	Low	7	37	29
50–59	High	26 +10	35 +8	44 +28
	Low	16	27	16
60+	High	39 +31	30 –13	34 +17
	Low	8	43	17

TABLE 5.8   Age Cohort Differences in Influence Perceptions: Administrators

	U.S.		Sweden		Netherlands	
	Under 50	50+	Under 50	50+	Under 50	50+
A. Breadth of Influence % who say they have "much" influence in:						
- 3 or more areas	20	20	7	7	15	17
- 1 or 2 areas 54	62	38	52	59	33	
- No policy areas	26	18	55	41	26	50
N	76	56	45	70	66	36
B. Type of Policy Areas In Which Administrators Have Influence % involved in social policy areas (of those with influence in at least one area)	34	37	80	61	61	61
N	56	46	20	41	49	18
C. Influence Distribution Index Scores						
- High (Score 11+)	23	24	8	6	14	21
- Low (Score 0 - 6)	32	29	78	70	42	53
Differential	–9	–5	–70	–64	–28	–32

Note: Age cohorts had to be combined for comparative analysis because there were too few cases of very young and very old administrators among the Dutch elites.

position. The least hierarchic (or most diffused) among the politicians are the two youngest American age cohorts. For them one finds a combination of a high percent with much influence and a small percent with low influence. The contrast is particularly striking for those in the 21-39 age group. Here are the differentials for the 21-39 groups:

U.S.	+36	Very Diffused
Sweden	+6	Mildly Hierarchic, or Balanced
Netherlands	–17	Quite Hierarchic

The administrators, however, old or young are "hierarchic" in their influence patterns in all three countries. All the scores are negative, *very negative* in the case of Sweden. (Table 5.8). There is a strong suggestion here that administrators are socialized to expect (and indeed do have) less influence than politicians in all systems, and age has little to do with it.

The contrasts by country and by role, therefore, are great. Using the "influence index" scores this basic composite summary emerges concerning the hierarchy-pluralism structure of influence.

	U.S.		Sweden		Netherlands		System Difference (Range)	
	Pols.	Adms.	Pols.	Adms.	Pols.	Adms.	Pols.	Adms.
High-Low Differentials								
Under 50	+33	-9	-6	-70	-3	-28	36	61
Over 50	+19	-5	-1	-64	+23	-32	24	59
Within System Differential								
Under 50		42		64		25		
Over 50		24		63		55		

Across systems there is less difference for politicians than for administrators, but the range is great for both. Within systems the Swedish elites are most similar in their tending to be "hierarchic". Dutch and American elites vary by age group: The American younger group of politicians least hierarchic, the Dutch older group least hierarchic.

Our data on length of tenure in public service (not presented here in detail) do not provide much confirmation of any "socialization" theory. There is evidence that longer service does lead to perceptions of *much* influence among politicians in Sweden, but this is not what we find in the Netherlands and the U.S. The data for administrators is even more inconclusive. U.S. administrators with long tenure do report some increase in influence, but this is not true for either of the European systems. Hence, expectations that more experienced or older administrators would be more positive about their influence roles than the newcomers are just not borne out by our findings.

How Cities Vary in Elite Influence Patterns

One might suspect from the previous analyses in this book that we would find considerable differences by city in all three countries on elite influence perceptions. Elites vary greatly in power perceptions, in problem perceptions, in their sense of responsibility for policy action, etc., and cities vary considerably in those aspects of elite "culture" which we have examined thus far. Hence, one might well expect variations in influence orientations also. And that is indeed what we find. (Table 5.9). In three basic respects the cities in these three systems vary: (1) in their breadth of policy area agendas, (2) in the extent of their influence in "social" policy areas (compared to "traditional" policy), and (3) in the degree of "hierarchy" in their influence patterns.

On the breadth of agendas (or conversely, specialization) it is clear that there are cities in all three countries where a high proportion of elites are "generalists" and cities where elites are very narrow in their policy areas (as measured by their self-reports of influence). Thus, in the U.S. cities range from zero to 70% in the proportion of elites who say they have much influence in three or more policy areas. And the same basic differences exist in Sweden and the Netherlands. Or, to put it in obverse terms, the percentage of "specialists" among elites (who have influence in one or two policy areas only) ranges for cities between 69% (U.S.) or 50% (Europe), to 8% (Netherlands) and 25% (U.S. and Sweden). Apparently elites vary by city greatly in the way they look at their roles, tasks, policy interests and their ability to make an influential contribution to the solution of their policy problems.

TABLE 5.9   Variations by Cities in Elite Influence Perceptions

	U.S.	Sweden	Netherlands
A. Breadth of Policy Areas In Which Elites Have Influence (% who say they have "much" influence in 3 or more areas)			
- Highest City	70	42	58
- Lowest City	0	8	0
B. Concern for Social Policy (% of elites who said they have "much" influence in 4 such areas—based on those who have influence)			
- Highest City	63	87	90
- Lowest City	0	63	43
C. Influence Distribution Index % High (Score 11+)			
- Highest City	57	33	57
- Lowest City	0	16	13
% Low (Score 0–6)			
- Highest City	38	63	56
- Lowest City	0	33	21
Range in Mean Influence Distribution Scores			
- Highest City Mean	11.7	8.5	10.3
- Lowest City Mean	7.4	5.9	6.1

This applies also with the preoccupation or concern of elites with social policy areas such as housing, health, social welfare, and recreation. As noted earlier, U.S. urban elites are much less involved with these problems or at least feel they are much less likely to have much influence in these areas than is true in Europe. However, we find American cities where 63% (of elites who have influence) assert influence on social policy while other cities where no (or few) elites are interested. Of course, in Europe there are no cities where fewer than 40% of the influential elites are concerned with social policy! The range among cities within the U.S. is greater than in Europe.

It is the pattern of influence structures and the way they vary by city, however, which is the most intriguing. Table 5.9 presents some of the relevant data, revealing the range within systems on the proportion of elites with high and low influence (using the scores of our "influence index" as a basis for measurement). One should keep in mind these rules of interpretation when using these scores by city:

High scores (11+):
  (a) a high percentage of elites with such scores (e.g. 25% or more) indicates influence is shared among a large number of leaders (suggesting a non-hierarchical structure).
  (b) a small percentage with high scores suggests a concentration of influence in a few (a hierarchical tendency.)
Low Scores (0 to 6):
  (a) a small percentage with limited influence (e.g. 25% or less) indicates a limited number who are excluded from influence (suggesting a non-hierarchical structure).
  (b) a large percentage with limited influence indicates many elites with marginal influential roles (a hierarchical tendency).

We may see, thus, four basic patterns for cities: (Williams 1976, 78).

1. Hierarchy: few with much influence, many with little influence
2. Democracy: many with much influence, a small percentage with none, and many in the "middle" with a moderate amount of influence.
3. Power Bifurcation: a large percent with influence at the top, but also a large percent with little influence at the bottom. (Perhaps a dispersed, pluralist system of influence).
4. Balanced Democracy: equal proportions with considerable influence (scores 11+), moderate influence (scores 8-10), and low influence (scores 0-6).

As Table 5.10 reveals, there is an abundant variation by cities in the type of influence structures based on our data, within each country and across systems. The Dutch cities exhibit all four types of structures, the U.S. three, the Swedish cities two. There are cities which are quite hierarchical, in Sweden and the Netherlands (none in the U.S.). There are also cities which have in appearance "pluralist democratic" influence structures (but not in Sweden). Two other democratic types—what is called here "bifurcated" democracy and "balanced democracy" are found in both the U.S. and the Netherlands. This in a sense summarizes our data in general theoretical terms. The contrast between the U.S. and Sweden stands out, with the Dutch influence configurations falling in between. This is due basically to the fact that all of the Swedish cities have a high proportion of elites who report little influence, i.e. with scores below seven: 100% of the Swedish cities, 20% of the U.S. cities, 60% of the Dutch. On the other hand, the percentage of Swedish cities where a high proportion of elites report a high influence score (of 11 or more) is small. Thus, if the criterion is 25% or more with high

TABLE 5.10 The Frequency of Four Influence Structures for Cities in the U.S. and the Netherlands

Elites' High Influence Scores By City (Score 11+)

Elites' Low Influence Scores By City (Score 0–6)	25% or more	Less than 25%
30% or more	Pattern: "Bifurcated Democracy" Percentage of Cities U.S. 25% SW 47% Neth 40%	Pattern: "Hierarchy" Percentage of Cities U.S. 0% SW 53% Neth 25%
Less than 30%	Pattern: "Pluralist Democracy" Percentage of Cities U.S. 50% SW 0% Neth 20%	Pattern: "Balanced Democracy" Percentage of Cities U.S. 25% SW 0% Neth 15%

Note: These characterizations are based on the scores for each leader, cumulated for each city, based on our "Influence Distribution Index." See Appendix for a description of this index.

influence scores, less than half of the Swedish cities qualify, while 75% of the U.S. cities do and 60% of the Dutch. Another way of summarizing differences is to look at the ratios of high to low influence scores by cities. If we do that we find that 100% of all Swedish cities have a *negative* ratio (a small percentage with much influence and a large percent with minimal influence), while this is true of 55% of Dutch cities and only 35% for the U.S.

There certainly may be a variety of meaningful explanations for why this is so. But clearly there seem to be cross systemic conditions in local government or local elite cultures which are determinative of these non-equivalencies. To explain these variations however, with available knowledge about these communities in influence patterns, is very difficult. We have attempted to do this by looking at the characteristics of cities based on aggregate data. There are no generalizations which emerge which hold up across systems. That is, if we take population size, for example, we find that there is some evidence that in the smaller cities in the U.S. a higher percentage of elites are likely to report more influence. But this relationship does not hold up for the two European countries. Second, partisan control differences do seem somewhat important in Europe, with cities where the elites of the "Left" are dominant indicating more influence than for the elites of the "Right" and "Center." In the U.S. it is cities where no party is dominant or where Independents have the dominant position which reveal elites with the greatest reported influence. Other variables on which we might distinguish cities on the basis of aggregate data have not revealed any uniform findings across systems. This suggests that there are more subtle factors at work, such as the problem contexts of these cities, their economic conditions, the recruitment of elites, the organizational conditions for politics, and the interaction patterns of elites, which account for these differences. Subcultural patterns clearly exist; to discover why, remains a formidable research task.

How Do the Top Influentials Differ from Other Elites?

In our analysis of influence perceptions two major groups of elites emerge in the cities of all three countries - those leaders who claim much influence in several policy areas, and those who admit to limited and no influence. The first group "the top influentials" constitute 30% of the U.S. sample, 24% of the Swedish and 29% of the Dutch samples. The second major group "the Peripherals" include about 20% of the U.S. sample, 40% of the Swedish, and 33% of the Dutch. It is interesting to note the differential characteristics of these two groups of local leaders. How do they represent or include leaders with different positions, from different parties, different generations, varying tenures in office? And what are their value orientations, and action profiles within their communities?

We present the contrasting profiles of "Top Influentials" and "Peripherals" in Table 5.11. In all three countries those who presumably are at the top of the influence structures in their communities are the elected councilors and party leaders. Only in the U.S. do the bureaucrats hold any claim to top influence status (37%) compared to 8% in Sweden and 18% in the Netherlands). And in Europe it is "Left" politicians who predominate. In the U.S. there is a balance between Democrats, Republicans and Independents. The younger generations have considerable status in the U.S. and the Netherlands among the "Top Influentials" (as well as the "Peripherals"), but in Sweden, as we noted earlier, the influentials are heavily controlled by the older generations. In fact, if one looks at the tenure in public service data, the dominance of the "old guard" is very conspicuous, but less so in the U.S. and the Netherlands. The characteristics of the top influential elites who are running the city government in the cities in these countries, therefore, are not necessarily the same. While politicians are clearly in charge, there is considerable variation by system in other top influential elite credentials.

Does having much influence in a city make a difference? We find that those who are the most influential exhibit certain background characteristics. But do they also exhibit different behavior patterns, or, to put it differently, do they seem to function in a different type of political context than those with little influence? We examine this in Table 5.12 in two different ways. First, by looking at the data on contacts which leaders *initiate* with community groups. In all countries the top influentials are in search of support from community groups. Much more so than are the "Peripherals". From 40% to 50% of the latter seem to have only a minimal interest in community groups. This is true of only one fifth to one-third of the most influential elites. They are the real "democrats", in contact with interest groups. The second type of data confirms this, by use of the extent to which elites are *contacted by* or pressured by community groups. Again, the differential for "Top Influentials" and "Peripherals" is striking, in all countries. From 70% to 80% of the former report very frequent overtures from interest groups, while only one-third to forty percent of the "Peripherals" do. Thus, one can visualize a large majority of the Top Influentials as existing in a vortex of community group communications, personal and by mail, attendance at group meetings, pressures at home and at office, and the existence of fairly regularized interaction between these top influentials and their constituent or clientele groups.

Additional data on the contacts the elites have with higher level leaders reveals their linkages to the system hierarchy. In every case the influentials

TABLE 5.11 Who Are the Influentials and the Peripherals? Political and Social Backgrounds

	U.S.		Sweden		Netherlands	
	Top Influentials N=80	*Peripherals N=54*	*Top Influentials N=98*	*Peripherals N=182*	*Top Influentials N=87*	*Peripherals N=102*
A. Role or Function						
- Politician	63	26	92	51	82	55
- Administrator	37	74	8	49	18	45
B. Party Affiliation*						
- "Left"	36	50	52	36	54	45
- "Center"	32	7	17	13	24	24
- "Right"	32	43	20	43	20	25
- Other	—	—	11	8	1	6
	(50)	(14)	(85)	(90)	(70)	(55)
C. Age Groups						
- 21–39	25	39	14	12	16	22
- 40–49	36	19	22	29	37	46
- 50–59	23	31	42	36	35	23
- 60+	16	11	22	23	13	9
D. Years In Public Service						
- 0–4	23	26	0	7		
- 5–10	31	20	14	18	34	31
- 11+	46	54	86	75	66	69
E. Class Mobility (% with working class occupational status)						
- Father of respondent	37	42	27	20	49	47
- Respondent	4	2	9	6	4	11

*Based on politicians only, since party affiliation was not secured for Swedish administrators

are more in touch with higher party officials, legislators at the national level, and higher administrators. This is particularly clear for the European systems, and documents the greater central-local ties and interactions of European systems. This becomes even more striking if we use the data for local administrators only, as follows:

TABLE 5.12 The Linkage of Influence to Behavior and Action (Politicians Only)

	U.S.		Sweden		Netherlands	
	Influ-entials	Peri-pherals	Influ-entials	Peri-pherals	Influ-entials	Peri-pherals
A. Extent to Which Elites Initiated Contacts with Community Groups (Based on leaders reports of such efforts)						
With 5 or more groups	54	43	39	15	27	18
With 3 to 4 groups	28	14	25	33	44	29
With 0 to 2 groups	18	43	36	53	29	53
N	(50)	(14)	(85)	(110)	(71)	(72)
B. Extent to Which Community Groups Pressure Local Elites (% of elites reporting such efforts)						
By 5 or more groups	68	35	80	38	83	43
By 3 to 4 groups	12	21	14	37	14	36
By 0 to 2 groups	19	44	6	25	3	21
C. Contacts of Local Elites by Higher Authorities						
By higher party officials	28	14	73	42	54	24
By members of Parliament (Congress)	44	29	65	28	36	9
By county, state, or provincial administrators	26	14	47	12	24	15
By national administrators ·	14	7	52	21	16	4
D. Evaluation of Effectiveness of Action on Policy Problems (Average % of all elites saying effective action has been taken or is being taken in 12 policy areas)	40	28	16	17	35	23

Note:
The influentials are the local leaders who scored high (Scores of 11+) on our "Influence Index;" the peripherals are the leaders scoring low (0 to 6) on the index.

	% of local administrators in contact with higher administrators					
	U.S.		Sweden		Netherlands	
	Influ-entials	*Peri-pherals*	*Influ-entials*	*Peri-pherals*	*Influ-entials*	*Peri-pherals*
1. Contacts Initiated By Local Administrators with National Administrators	30	15	88	43	63	70
2. Contacts Initiated By National Administrators with local Administrators	27	18	88	65	56	52

Finally, it is interesting to note also the top influentials are more likely to feel that effective action is being taken on community problems than are those with limited influence (Table 5.12). This is true for the U.S. and the Netherlands, but not for Sweden. In Sweden as we noted earlier, local elites seem fairly consistently pessimistic and negative about the extent of progress being made on community problems. If there are optimists in the U.S. and the Netherlands, they are found among the Influentials.

Conclusions

To summarize these findings on elite influence perceptions is difficult. These three Western democracies reveal much variation among elites in the degree of influence, the focus of influence, and the structure of influence in communities. On the big question of whether elite influence is pyramidal and unitary the answer seems clear. It is not, it is diffuse and pluralized, although in some communities hierarchic influence structures do exist. It is a particularly diffuse and pluralistic influence structure in the U.S., lending support to the earlier pluralist position in the study of "community power structure."

We can return to the six questions posed at the outset of this chapter. Obviously one is struck by the finding that many local leaders in our surveys report no influence or a minimal portion of it - from one fifth in the U.S. to two-fifths in Europe. And the indication that this denial of influence is found particularly among bureaucrats can not be overlooked. When 47% (Sweden) or 34% (Netherlands) or 23% (U.S.) of local administrators say there are no policy areas in which they have influence, one wonders. And indeed, one wonders even more about the status of local government when similarly large proportions of elected officials deny much influence in any policy area. What may be disturbing is that these leaders are much more likely to say their city has the power to deal with these policy problems, *and* that they should have (or do have) responsibility, but much fewer say they have much influence. The disjunction is very high in all three countries. This is not perceived powerlessness of the city which is the root cause of the problem. The cause may lie, as we indicated earlier, in the constraints on influence, and on leadership generally, imposed by the structure of local government. And this may be linked to a lack of drive to seek influence, or a feeling of lack of possible efficacy, outside a narrow policy specialization.

A particular concern in the U.S., of course, is the lack of attention to social policy, the problems of housing, social welfare, etc. What really makes the U.S. stand apart from Europe is that less than half of all U.S. elites are by their own admission involved in such social policy problem resolution while 70% to 80% in Europe are. In this connection, the different value positions of elites in the three systems on the matter of economic equality is of relevance. In a later chapter the values of elites are analyzed in detail. Here it is important to note the differences between local elites in the U.S. and Europe, particularly the top influentials, on economic equality. Our economic equality scale reveals these contrasts:

	Top Influentials			Peripherals		
	U.S.	Sweden	Netherlands	U.S.	Sweden	Netherlands
% Positive on Economic Equality	23	64	47	24	52	40

In Europe those with most influence are the leaders more likely to be committed to equality; in the U.S. influence status is irrelevant for value orientations on equality. The overwhelming majority of U.S. elites are not believers.

We find much specialization in policy agendas and influence. Among those who say they have much influence, 60% in all three countries report influence in one or two policy areas. Among administrations the proportions of specialists (for those who say they do have influence) are particularly high: 75% (U.S.), 87% (Sweden), 76% (Netherlands). This of course is to be expected for administrators. The high frequency of specialization among the elected politicians with influence may not be clearly expected. Actually, we can divide the *elected leaders* as follows:

	U.S.	Sweden	Netherlands
Policy Specialists	47	53	45
Policy Generalists	53	47	55

This even split in all countries suggests a diverse, composite image of local elites' involvement with policy problems — much specialization but also a large core of generalists preoccupied with and having influence in many policy areas.

The structure of influence in local governments is fascinating to study. Using our "Influence Distribution Index" we determined the influence pattern in each city. We find great variations within systems as to the incidence of the "hierarchic", "pluralist", "bifurcated", and "balanced democracy" models. The Dutch cities illustrate all four patterns, the U.S. three and Sweden two. One fourth of all the cities in this study are basically "hierarchic" (primarily Sweden). One fourth also have basically "pluralist-democratic" structures (primarily American). The balance illustrates the other two models. Hence, again, there is a great diversity at the community level in types of influence structures.

The characteristics of the influentials which emerge from our study can be fairly precisely identified, and compared across systems. Bureaucrats do not appear to have the greatest influence in these cities but rather seem to be specialists who work with politicians, apparently less influential and somewhat dependent. The elected officials claim much more total influence. But systems do differ — administrators seem to play a larger influence role in the U.S. than in Europe. There is, however, much "within system" uniformity for politicians and administrators. For example, both types of leaders in the U.S. have less interest in "social" policy areas than do both types of European leaders. System differences for partisan groups among elites also exist: while the "Left" is dominant in Europe it is the "Independents" among elites in American cities who are distinctively influential. As for age cohorts, the U.S. and Dutch influentials are very young compared to the Swedish.

Our data on influence perceptions, therefore, reveal both empirical uniformities and contrasts. Several observations perhaps stand out. The considerable specialization in all systems, the relatively small proportion asserting much influence as generalists in several policy areas, and the disjunction between power, responsibility, and influence — these are major patterns of findings which prevail in all three systems. On the other hand, the differential influence roles of the young and the old elites, of the socialist or center or conservative elites, of the relatively recent recruitees to local position as compared to those of long tenure — these differences by system are striking. Certainly institutional and cultural factors are important in understanding these contrasts.

Above all, the great variation by city in each system demands out attention. In democratic systems elites' influence varies from little or none to very much. Communities vary from much pluralism and diffusion in elite influence to much concentration of influence. Cities can be "hierarchic" or "democratic" in the distribution of influence. This suggests that there are indeed city elite subcultures which may be more important in these democratic systems than the national elite culture. We can well devote more research to this major question.

6

The Political Contacts of Local Elites

A central concern of elite analysis is elite interaction. The contact patterns and networks of elites presumably tell us much about how they function as well as about their political systems. Data on such contacts tells us who elites see as influential in their communities, with whom they try to develop coalitions, with whom they feel their job requires them to maintain communication, and how they seek to mobilize support for their policies.

One of the theoretical preoccupations of scholars has been the question of the "integration" of elites. Early classical scholars (such as Michels and Mosca) described elites as unified, coherent, even conspiratorial as a group (Meisel 1962). Other scholars have followed with arguments in favor of the conception of elite cohesion or contradicting it. Although the controversy has subsided today, the basic theoretical concern remains. And the research on elite contact patterns, although only one type of evidence of "integration" (or the lack of it), has direct relevance. What has emerged from whatever research we have is the sense that political systems vary considerably in the extent of elite interactions with other actors in the system. The assumption that because elites work together on the same problems and in relatively close proximity, therefore they all have a "dense" set of significant interactions is not borne out by much of the research that has been done. In some systems, the relations between national bureaucrats and politicians are close and frequent (the U.S. and W. Germany, for example), while in other systems they are more distant and infrequent (Britain and the Netherlands, for example) (Aberbach 1981). In an early (1966) study of local government there was some preliminary evidence that the leaders of cities varied considerably in the extensiveness and character of their contact patterns with local leaders and groups (Jacob 1971). A 1979 Swedish study also revealed considerable local elite interactions, particularly contacts (Wallin, Back, Tabor 1981, 17; Strömberg and Norell 1982). No analysis of the meaning of these findings was undertaken, however.

The interesting question is why there are these variations in the interaction behavior of elites, *by systems* and *within systems*? It is our aim in this chapter to explore for local elites those factors or conditions which facilitate, indeed probably require, elite interactions and, on the other hand, those conditions which constrain or constitute barriers to such interaction. First one must recognize, of course, that *systems* may have particular character- istics which contribute to the variance. In studying local elites in the three democratic systems investigated here it is likely that different central-local governmental contexts (Federal vs. Unitary relations) may be relevant for the extent of hierarchical contacts. Also, the emphasis on party government in European local government clearly suggests a difference in specific types of elite contacts. And, on the other hand, the reputed importance of interest groups in the U.S. must be considered as possibly distinguishing American from European systems. Finally, system differences in elite contacts may be the result of political-cultural patterns which may be distinctive. The traditional, or expected, ways of elite communication or of mobilization of support, a product of long experience, may be the explanation which is most acceptable. Leaders' roles, decision making processes, and hence contact patterns may be culturally defined.

When we consider variations in elite contact patterns *within systems*, there are certain variables which are probably useful to explore. First, the leader's position (e.g. as bureaucrat or elected councillor), or the way leaders see their governmental role, may be relevant. Administrators may have a more specialized set of contacts. Second, the collegial environment or background within which the leader works (the type of partisan group, the age cohort, even the social class) may influence the pattern of contacts. There is also some speculation that the numerical size of the elite group may be linked to the degree of elite cohesion as revealed by the contacts engaged in (Eulau and Prewitt 1973, 187-188; Presthus 1964, 408). Third, the type of city (or commune) may be important, the relevant characteristics being: its size, partisan character, and the social or economic character of the popula- tion. We may find, indeed, particular city "subcultures" which have a highly interactive set of elites, as well as those relatively inactive or quies- cent. Fourth, the basic outlook of leaders, or of a collective elite, may provide insights explaining variance in elite contacts—their problem orientations and their conflict perceptions about their communities, their sense of responsibility toward solving problems, as well as their basic values. The linkage of contacts to political beliefs and perceptions is a set of associations we hope to explore.

Our data concerning the total interactional context of local elites consist of responses to two types of questions. We deal with both of these in this chapter. The questions are:

"When you as a public official or community leader need support from others, to whom do you usually turn among the following?"

"Do any of these contact you about their interests and views?"

Seventeen actors and groups, comparable for all three countries, are then listed for each question, including party leaders (local and higher) and a set of seven local community interest groups, plus the media, and "the public" or "close friends and supporters."

In presenting these data we can look at the findings for contacts with particular actors (as party leaders, business groups, etc.), and we also can combine the responses in order to identify particular patterns, such as the "specialists" in contrast to the "cosmopolitans." The extent and various types of contact activism can be described, then, and hopefully, explained.

System Similarities and Differences in Elite Contacts: An Overview

Our questions generated responses which provided us with a considerable body of data on the interactions of elites, presented in the accompanying tables and charts. The most important descriptive findings can be summarized quickly. First, we found certain uniformities across all three systems. (See Tables 6.1 and 6.2) Few of these leaders were completely isolated or specialized, approximately four percent. Local government leaders in these

TABLE 6.1   System Comparisons in Contacts Initiated by Local Elites (Summary of Major Findings)

	United States	Sweden	Netherlands	System Differences (Range)
A. Total Contact Patterns				
(Based on all elite contacts)				
1. "Cosmopolitans"				
(Had contacts with 8 or				
more actors or groups)	50%	42%	31%	19%
2. Moderately Active				
(2 to 7 contacts)	45	56	65	
3. "Isolates" or "Specialists"				
(0 to 1 contact)	4	2	4	
B. Contact Patterns in the				
Community				
(Based on 10 local groups)				
1. "Cosmopolitans"				
(Had contacts with 5 or				
more actors or groups)	40	21	17	23
2. Moderately Active				
(3-4 groups)	31	25	31	
3. Minimally Active				
(1-2 groups)	23	40	42	
4. Completely Isolated	6	14	10	

TABLE 6.2   The Types of Contacts Initiated by Local Elites

% saying they have sought support from the following types of leaders or groups	United States	Sweden	Netherlands	Range In Country Differences
A. Party Leaders				
1. Local leaders	25	69	76	51
2. Higher leaders	13	38	36	25
B. Elected Legislators*				
1. Local	85	79	65	20
2. MPs (National Legislative)	48	39	35	13
C. Administrators				
1. City	84	73	76	11
2. County (or State)	44	27	37	17
3. National	22	33	41	19
D. Community Groups				
1. Business	71	26	41	45
2. Civic/Reform	36	6	19	30
3. Religious	34	14	9	25
4. Unions	22	22	17	5
5. Ethnic/Racial (Immigrant)	23	13	14	10
6. Neighborhood	53	18	22	35
7. Public Employee Unions	19	30	12	18
E. Local Media	66	44	37	29
F. Friends and Supporters/ "The Public"	68	33	32	36
Average for 16 Actors and Groups	44.6	35.3	35.6	
Average for Community Groups (7)	36.9	18.4	19.1	

*State and county, or provincial, legislators are not included because of the difficulty of getting equivalent data.

democratic societies do initiate contacts with other political actors as an imperative of their roles, (and over 50% of them are subjected to considerable pressure from others who are involved in local politics). Indeed, our diagrams of the percentages reporting contacts with or pressures from other sources reveals that the interaction networks are very diverse. What strikes one is the existence of a variety of contacts for both administrators and councillors. There are differences by system and by type of leader, which we will shortly describe. But it is clear that both types of leaders are centerpoints in a complex network in their communities including parties, interest groups, media, and the public, to say nothing about their linkages to other elective and appointive officials in their own communities or upward in their systems. (See Figures 6.1, 6.2, and 6.3)

Differences across these three systems exist, however. Local elites from country to country engage in different types of contact behavior. One observation is that they vary by system in how active they are, that is, how extensive and diverse their contacts are. We have looked separately at all their contacts with political leaders and groups as well as a subset of contacts with those actors of groups which exist exclusively in the community. From this we have identified the "cosmopolitans," those with many, wide-ranging contacts. The U.S. has the highest percent of cosmopolitans (50%) while the Dutch reveal the least evidence of such activity (31%). What our data reveal is that local Dutch leaders are much more likely to be in contact with one or two groups at most (the local party, and/or one other group) while half of the American leaders have multiple connections to local groups. Swedish leaders are moderately active, with 42% having eight or more contacts. It is the relatively specialized character of Dutch elite interactions and the cosmopolitan character of the Americans, which, thus, stand out. In sum we have a "system difference" in this regard of about 20 percentage points.

FIGURE 6.1 The Interaction Patterns of the Elites with Party, Interest Groups, the Media, and the Public: U.S.

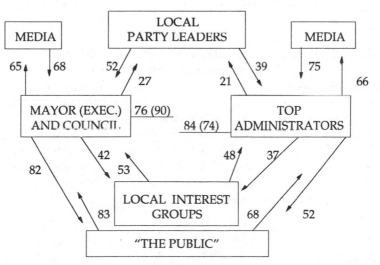

Each % is the proportion of respondents (either politicians or administrators) who say (1) they contacted a particular actor or group, or (2) they were contacted by a specific actor or group.

Figures in parentheses are the responses of the opposite set of elites.

FIGURE 6.2 The Interaction Patterns of the Elites with Party, Interest Groups, the
Media, and the Public: Sweden

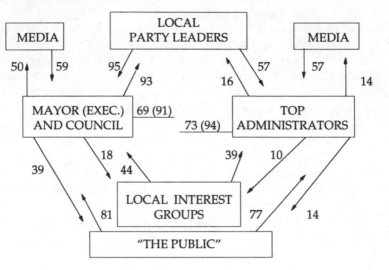

Each % is the proportion of respondents (either politicians or administrators)
who say (1) they contacted a particular actor or group, or (2) they were contacted by
a specific actor or group.

Figures in parentheses are the responses of the opposite set of elites.

The data on the extensiveness of contacts which certain actors and
groups initiate (Table 6.3) reveal less pressure on Dutch elites than on U.S.
and Swedish leaders (a 21 percentage point difference). But in all three
countries there is more pressure on local elites than contacts initiated by
local elites—a 20 to 30 point differential.

In terms of contacts with specific actors these three systems differ
strikingly. (Tables 6.2 and 6.3) As indicated above, the contact with parties
is one of these. The contact with local interest groups, local media, and the
public are other contrasts. To indicate the size of these system differences
the following summary is helpful.

	Comparison of:		
	U.S. and	*U.S. and*	*Sweden and*
Difference between	*Sweden*	*Netherlands*	*Netherlands*
two systems in:	*Difference*	*Difference*	*Difference*
1. % contacting local parties	44	51	7
2. % contacting local interest groups	19	18	1
3. % contacting "the public"	35	36	1

FIGURE 6.3 The Interaction Patterns of the Elites with Party, Interest Groups, the Media, and the Public: the Netherlands

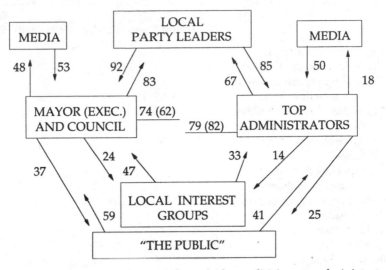

Each % is the proportion of respondents (either politicians or administrators) who say (1) they contacted a particular actor or group, or (2) they were contacted by a specific actor or group.

Figures in parentheses are the responses of the opposite set of elites.

Thus, for contacts initiated by elites, the two European countries are very similar in contact patterns with local groups, while the U.S. differs sharply with both countries. The U.S. is low in party contacts, high in interest groups, media, and public contacts. For pressure on elites, however, except for the role of parties again, the countries are quite similar. Business, civic, and neighborhood groups exert almost as much pressure on local leaders in Europe as in the U.S.. The European leaders, however, do not reciprocate as much as in the U.S., although business groups appear particularly prominent as pressure groups in both these countries.

A final difference across the three systems has to do with the relations of local leaders to national leaders. The question is whether hierarchical contacts are greater in unitary systems, such as Sweden and the Netherlands, than in the U.S. with its federal system and limited central government control over municipalities. The answer is that there are differences. As Table 6.4 reveals, local leaders in the European countries are much more in contact with national administrators and also national party leaders than is true for the U.S. In American cities, leaders are more likely to contact U.S. Congressmen than national administrators. In Sweden and the Nether-

TABLE 6.3   System Comparisons in Pressures on Local Elites (Contacts initiated by different actors seeking to influence local elites)

	United States	Sweden	Netherlands	Range In Systems
General Overall Patterns				
A. "Heavily Pressured" Elites (% of elites reporting 8 or more actors contacting them)	65	73	52	21
B. Moderately Pressured Elites (% of elites reporting 2 to 7 actors contacting them)	32	25	45	
C. "Isolates" (% reporting none or one actor contacting them)	3	2	3	
Specific Types of Pressures on Elites				
1. Party Leaders				
a. Local Party	43	83	88	45
b. Higher Party	20	47	38	27
2. Business Groups	76	53	68	23
3. Civic/Reform Groups	60	56	70	14
4. Religious Groups	37	39	17	22
5. Trade Unions	27	34	34	7
6. Ethnic/Racial (or Immigrant Groups)	33	33	27	6
7. Neighborhood Groups	70	53	50	20
8. Public Employee Groups	37	56	23	33
9. Local Media	72	63	51	21
10. "The Public"	76	79	52	27
Averages for 7 Community Interest Groups (#'s 2-8)	48.6%	46.3	41.3	

lands the contacts are through the administrative hierarchy. If we turn the question around and ask to what extent national leaders contact local politicians and administrators we find essentially a reciprocal set of results. National administrators in Sweden and the Netherlands are much more interested in initiating contacts with local administrators (69% and 54% do, respectively) than in the U.S. (only 27% are contacted). And higher party leaders contact city councillors in Europe (57% in Sweden and 45% in the Netherlands) while in the U.S. only 25% are thus contacted by national (or state) party leaders. There thus are apparently three "vertical channels" of central-local contacts for elites:

1. Local councillors and national legislators (all three countries);
2. Local councillors and national party leaders (Sweden and the Netherlands);

TABLE 6.4 Local Leaders Interactions with National Leaders

	United States	Sweden	Netherlands	System Differences (Range)
A. Contacts of Local Councillors with:				
1. Higher Party Leaders	14%	49	43	35
2. National Legislators	51	50	48	3
3. National Administrators	15	27	29	14
B. Contacts of Local Administrators with:				
1. Higher Party Leaders	12	5	25	20
2. National Legislators	45	13	12	33
3. National Administrators	39	49	65	36

3. Local administrators and national administrators (Sweden and the Netherlands).

There is actually a fourth vertical pattern also—between local administrators and state (or provincial) administrators (57% in the U.S., 40% Sweden and 60% the Netherlands). This body of data suggests overall, that there is much more hierarchical central-local "integration" in European systems. Summing our data yields these findings to support that conclusion.

	Mean contact between:	
	Local Councillors and National Party Leaders	Local administrators and National administrators
U.S.	20%	28
Sweden	53	59
Netherlands	44	60

Bureaucrats and Politicians Compared

There has long been a controversy about the relationships between bureaucrats and politicians, ideal and real. There are many nuances and variations in the theoretical positions advanced, but a major aspect of the argument concerns the role perceptions and political interaction patterns of the two types of leaders. Is there mutuality in roles and associations? Do bureaucrats work with politicians in the performance of functions; do politicians interact with bureaucrats in their key decision making activities? In Weberian theory, long accepted, the ideal relationship was a separation of bureaucrat and politician, in function and role. Modern theory emphasizes the blurring of role, the development of overlapping functions, and a convergence of bureaucracy with politics. Not all scholars, however, accept this position as necessarily generalizable across time and space. Ironically, it comes close to the theory of "the cohesion of elites" which the early classical scholars such as Michels and Mosca developed (Aberbach 1981, 4-23).

The Michigan study of national bureaucrats and politicians actually revealed three different system models so far as actual interactions are concerned (Aberbach 1981, 234). The first type is exemplified by the American (and German) systems where there is close and frequent contact by the two types of leaders. There seems to be a high degree of mutual dependency of bureaucrats and members of Congress. This is, then, the convergence model. The second model is illustrated by the Dutch (and British) systems where there is limited contact initiated by bureaucrats with MPs (although in the Dutch case a majority of MPs do make overtures to top civil servants). This is closer to the Weberian conception of an encapsulated bureaucracy, with a high frequency of administrative contacts but with bureaucrats attempting to keep the politicians at arms length. In a sense it is part of the earlier "accommodationist" theory which allegedly existed in the Netherlands until the Seventies. As Weber predicted, however, it has been impossible to completely separate the politician and the bureaucrat, functionally or behaviorally. The third, intermediate, model is the Swedish, in which the top bureaucrats are divided into two groups, the Ministries and the Boards. The former have close contacts with the politicians, the latter very little contact. This is a "functionally bifurcated" model. In Sweden, Anton argues, the roles of elites are quite specialized. Politicians initiate political discourse with bureaucrats, some bureaucrats (the Ministries) are deeply involved in politics; others (the Boards) are not (Anton 1980, 95-98, 152).

These model distinctions at the national level do not have much applicability at the local level. Table 6.5 compares the national and local elites' contacts with each other at the same governmental level. It is clear that bureaucrats and councillors are very "convergent" in all three local systems; they both initiate contacts with a high degree of frequency. Indeed, if we cumulate all the responses we have which report on the initiation of contacts (by self or by others) we find that these are remarkably similar patterns of behavior: 82% of the U.S., 70% of the Swedish, and 75% of the Dutch leaders report close contact. Thus, interactions are more dense at the local level in all systems. The Netherlands' contrast is particularly striking: the national bureaucrats (in the earlier study) tended to isolate themselves from MPs, but this tendency (of separation of politicians and bureaucrats) is certainly not so in Dutch local government today.

While we found uniformity across systems in the integration of councillors and administrators, American local elites are more actively in contact with most groups except for local parties. (Table 6.6) The highest percentage of contacts for the U.S. local leaders is with business groups and the media. For European leaders it is the local party groups and the media. On average the administrators are less likely to initiate contact with these local groups.

TABLE 6.5 Comparisons of Political Elite Contact Patterns at the National and Local Levels

	U.S.	Sweden	Netherlands
Contacts Between Legislators and Administrators at the Same Governmental Level			
1. National MP's with National Top Level Civil Servants (Studies in the Seventies)			
-Initiated by MP's	55%	54	66
-Initiated by Administrators	64	17(86)	16
2. Local Councillors with Local Administrators (Studies in the Eighties)			
-Initiated by Councillors	76	69	74
-Initiated by Administrators	84	73	79

Sources for National Elite Data:
The seven-nation comparative elite study conducted in 1970-71 (U.S. and Sweden) and 1973 (Netherlands). See Aberbach et al., 1981, pp. 230-34; Eldersveld, 1981, pp. 137-45; Anton, 1980, pp. 95-100.

1. The contact question was phrased somewhat differently. In the national study respondents were asked "how frequently [do] you have contact with [each actor]?" The response categories were: more than weekly, weekly, not weekly but regularly, often, seldom, never. We combined here "very often" and "often" with "regularly" or more often. In the local elite study the question was: "When you [as leader] need support from others to whom do you usually turn?" No frequency categories were used, beyond "usually."

2. The top civil servants in Sweden in the national study were located in either the ministries or the Boards and authorities. Their response could differ, as they did in the proportions reporting contacts with MP's: 17% for Boards and 86% for ministries—the latter figure is placed in the parenthesis in our table.

3. The national elite N's were:

	U.S.	Sweden	Netherlands
MP's	77	44	44
Bureaucrats	126	315	93

Swedish administrators particularly do not contact party leaders, but this is not true for the Dutch administrators.

A special analysis of American cities contrasting those with partisan versus nonpartisan election systems provides a partial explanation of one system difference—the contacts of elites with local parties. In partisan cities in the U.S. this contact is much higher, as the following summary reveals:

	Nonpartisan Cities	*Partisan Cities*
Contacts with Local Parties		
% of elites initiating contacts	22	43
% of elites contacted by local party leaders	38	66

The partisan environment appears very relevant. It even increases the contacts of so-called "independent" elites from zero (in nonpartisan cities) to 38% (in partisan cities). American partisan communities thus have elites

TABLE 6.6   Comparisons of Politicians and Administrators: Their Contacts Which They Initiated with Particular Groups at the Local Level

	U.S.		Sweden		Netherlands		*Differences Across Systems (Range)*	
	Pols.	*Burs.*	*Pols.*	*Burs.*	*Pols.*	*Burs.*	*Pols.*	*Burs.*
Interest Group (Averages for seven local groups)	38%	35	20	14	22	15	18	21
Special Examples								
1. Business	76	66	27	21	46	35	49	35
2. Religious	36	32	16	6	11	6	25	26
3. Unions	26	18	27	9	20	14	7	9
4. Neighborhood	60	47	19	14	27	14	41	33
5. Civic/Reform	37	34	7	5	23	13	30	29
6. Ethnic/Racial	18	26.5	14	6	17	9	4	20
Local Party Organizations	27	21	93	16	83	67	66	51
Local Media	65	67	50	28	48	18	17	49
Summary: Within Country Differences for Politicians and Administrators								
1. On all contacts	.4		11.8		3.6			
2. On interest group contacts	2.7		5.3		6.8			

who are somewhat closer to the European model in this respect, although still not as active in partisan interactions as in Europe.

What stands out in this analysis is the similarity of contact behavior for politicians and administrators within each system, with only a few exceptions. The intrasystem differences (for bureaucrats and politicians) for interest groups, for example, are small (2.7%, 5.3%, 6.8%) while the cross-system differences are larger (18%, 21%). (See Table 6.6) The cross-system scores are very large for certain groups. Perhaps we have three different models for elite relationships at the local level. While councillors and administrators work closely together in all systems, their contacts with other groups vary. Model 1 is the U.S.: minimal party contact but extensive contact with local interest groups and the public for all leaders. Model 2 is the Dutch case: Maximal contact with parties but much less contact with interest groups and the public, for all leaders (although councillors tend to be in touch with business leaders to some extent). Model 3 is the Swedish system: Maximal contact with parties for councillors but not for administrators, and generally low contact with interest groups for all leaders. Local elite contact relations vary, thus, by the political culture of the country.

Factors Explaining System Differences in Elite Contacts

We have discovered thus far certain system similarities but also system differences. The major similarities are: (1) the extent of interaction between local councillors and administrators (contrary to national data these interactions are extensive in all three systems) (2) the extensive pressures which local interest groups, aside from political parties, bring on local elites (in all three systems.)

Our task, however, is to explain the system differences. There are three major types: (1) the proportion of elites who are very active in initiating contacts is decidedly higher in the U.S., particularly for certain types of local interest groups (business, neighborhood, civic, religious) as well as for overtures to the media and to the public; (2) the Netherlands and Sweden elites are much more in contact with local and higher party leaders; (3) the Netherlands and Sweden are much more in touch with national administrative officials.

Some of the major findings on differences of systems in elite contact patterns are summarized in Table 6.7. In order to explain these system differences is a complex task. We have already suggested that basic institutional differences may help explain the party and the national-local administrative contact differences. Yet, beyond these differences there is strong evidence that generically and specifically local elites in Europe are just not motivated or expected to, seek out and attempt to mobilize support from interest groups, the media, and the public as is the case in the U.S. In a sense this is surprising because local European leaders are apparently operating in much the same type of high pressure environment as are the American leaders. From 55% to 70% report contacts by, and pressure on them from, local political pressure groups, very similar to the proportions reported by U.S. leaders.

There are several types of factors, aside from the institutional system, which we will explore here as possible determinants of these system differences. First, there may be differences in elite subgroups (partisan, generational, positional) which are distinctive across systems. For example, younger elites may be much more active in the U.S. (than older elites in the U.S. and the younger elites in Sweden and the Netherlands), and this then could be the key answer. Second, elite attitudes and values may be linked to their motivations to contact community groups for support, attitudes and values which may be more prominent in one country (the U.S.) than in the others. Third, the subcultural context of the city may be linked to elite contact activism (the city's type of population, its special types of problems, its party politics, its type of leadership with particular value priorities, etc). Certain types of city subcultural environments may be more frequent in one society than in another and, hence, explain the basic pattern of differences in elite contact behavior. Finally, it may be again necessary to fall back on the residual explanation of "culture" and agree that there is a persistent and pervasive political culture of elite contact behavior which has developed in these societies accounting for the different empirical findings we have discovered.

TABLE 6.7 A Summary of Major System Differences in Elite Initiated Contacts

	U.S.	Sweden	Netherlands	System Differences (Range)
1. Total Contacts				
% of local elites very active in initiating contacts (8 or more)	50	42	31	19
2. Community GroupContacts				
% of elites very active in initiating contacts (5 or more)	40	21	17	23
3. Examples of Specific Types of Contact:				
- The Public	68	33	32	36
- Local Parties	25	69	76	51
- Local Media	66	44	37	29
- Business Groups	71	26	41	45
- National Administrators (by local administrators)	29	49	65	36

If we begin with the so-called "collegial environment" factors, it becomes clear that although subgroups may differ, this is an inadequate explanation. Subgroup differences are not much help in explaining overall cross-system differences (Table 6.8). We use here to demonstrate this, the extensiveness of contacts initiated with community interest groups. (If we had used total contacts with all actors the findings would be very similar). We note two facts at once in perusing these data: (1) The only cross system uniformity is that administrators in all countries tend to be less active than councillors; (2) all of the American subgroups are much more active than their counterparts in Sweden and the Netherlands. Thus, one cannot generalize across the three countries that "left" elites are always more active or that the older elites are less active, etc. Such generalizations are just not tenable. Rather, one must generalize that American elites, regardless of party, age, years of service, or position, are always more active than are European elites. And

TABLE 6.8   Subgroup Variations in Local Elite Contact Activism (% of elites in each group initiating contacts with five or more community interest groups)

	U.S.	Sweden	Netherlands	Cross-National Difference (Range)
Subgroups:				
A. Party Affiliation of Respondent:				
"Left"	40%	26	19	22
"Center"	48	35	13	35
"Right"	49	20	11	38
Within System Difference—				
"Left" vs. "Right"	8	6	8	
B. Positions:				
Councillors	47	26	21	26
Administrators	34	9	11	23
Within System Difference	13	17	10	
C. Age Cohorts:				
Under 50	40	17	17	23
50 +	40	24	18	22
Within System Difference	0	7	1	
D. Years in Public Service:				
10 or less	40	16	18	24
11 or more	40	22	15	25
Within System Difference	0	6	3	

The data on party are confined to the politicians only because no party data were available for Swedish administrators. The "Center" for the Americans are those saying they belonged to no party or were Independents.

this is not due to a matter of proportions (i.e., the percentage of young or old, or councillors or administrators, or particular partisans in the samples we were using here). It is true that the national samples were different (as we pointed out earlier). For example, on position, the U.S. proportions are 49% councillors, 51% administrators; for Sweden 70% councillors, 30% administrators; for the Netherlands 66% councillors, 34% administrators. However, ironically, if one would weight the administrators more in the Dutch and Swedish samples the extent of activism would be even lower than it is! Hence, neither "proportional" explanations, nor specific subgroup differences across systems can be considered explanatory. We are left for the time being, therefore, with something akin to an institutional-cultural explanation. We will pursue our analysis further, to test other theories.

We explored in detail the relationship between problem perceptions, value orientations, and elite contact behavior. A consistent finding across countries was that those local elites who saw problems as serious were inclined to be more active in working with local groups. More important perhaps is that we also found in all systems that elites who were strongly committed to the values of equality and participation were more likely to engage in contacts with community groups (Table 6.9). This was particularly true in the European countries on the equality scale. Positive value orientations to economic equality and political participation thus seem linked (Sweden and the U.S. only) to elite contact activism. But, although this is true, it doesn't explain completely the basic differences across systems and within systems. We will explore this further in our analysis of city variations.

How Cities Differ in Elite Contact Patterns

We are preoccupied here again, as in previous chapters, with the conviction that it is the city as a political microcosm which must be understood. While there are indeed differences at the macrolevel of the system, the national culture of local elites is in the last analysis a composite of great differentiation by community. We see that clearly when we look at elite interactions with other leaders and groups by city (Table 6.10). The data demonstrate the great range in elite behavior for cities within all three countries: cities with three-fourths of the leaders actively contacting many other leaders in contrast to cities where one-fourth or less of the leaders are initiating contacts. While the contrasts among cities is somewhat greater in the U.S., the variations are considerable also in Sweden and the Netherlands.

The extent of elite homogeneity or cohesion in contact behavior by city varies. Among the 20 U.S. cities, for example, (where on the average 50% of elites are quite active) eight cities have very interactive elites, three have leaders who as a group are not very involved, and the remainder are

FIGURE 6.4 A Model to Explain Elite Contact Behavior

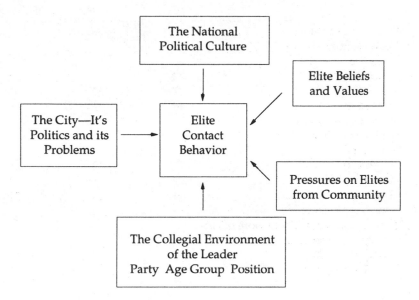

TABLE 6.9 The Link Between Elite Values and Elite Contact Behavior (% reporting 5+ contacts with community groups)

	U.S.	Sweden	Netherlands
Value Scale			
A. Economic Equality:			
Very Pro	45	27	25
Somewhat Pro	40	24	18
Somewhat Anti	41	16	16
Very Anti	39	16	13
Within System Difference	6	11	12
B. Participation:			
Very Pro	45	22	20
Somewhat Pro	39	22	14
Somewhat Anti & Very Anti	35	13	17
Within System Difference	11	9	3

The value scales items used here are presented in the Appendix. Six agree-disagree items were used for each value scale. Those considered "very pro" or "very anti" were the extremes on a four-point agree-disagree continuum. The last two categories of the participation scale had to be combined because there were so few cases in all three countries of elites who were very negative on these items.

TABLE 6.10 Variations by Cities in Elite Contact Patterns

	U.S.	Sweden	Netherlands
A. Total Contact Patterns			
High Number of Contacts (8+)			
% of elites			
- High City	73	71	54
- Low City	27	22	0
Difference	46	49	54
B. Community Group Contacts			
High Number of Contacts (5+)			
% of elites			
- High City	73	40	33
- Low City	9	11	0
Difference	64	29	33
C. Summary Measure			
% of all cites with 50% or more of elites			
very active in contacts:			
a. Total Contacts (8+)	60	13	5
b. Community Contacts (5+)	25	0	0

moderately active in initiating contacts. In the Netherlands, on the other hand (where on the average 31% of elites are very active), four out of the 20 cities exceed that mean considerably, another four have leaders who are very inactive, and the remainder are moderately active (in relative terms). The same differential patterns are found in Sweden. Thus, overall, elite cohesion varies by city. If we use a measure of "the largest majority" in each city (trichotomizing each city's elite into those very active, moderately active, and minimally active), we find that following averages for the highest majority across cities: U.S. 53.8%, Sweden 44.8%, Netherlands 46.5%. Such averages suggest a very similar cross-national finding. Yet, more important is the fact that all systems reveal diversity in elite contacts by city. There are cities whose elites are clearly very active and cities whose elites are not very active. What factors explain these community differences?

The first question is whether certain characteristics of cities are related to the activeness of elites in seeking support from community groups? After examination of a variety of factors the only aggregate variable which emerged as possibly important was population size (Table 6.11). Elite contacts are considerably more frequent in the larger cities in the U.S. and Sweden, but there is no relationship in the Netherlands. The distribution of Dutch cities in our sample by population size may be a reason for this finding: only one large city (over 90,000) compared to four in Sweden and five in the U.S.; and many (10) small cities in the Dutch sample (under 40,000), compared to only three in the U.S. and four in Sweden. The fact that the larger cities in two of these countries have more active elites may attest to the types of problems in these cities, the types of leaders elected, the strength of "Left" parties, and the type of pressures these leaders are subjected to.

Among the many ways that we might classify cities for the purpose of this analysis there are three, aside from population size, which appear to be relevant: the partisan character of elite control, the values of elites (especially the extent to which they feel positive toward citizen participation), and the pressures on elites from community groups and actors. In Table 6.11 the data for all of these are presented. All three seem significantly related to elite contacts (i.e. contacts initiated by elites) in the U.S. and Sweden. Only the pressures variable is significant for the Netherlands.

TABLE 6.11 Characteristics of Cities Which Might Be Linked to Elite Contact Activity (% initiating contacts with 5 or more community groups)

	U.S.	Sweden	Netherlands
1. Population Size			
- Largest Cities (upper third of sample of cities)	50.5	27.4	16.0
- Medium Cities	36.3	17.2	19.9
- Smallest Cities	35.3	18.8	14.9
2. Partisan Character of Elite Structure			
(based on our sample of elites)			
- Cities in which "Left" parties were dominant	43.1	24.3	15.4
- Cities in which "Right" parties were dominant	41.0	20.5	20.2
- Cities where party control was split			
(including "Independents" in the U.S.)	33.7	16.8	15.7
3. Pressures from Community Groups on Elites			
- Cities ranking highest on pressures			
(top third of sample of cities)	59.2	27.8	22.2
- Cities ranking in the middle on pressures	32.4	20.0	20.4
- Cities low in pressures on elites			
(lower third of city sample)	31.9	15.6	9.0
4. Elite Value Orientations—			
The Participation Value Scale			
- Cities with elites very high in support			
for participation	49.7	25.6	19.5
- Cities medium in support for participation	33.5	18.6	17.7
- Cities lowest in support for participation	37.3	19.2	19.3

The Pearson correlations document clearly the relations between these three variables and elite-initiated contacts:

	U.S.	Sweden	Netherlands
1. Party Strength in City (% left)	.156	.282	-.088
2. Pressures from Community Groups			
(% of elites reporting heavy pressure)	.633	.563	.432
3. Elite Belief in Citizen Participation (% pro)	.138	.169	.097

The strongest variable is the pressures on elites, for all countries, and for Sweden and the U.S. there is a small relationship for the other two variables. If we control by population size we find that the amount of pressures from community groups is still a discriminating variable, although least relevant for the largest Swedish cities.

When we analyze the explanatory relevance of the pressure variable by individuals, rather than cities, we find correlations between pressures on leaders and contacts initiated by leaders to be close to .500 for Sweden and the U.S., for both politicians and administrators, with the Netherlands even higher (.583) for administrators but a bit lower (.390) for politicians.

A summary of our findings, then, is as follows:

1. Elites in cities where parties of the "Left" are in control are most active in initiating contacts, followed by cities with conservative party dominance. Cities with split party control are places where elite activism is lowest. (This is not true for the Netherlands.)
2. There is a reciprocal relationship between pressures on elites and contacts initiated by elites in all three countries. The more evidence of pressure, the more self-generated elite activity to mobilize support.
3. Cities with elites most positive in their belief in political participation and economic equality tend to be cities with the greatest elite contact activism. (But this is not true for the participation value in the Netherlands).

The differences among cities on these variables are great. On pressures, the percent of elites reporting pressures by five or more community groups ranges from 82% to 30% in the U.S., 83% to 32% in Sweden, and 77% to 43% in the Netherlands. On the value of participation cities range in percent who are very pro-participation from 54% to 5% in the U.S., from 65% to 42% in Sweden, and from 55% to 26% in the Netherlands. And the strength of the "Left" parties in these cities ranges in the U.S. (the Democrats) from 94% to 7%, from 64% to 30% in Sweden, and from 82% to 27% in the Netherlands. And at least in the U.S. and Sweden these differences appear to be linked to elite contact activism.

To demonstrate that these factors are indeed very relevant we have analyzed the joint determinacy of two key variables: the level of pressures on elites from community groups, and the level of personal value commitment to public participation in politics. (Table 6.12) We have developed measures for each of these two variables for the total elite group of each city and then determined the relationship of these to the aggregate elite contact score for each city. The findings reveal that in all three countries the same pattern is observed: elites in cities with high scores on interest group pressures plus high scores on elite belief in participation rank high in elite activism. This is clearly true for U.S. and Sweden and partially true for the Netherlands. Since community interest group pressure is greatest in the U.S. the contrast is more striking in the U.S. and the explanatory theory more powerful in the U.S. Note these country findings:

Average % of contacts initiated by elites in:	*U.S.*	*Sweden*	*Netherlands*
1. Cities high on group pressure and high on elite support for participation.	49.4	32.0	19.0
2. Cities low on group pressure and low on elite support for participation.	26.8	18.5	12.8
Difference:	22.6	13.5	6.2

Although the relationship holds cross-culturally, it is clearly a very strong one in the U.S. and least strong in the Netherlands.

The political life of the city and the character of political leadership in the city varies and obviously are very important to understand in order to comprehend the variance across cities in elite contact behavior. One final type of analysis documents this theoretical position further, and that is the "breakage" theory that we utilized previously. That is, the theory that the behavior of the dominant (partisan) elite group influences the behavior of other elites. If there is a dominant group which is very active in mobilizing support, the contagion will spread to other elites, so the theory goes, who will also seek to mobilize support. A "bandwagon effect", so to speak. Cities vary significantly in the existence of a dominant group active in mobilizational contacts. Our analysis reveals that there is a sharp distinction in elite contacts in cities with such a dominant, active elite and other cities. (Table 6.13) All the differences for all three countries are in the same direction, although the magnitudes of the differences vary. The Dutch system does not reveal as much of the bandwagon phenomenon as is true for the U.S. and Sweden, but the difference does still exist. In cities where all elites are relatively in a state of inactivity or inertia, the apathy is generalized for all leaders. Where one group of leaders reveals considerable activity in contacting local groups, other elites follow with their own contact efforts. We thus have the convergence of certain community characteristics which help to

TABLE 6.12 The Joint Determinacy of Values and Pressures (for Each City) as Explanations of Elite Contact Activeness (% of elites initiating 5 or more contacts with community groups)

	United States	
	High on Support for Participation	*Moderate or Low on Participation*
High Level of Pressures on Elites from Below	49.4	57.2
Low Level of Pressures on Elites	29.6	26.8
	Sweden	
	High on Support for Participation	*Moderate or Low on Participation*
High Level of Pressures on Elites	32.0	22.0
Low Level of Pressures on Elites	14.8	18.5
	Netherlands	
	High on Support for Participation	*Moderate or Low on Participation*
High Level of Pressures on Elites	19.0	24.2
Low Level of Pressures on Elites	16.5	12.8

The percentages are averages for cities. Thus, in the first table, 49.4% of the leaders in cities where elites reveal a high support for the value of participation and who also report great pressure from interest groups, are active in initiating contacts with local groups and other actors (out of 10 local groups).

explicate variation in elite behavior across cities in all three countries: pressures on elites, value orientations of elites, party affiliation of elites, and predispositions of elites to imitative or competitive behavior. These components of city political culture cumulatively help understand elite behavior.

Conclusions

The analysis of these data tells us a great deal about the state of local elite interactions with political groups and leaders in Western democracies. We have discovered a considerable, although varied, amount of such interaction. There are many pressures on such leaders as well as many contacts

TABLE 6.13 The "Contagion Effect" of Dominant Party Behavior in Cities: The Relevance of Elite Culture in the City for Elite Contact Behavior (Basic measure: % of elites contacting 5 or more community groups)

	U.S.	Sweden	Netherlands
Basic Categories of Cities			
A. Cities where there is a dominant party whose elites are active in initiating contacts with community groups			
1. Average % of elite contacts for the dominant group	60	49	43
2. Average % of elite contacts for the elites of other parties	47	42	18
B. Cities where the elites of no party are very active % of elite contacts for elites of all parties	27	21	14

initiated by such leaders. Across these three systems we found uniformity in the level of such pressures, as well as in the intensive contacts between the politicians (city councillors and party leaders) on the one hand, and the administrators (Department functionaries) on the other hand.

The differences between these systems in elite contact behavior are quite apparent, however. They differ strikingly in the contacts of local elites with party leaders (much more in Europe), and with upper level administrative leaders (also much more in Europe). On the other hand American leaders have more contact with interest groups, and overall have a generally higher level of elite contacts.

We attempted to test a variety of theoretical propositions to explain these differences. Obviously institutions make a difference. The unitary European systems seem naturally to lead to more hierarchical contacts between local and national authorities then in the U.S.. And the heavy emphasis on partisan government in Europe at the local level also leads to more contact with party organization leaders (as it does in the U.S. in cities with openly partisan systems). But institutional explanations are not enough and we are really left with systems which appear to be "culturally" different, that is different in the politically cultural patterns of elite behavior. In an aggregate, macro-descriptive sense this is true.

Our comparative analysis is improved greatly, however, when we dig into city differences in elite contacts and then try to explain them. It is uniformly true in all systems that there are striking differences by city in the level of elite action to mobilize support from other groups. Within the overall cultural constraints of each macro-system we find great city variance.

In testing theories to explain city variance, we find some limited support for the relevance of city size. In the U.S. and Sweden it is the larger cities where elites are more active, but this does not hold for the Netherlands. Similarly the partisan character of the city also seems a factor marginally linked—cities with "Left" parties which are dominant (the Social Democrats in Sweden and the Democrats in the U.S.) tend to have the most active elites (but not in the Netherlands). To generalize for the utility of these two factors, therefore, is not possible.

It is when we combine two other factors—pressures on elites and the degree of elite belief in citizen participation—that we have a cross systemic finding of real power. Although the Dutch data are not as impressive, in all three countries it is clear that where there is a convergence of considerable pressure on elites from other actors and groups, and the existence of high pro-participation value orientations—then elite contact behavior escalates. Comparatively this finding provides genuine empirical support for a key characteristic of the democratic process at the local level in Western democracies.

As we argued in other chapters it is our conviction that cities are microcosms of political practice, belief, and behavior, particularly of special patterns of elite orientations to political life. We find that to be true here again, and document it with a "breakage analysis" which demonstrates that where and when the dominant elite in a community decides on a particular pattern of contact behavior (activist or apathetic), responsive no doubt to local pressures, problems, and conflicts, other (oppositional) elites seem to engage in behavior which is reactive and imitative. This "bandwagon" phenomenon illustrates again the distinctiveness of the cultures of our cities.

7

The Political Values of Local Elites

In our three Western systems the elites we study hold the top political positions in the community. Such elites presumably "drive" their local government in the directions they feel it should go. It is important then to ask what values "drive" these political elites. What normative preferences about the political system and process dominate their thinking? We assume that elites have fundamental value orientations, which are stable over time, and which are relevant for their attitudes, policy preferences and behavior. We gave considerable space in our questionnaire to the inquiry about values because we believe they are critical elements in elite political cultures. Values are considered by many to be central to understanding cultures and, thus, political behavior (Inglehart 1990; Thompson et al. 1990). What these values are, then, requires careful systematic analysis.

We have used five value scales in this study. The first two are central to the political functioning of democratic systems: the commitment of elites to meaningful citizen participation in the political process, and the acceptance by elites of the necessity and legitimacy of political opposition and conflict. As other scholars have argued, these are two essential characteristics of a competitive democratic order. They are similar to the two dimensions used by Dahl—political "contestation" and political "participation" (Dahl 1971, 4-5). In the national study of Western elites the same two dimensions were used—referred to as political "liberty" ("contestation") and equality ("participation") (Aberbach 1981, 172-173). In operationalizing these two values we have focused on certain specific components. The items used for the participation scale inquire of our elites: how inclusive, or exclusive, are their values about the right to vote; how open, or restrictive, do they feel about free speech and the right to express opinions on issues; do they believe participation leads to undesirable conflicts; and to what extent do they believe that political decisionmaking is the province of competent experts without the need for citizen participation.

The conflict value scale includes items which ask the respondent to appraise his or her role as a leader in a community confronted with opposition. A leader is often faced with the need to make proposals for action, and to implement these actions, which are not necessarily supported by significant sectors of the population in the community. In such a context how much consent is necessary? How important is communal harmony? Is the resolution of conflict of greater importance than action on important programs? Should leaders "modify actions to keep consensus"? Basically the scale seeks to measure whether these leaders prefer to avoid conflict or believe that conflict is functional to progress.

In addition to the "Participation" and "Conflict" scales three other value scales are included in this study. One deals with national versus local elite orientations. This was considered to be of special relevance in our study because of the differential institutional context for local government in these countries—the U.S. a highly decentralized system, and the Dutch and Swedish systems exhibiting moderate to considerable central government influence over local government decisions. Hence our scale items deal with leaders' views about the importance and priority of national or local problems, as well as the expectation that they should have to modify local government goals and actions to fit national government goals and preferences.

The fourth value scale dealt with the change orientation of leaders. The items query whether traditional ways of doing things in the community should be maintained or, at the other extreme, whether changes should be adopted even if they do not seem to contribute much. In between these extremes leaders are asked whether progress means that new solutions are essential? The contrast between continuing "the old ways" and the necessity for innovation was central to this battery of value items.

The final value scale dealt with economic equality, focusing exclusively on "economic" rather than "political" equality (which was implicitly tested in the first two scales). Again, for our three countries, with their great differences in social welfare policy, this scale was not only relevant but could be expected to evoke contrasting patterns of responses. The items tested respondents' preferences concerning ceilings on incomes, the need to equalize salaries, the need for the rich to pay more, and the need to provide more opportunities for the poor. It is interesting to see on the basis of these tests of egalitarianism how these three democratic systems differ.

These value scales were first developed and tested in the 1966 study of community leaders in the four nation study of *Values and the Active Community* (Jacob 1971). The items conceptualized and validated then have been incorporated in research on local elites in many countries since then.

In presenting the data on these values, our discussion will be divided into four basic sections. First, since our focus is a cross-system analysis we will describe the findings comparatively, particularly the level of elite commitment and value cohesion across systems. We will highlight system uniformities and variations. Second, the *within system* differences for the cities and communes of each country will be described and analyzed. Third we will present a subgroup analysis (by elite position, party affiliation, age cohort, educational level, and socioeconomic status) comparatively. Finally, our intent is to explore the linkages between values and other elite attitudes, perceptions, and group contact patterns. Underlying the presentation of these four types of analyses is our interest in discovering whether distinctive elite value cultures exist, how they differ by system, what the socialization processes seem to be which explain the emergence of such cultures, and how important they are for explaining how elites think about the problems of politics in their communities as well as how they function as leaders in their communities.

From classical scholars of elites to the present the beliefs, agendas, formulas, and values of elites have been the subject of much speculation and some investigation. Early theorists emphasized the like-mindedness of elites, or their congruence on basic beliefs. A position was elaborated which contended that elites coming from similar backgrounds, engaging in close and frequent interactions, and engaging together in the same "power game" presumably would result in elite value and ideological cohesion. Revisionists have argued otherwise, however, that elite backgrounds vary significantly, their roles and positions in the authority structure are specialized, their socialization influences differ considerably, and intra-elite conflicts over values may be very probable. Rather than consensus, it is argued, the elite is naturally dissensual, competitive, and even combative. And this lack of unity in agreement includes their values about democracy—such as the role of conflict, the importance of citizen participation, and the pursuit of economic equality.

The revisionist position is surely the theoretical expectation one is inclined to operate with these days. But the answers based on empirical research are not yet all complete. The comparative research on elite values has made important contributions in recent years. The lack of elite congruence within system at the national level is strongly suggested by certain studies (Aberbach 1981). That elite values vary by system has been documented in national and local elite studies (Jacob 1971; Putnam 1973). What the key factors are which explain elite non-congruence and system variance have not been adequately explored. However, the linkage of elite values to other attitudes and to elite ideology has been strongly argued and has found some support (Putnam 1973; Aberbach 1981). But the generalization that elite values have an impact on elite behavior and on community activeness and development has been more difficult to demonstrate convincingly. In fact, the Jacob study found that elite values did seem to have a role in explaining community development in India, some secondary role in the U.S. and Yugoslavia, and no meaningful role in Poland (Jacob 1971, 299-

303). There is thus a significant body of theory and research on elite values relevant to our undertaking here. But more comparative knowledge is necessary. We build on this work to investigate elite values in the communities of these Western democracies.

We should note here the methodological approach used, and thus, the limitations of this analysis. Five basic value scales were developed, as indicated. In our data collection we included 31 short answer agree-disagree items (see Appendix for these). These items originally were developed in the 1966 Jacob study, validated for cross-national use. Not all of them were finally included in our scales here. Factor analysis revealed that certain items did not scale well; therefore in the construction of the scales six of the 31 items were dropped. While relying here heavily on the value scale scores (based on the 25 items), we will refer to the other items from time to time to illustrate the range of support for value components. In presenting our information we will use mean value index scores (based on factor analysis), as well as simple percentages of average support for a particular value.

An Overview of Elite Values Across Systems

Local elites in these three countries are the mirror images of each other on four of these value scales. They are "democrats," and "innovators," and marginally also "localists." Their strong commitment to the democratic values of citizen participation and the legitimacy of conflict is apparent (Table 7.1). Only small minorities, of 25 percent or less, reveal a limited commitment to these values. This confirms at the local level the expectation of Dahl for "polyarchy." Indeed, it is stronger support than was found in the study of national elites (to be discussed subsequently).

The question of whether local or national priorities and goals should prevail is only marginally resolved in favor of localism (unless one eliminates certain scale items for the U.S. and the Netherlands—which will be discussed later in more detail). This finding is perhaps somewhat surprising for the European systems, although as we described in Chapter I, movement toward decentralization in these countries recently may help understand their localist orientations today. Local elites in these unitary European systems certainly have a great deal of orientation and loyalty to their own cities and communes. On balance 55-60 percent are locality focused, as in the U.S.

It is on the value of economic equality that the systems diverge. The contrast is quite striking, with the Swedish leaders much more committed to equality (over 50%) compared to 10-20% in the U.S. (depending on which items are used). The Dutch also are more egalitarian than the Americans. These findings should come as no surprise to those who are familiar with previous research on economic equality in these countries. In their American study Verba and Orren demonstrated the low level of support for this

TABLE 7.1 Value Profiles of Local Elites

	U.S.	Sweden	Netherlands
Value Scale (% favoring)	(1984)	(1985)	(1989)
Political Participation	79	90	85
Political Conflict	78(84)	75(75)	72(80)
National (vs. Local) Commitment	38(53)	43(45)	39(53)
Innovative Change	77(74)	85(81)	74(77)
Economic Equality	23(11)	57(61)	41(33)

These are the average percentages of the elites supporting each value, utilizing all the agree-disagree items included in the questionnaires for all countries. The number of items included in each scale was 6, 7, 6, 5, 5. The figures in parentheses are the average percentages if we utilize only those items included after the factor analysis was completed: 6, 4, 4, 3, 4.

value (Verba and Orren 1985, 255-256). A Gallup Poll in 1968 revealed that only 9 percent of the public favored an income ceiling (17% of Democratic leaders, 2% of Republican leaders). However, three-fourths of the Democratic leaders (only 14% of the Republicans) favored some government action to reduce the income gap between rich and poor. In their special study comparing U.S. and Swedish party and union leaders they reveal large differences, as follows:

	*"Left" Party Leaders**	*Union Leaders*
1. % favoring a limit on income:		
Sweden	44	51
U.S.	17	13
2. % favoring equal pay:		
Sweden	58	68
U.S.	12	11

* U.S.: Democrats; Sweden: Social Democrats.

These differences are consistent with our data.

Another general finding is that the strength of commitment (or, for economic equality, of opposition) varies by country (Table 7.2). The strength of support for participation is extremely high in Sweden, higher than in the U.S. (as is true of the Netherlands also). Sweden also has elites with stronger commitment on the conflict and economic equality scales. The Americans, however, are very committed to change. The marginal character of the support for localism is seen in all these countries.

A broader global and developmental perspective can be employed in order to see the meaning of these data. Since these same value scales were used in four countries in the 1968 Jacob study, as well as more recently in a Polish study (and in two states in India), comparisons of various types are

TABLE 7.2   Variations in Strength of Elite Commitment to Democratic Values

Value Scale	U.S.	Sweden	Netherlands
1. Participation:			
- Very strongly support	26%	58	42
- Moderately support	53	32	42
2. Political Conflict:			
- Very strongly support	19	33	20
- Moderately support	66	42	59
3. Economic Equality:			
- Very strongly support	2	26	8
- Moderately support	8	33	25
4. Innovation:			
- Very strongly support	39	21	25
- Moderately support	35	60	52
5. Local-National Scale (% pro national):			
- Very strongly support	11	19	11
- Moderately support	42	26	42

These percentages are the proportion of *all responses* on a given scale which were "very strongly" or "moderately" supportive.

possible (Table 7.3). We focus here particularly on the key values of participation, conflict, and equality. The Western democracies are clearly much more supportive of citizen participation than the non-western systems. And over time the Polish and Indian systems have made only marginal progress on this value. Further, the Western elites are much more tolerant of conflict than elites in developing systems, although India, based on these data, reveals a significant movement toward the acceptance of conflict recently as a necessary component of a democratic order. But on economic equality the U.S. ranks lowest, even lower than Poland in 1991. The most egalitarian system is the Indian (as of 1966), much more egalitarian than even Sweden.

The findings in 1966 that the Indian, Yugoslavian, and Polish elites were much more accepting of economic equality than the U.S. evoked the following harsh observation by non-American scholars published in the 1971 book:

> The extraordinary social conservatism of American [leaders] comes to the fore. [Few American leaders] are even modestly committed to change in the direction of economic equality. (Jacob 1971, 92).

The pro-innovation scores in 1966 were: U.S. 60%, India 84%, Poland 78%, and Yugoslavia 76%. While local elites in the U.S. are now more in favor of change (77% in 1984), their support for economic equality has actually declined.

It is difficult in these cross-national data to see any clear linear or non-linear pattern, a meaningful comparative structure in which these data fit, by developmental status, or degree of democracy, or any other system level criteria or dimensions. True, the three Western systems are similar on the participation and conflict values, but not on economic equality. Developing systems may be very egalitarian or not at all. Poland's movement toward a more free-market economy recently apparently is linked to less interest in economic equality (58% in 1966, 22% today). There is no progress toward elite support for citizen participation in Poland after the demise of communism. There is much more evidence of change in India. Thus the overall country-by-country findings are very diverse and the explanations seem system-specific. No quick comparative rationale suggests itself.

One way of attempting to locate these countries is by using two value dimensions based on these data: commitment to political democracy, and commitment to economic equality. (See Figure 7.1) One can see from this arrangement of the findings that each system occupies its own space in this fourfold diagram. Poland and Sweden are at extremes of one diagonal; India and the U.S. are at the extremes of the other diagonal. The Netherlands

TABLE 7.3   Local Elite Value Profiles of "Western" Democracies in Comparison with "Non-Western" Systems

	Three Western European Systems			Poland		Yugoslavia	India	
	(means) 1984–1989			1966	1991	1966	1966	1979
Value Scales (% favoring)								
Participation		84		42	44	58	37	47
Political Conflict		75		53	54	38	28	49
Economic Equality	U.S.	SW	Neths					
	23	57	41	58	22	38	85	—

The 1966 data come from Jacob, et al., *Values and the Active Community* (1971). A comparison of the U.S. 1966 and 1984 is as follows:

	1966	1984
Participation	58	79
Political Conflict	63	78
Economic Equality	24	23

The 1991 Polish data come from the study conducted by the Institute of Sociology, University of Warsaw, and used by permission of Renata Siemenska.

The 1979 India data come from a study of elites done in 1978-79 by Subrata Mitra in Gujarat and Orissa and reported in Mitra (1992), pp. 163 and 253-54.

is close to Sweden but considerably less supportive of economic equality. India appears to be moving toward the Swedish model; Poland is diverging more from any of the other systems. Each system has local elites, thus, who espouse democratic values in a combined pattern which makes these systems rather unique, and different, elite "value cultures."

A Comparison of National and Local Leaders' Values

In the early Seventies a study of national politicians and bureaucrats was completed in these three countries, as part of a seven-nation study (Aberbach 1981). The seven nations were: Britain, Sweden, Netherlands, West Germany, France, Italy, and the United States. Special attention was given to the democratic values of elites, particularly mass participation (or political equality), and political conflict or contestation (or pluralism). Although the questions used were different than the items in our value scales, the content and focus of the questions were similar enough to permit a comparison at the two elite levels. On the values of citizen participation, here is a summary of the data (only for our three countries):

	Averages	
	National Elites	*Local Elites*
Citizen Participation (% favorable)		
All leaders	48	84
Politicians	79	87
Bureaucrats	39	83

The politicians were committed strongly to political equality at both levels, but there is a striking difference for the bureaucrats. Top national civil servants in the Seventies were not very interested in citizen participation in these three countries (true also for the other countries in the seven-nation study—only 44% were favorable over all).[1] The distance between politicians and bureaucrats at the local level is virtually nonexistent. It is a large gap, however, at the national level. This is particularly true for Sweden and the Netherlands. For our three countries, here are the comparisons:[2]

	% Supportive of Citizen Participation		
	U.S.	*Sweden*	*Netherlands*
National Elites			
Politicians	80	94	63
Administrators	56	26	35
Local Elites			
Politicians	81	91	86
Administrators	77	87	82

For the second democratic value, political conflict (or contestation) we used national study responses which probed how the respondent evaluated the role of conflict in society and politics, including the response to the question "Do you consider social conflict healthy or harmful?" (Only 44% of the national bureaucrats and 50% of the politicians were coded "positive" on this evaluation) (Aberbach 1981, 177. 40-42). Comparing these national data with our local value scale data is again interesting:

% of Elites Favorable on Political Conflict

	U.S.		Sweden		Netherlands		All Countries (Means)	
	Nat'l	Local	Nat'l	Local	Nat'l	Local	Nat'l	Local
Politicians	34	83	42	77	50	74	42	78
Bureaucrats	45	85	39	74	39	70	41	77
All Leaders (Means)	40	84	41	75	45	72	42	78

On the values of political conflict, politicians at the national level are surprisingly ambivalent and even negative. One might have expected negative evaluations by bureaucrats to be much higher than they are, and higher than for politicians. The three sets of national elites are very close, and their low percentages much lower than those for both types of elites at the local level. While it is true that the seven-nation study found higher support for pluralist politics among politicians than bureaucrats, on the specific measures of approval or disapproval of conflict, the responses were more negative than positive. As the authors of a special study of the American data reported, "American federal executives are less inclined than Congressmen to see conflict as socially deleterious. The executives are especially likely to think that conflict is beneficial for bringing new problems onto the public agenda and for widening the diversity of ideas in society." While 55 percent of Congressmen are concerned that conflict will lead to social chaos, this is true of only 24 percent of the American federal executives (Aberbach and Rockman, 1977, 40-42).

Why should there be this difference in support by elites for democratic values at the national and local levels? Why are (were) national bureaucrats so skeptical of citizen participation while local bureaucrats were not? Also, why should local politicians be so much more accepting of the legitimacy of political conflict than national politicians? The answer is not clear. But conceivably the 13-16 year time difference in the studies may be critical. The national studies were done in 1970-71 (U.S. and Sweden) and 1973 (Netherlands). At that time and during the Seventies there were major "democratic" crises occurring in all three societies and popular movements emphasizing a greater citizen role in the political process as well as a recognition of political conflict as inevitable and functional. Thus, by 1984-85 when the local studies in the U.S. and Sweden were completed, and 1989-90 in the Netherlands, new leaders were exposed to new democratic currents and conceivably other leaders at that time were to some extent resocialized. We will go into more detail in analyzing this question when we discuss the factors related to elite value positions in a later section of this chapter.

Other explanations of course must also be considered for this disjunction. The basic conclusion in our study of strong support of both bureaucrats and politicians for these values at the local level is significant. Theoretically one might expect less support at the local level, particularly for bureaucrats. The fact that we find the two types, bureaucrats and politicians, highly supportive at the local level in contrast to national elites, may be due to the different institutional environments of these elites at the two levels, their differing role orientations, their distance from the public in day-to-day activities, or the different recruitment and socialization processes. Mass-elite relations, which vary for these two sets of leaders, may be very relevant. These hunches need further empirical exploration. As we examine the value orientations of various subgroups (party, age, SES, education), and compare such analysis with that at the national level, we may be able to cast more light on this disjunction between national and local elite value orientations.

Variation in Elite Value Responses for Scale Components

If we disaggregate the value scales we can see that in each system the agree-disagree items in these scales evoke different responses. This is to be

FIGURE 7.1 The Location of Systems on Two Democratic Value Dimensions

		*Political Democracy Value Support**	
		High	Low
Economic Equality Value Support	High	Sweden (1985) Netherlands (1989)	India (1966) India (1979) Poland (1966)
	Low	U.S. (1984)	Poland (1991)

* This dimension is a composite of the level of support for the two values of citizen participation and political conflict.

expected because these items tap different components of the value. Value scale percentages are absolutist and suppress these variations within the scale. This point is not only an explication but also a caution. Further, if one wants to know what the essential basis for system differences or uniformities is, one must look specifically at all the components. Factor analysis, of course, excludes components which do not "fit in." It is useful to look also at these excluded items to see the ranges in support for possibly relevant value components.

The Participation Scale revealed high agreement for most of the components. Yet, even for this scale there is no unanimity of support for all components. When one looks at elite responses to the query whether citizen participation leads to undesirable conflicts, barely 50 percent of the American and Dutch respondents are pro-participation. Note these contrasts:

	% Pro-Participation		
	U.S.	Sweden	Netherlands
"The complexity of modern day issues requires that only the more simple questions should be considered publicly" (% disagree)	89	95	96
"Wide spread participation in decisionmaking often leads to undesirable conflicts" (% disagree)	52	79	55
Difference:	37	16	41

In the U.S. and the Netherlands, although there is commitment to the basic idea of public involvement, ambivalence is manifested because of a concern for dysfunctional consequences, that is, conflicts.

As for the Political Conflict Scale, we find similar variations. In fact the response patterns can be construed as very puzzling and certainly not consistent. Note these comparisons:

	% Pro-Conflict		
	U.S.	Sweden	Netherlands
"A good leader should refrain from making proposals that divide the people even if these are important for the community" (% disagree)	91	92	90
"A leader should modify his actions to keep consensus" (% disagree)	62	50	68
Difference:	29	42	22
"Leaders who are overconcerned about resolving conflicts can never carry out community programs successfully" (% agree)	41	48	62

On the one hand there is overwhelming support for leaders actively pursuing community goals despite conflict, but keeping consensus is also important to many of these leaders. And the third item listed above was so poorly associated with the other two that it was excluded after the factor analysis. Including items two and three, however, would have certainly decreased the level of support for political conflict.

The Economic Equality Scale reveals wide variations by components. It makes a great deal of difference whether one probes for preferences generally (such as whether "the rich should pay more") or bluntly and specifically asks about income ceilings and salary discrepancies. Here are examples:

	% Pro-Economic Equality		
	U.S.	Sweden	Netherlands
"Rich people should pay more for the support of community projects than poor people" (% agree) (Swedish substitute: "Communal taxes should be progressive")	67	42	73
"There should be an upper limit on incomes so that no one earns very much more than others" (% agree)	4	21	24
"Discrepancies in salaries should be continually reduced" (% agree)	32	66	27
Difference:	63	45	49

While a majority of American leaders accept the abstract principle embodied in the first item, they strongly reject income limits *and* reduction in salary differences. The Dutch and Swedish leaders also reveal a considerable range in support. They are much more supportive of economic equality, as their total scores reveal, than the Americans. Yet, they too reveal large majorities which reject income limits. Item one was excluded from the scale after the factor analysis, as a poor test item, but the others were included.

Another scale with components which reveal some puzzling differences by country is the National-Local Scale. Here are the responses for two of the items:

	% Pro-Local		
	U.S.	Sweden	Netherlands
"Although national affairs are important people should first worry about the problems of their own locality" (% agree)	63	69	31
"Community progress is not possible if national goals always have priority" (% agree)	41	61	75
Difference:	22	8	44

It is somewhat difficult to understand why the Dutch are anti-local on the first (but not on the second) and the Americans anti-local on the second (but not on the first). The Swedish responses are quite consistent throughout.

In short, by studying carefully the responses to the item-components of scales we discover elements of system variation which may be enlightening. In summary form these seem to be:

Participation: All countries have elites which generally are very supportive. However, the consequences for community conflict are troubling to both the U.S. and the Netherlands, but not to the Swedish.

Conflict: Although all countries have scale scores indicating strong support for the legitimacy of conflict, there is genuine concern over the breakdown of community consensus.

Economic Equality: Even in Sweden the range on these items is considerable. There is in fact no cross system uniformity nor within system consistency. The U.S. is the least egalitarian if one cumulates responses to all items. But it depends on what aspect of economic equality one is emphasizing: progressive taxation, or income ceilings, or salary discrepancies, or the government's role to provide more opportunity for the poor, etc.

National-Local Commitment: These elites are marginally pro-local, but the rationale for the acceptance and rejection of components is not at all clear, for the U.S. and the Netherlands.

The variations in level of elite support for components in each scale suggest that one must be careful in generalizing too dogmatically across these three countries about their belief in participation, conflict, economic equality, and their localist commitments. There are reservations which the elites in each country have in accepting each basic value, and these reservations may vary by country. Or, to put it differently, there are certain conditions on which these elites accept these basic values. And an inspection of their responses to the specific components is very useful in order to understand these reservations and conditions.

Variations in Elite Values Within Systems—By City

Although we have been treating the findings presented here thus far as system level value orientations—American, Swedish, Dutch—in fact if we look below the national level at the municipal units in our study we find differences in elite support for these values. This is particularly true for the values of political conflict and economic equality. Elite support for participation does vary by city, but in no city does it drop below the 70 percent level in any country (Table 7.4). Yet one notices from these data that the leaders in some cities can drop considerably below the average, whether it is in support for economic equality in Sweden and the Netherlands, or in support for political conflict in all countries. Almost a hundred percent of the leaders of one city in each system are committed to participation, while in another city 30 percent are not believers. Eighty to ninety percent of the leaders in one city are committed to the need for conflict while 35-50 percent in another city may have negative orientations to conflict. However, one should not exaggerate these ranges in elite support by city. The "low" scores are usually not very low in actuality, except for economic equality.

One wonders, however, whether certain cities have elites with a more consistently pro-democratic orientation than other cities, on the three values of participation, conflict, and economic equality. If we look at our data carefully it is possible to identify communities which appear to fit such an analysis—cities which have a relatively highly developed elite democratic value subculture, in contrast to cities where the elite democratic value subculture is more poorly developed. The results can be seen in Table 7.5. In some cities there does indeed seem to be a pattern of consistently strong pro-democracy orientations while in other cities a consistently weaker set of democracy orientations. The average deviations from country means are highest in European systems. These extremes are found for only two or three cities at each end of the democratic value continuum in each country. Most cities have elites which do not exhibit a consistent syndrome.

What community variables may help explain these city differences? Among the many that could be used we examined four carefully: population size, median family income, unemployment rate, and party affiliation

TABLE 7.4   City Differences in Elite Value Orientations

Value Scales	U.S.	Sweden	Netherlands	System Differences (Range)
1. Participation (% Pro)				
High City	98	97	92	
Low City	70	81	72	
Average All Cities	79	90	85	
Difference (High and Low)	18	16	20	4
2. Political Conflict (% Pro)				
High City	88	76	82	
Low City	66	57	50	
Average All Cities	77.5	69	70	
Difference (High and Low)	22	19	32	13
3. Economic Equality (% Pro)				
High City	25	68	67	
Low City	2	44	31	
Average All Cities	10	56	43	
Difference (High and Low)	23	24	36	13

TABLE 7.5 Examples of Contrasts in Elite Value Cultures for Cities

	U.S.		Sweden		Netherlands	
	City A	City B	City E	City D	City E	City F
Participation Value Score	85	74	97	80	90	71
Conflict Value Score	85	78	72	58	79	50
Economic Equality Value Score	14	2	68	52	50	40
Average Deviation from Country Norm	+ 6.0	- 4.3	+ 7.3	- 8.3	+ 7.0	- 12.3

TABLE 7.6 Community Variables Linked to Elite Economic Equality Value: Population Size and Party Control (% of elite favoring equality)

	U.S.		Sweden		Netherlands	
	Large Cities	Small Cities	Large Communes	Small Communes	Large Cities	Small Cities
1. The Basic Scale on Economic Equality:						
- Cities where elites of the "Left" are dominant	16	9	63	58	45	50
- Cities where the "Left" is not dominant	8	9	52	52	37	37
2. Supplementary Example: "Rich people should pay more for the support of community projects than poor people"* (% of elites who agree) Party Strength:						
- Cities where the "Left" is dominant	71	71	46	47	76	81
- Cities where the "Left" is not dominant	57	69	42	32	64	73

* The Swedish version was: "Communal taxes should be progressive."

(specifically the percentages of elites affiliated with parties of the "Left"). Of these, population size by itself was not significantly linked, but party strength was. We can illustrate this best by using economic equality value orientations as the test case (Table 7.6). Population size is clearly not the primary factor. Rather we find, particularly in Europe, that in cities where the Labor and Social Democrats are in control there is the highest elite support for economic equality. This is true also in the U.S. for large cities but not in the smaller cities. The European finding of course makes sense because of the ideological differences between "Left" parties and the opposition parties on social welfare issues. Yet, in European cities controlled by Center and Right parties there is significantly higher elite support for economic egalitarianism than in any American cities. Cities with a low median family income in the U.S. and Netherlands also have elites which are marginally more egalitarian; there is no consistent evidence of this in Sweden.

The Social and Political Correlates of Elite Values

The analysis and discussion up to this point has demonstrated (1) high congruence in local elite support for political values but important differences in local elite support for economic equality across systems; (2) considerable differences in elite values between national and local levels of systems; (3) to some extent cities can be differentiated by levels of elite support for values. The next question is whether we can discover variations in elite values as a result of early or later socialization and exposure experiences in family, party, position, and age or generation.

We operate from the same basic assumptions here of other scholars such as Verba that "political cultures are learned." The beliefs of elites (as of citizens) are the product of non-political exposures in the family, school, peer group, etc. They are also the result of observing (and participating in) the political process in their nation and community. And, as Pye added, "each individual must be seen in his own historical context" (Pye and Verba 1965, 7, 550). The earlier national studies of bureaucrats and politicians were preoccupied with most of these same variables also (with the exception of family economic status or origins). They concluded that age, ideology, role (as politician or bureaucrat), and "system involvement" (frequency of contacts) were all relevant for explaining why elites varied in their support for democracy (Aberbach 1981, 198-205). We will explore these "determinants" also as well as other variables. But rather than lump all elites together for all systems we will present the data separately for each country because of the clear indication that these systems differ significantly on what determinants are most relevant.

Beginning with role, it is already clear that local elites diverge from the national finding on this variable. The national study stated that "bureaucrats are in fact less enthusiastic about political equality" (Aberbach 1981, 198). We find no evidence of this in our study of local elites (Table 7.7). We find remarkable congruence for both sets of elites on all value measures. It is as if they were brought up in the same political community and exposed to the same political influences. Working side by side in local government they seem to be cut from the same democratic cloth. As administrators and politicians, they are both either strongly in favor of citizen participation (equality) and political conflict (liberty) or equally marginally supportive (Sweden and Holland) or equally negative (U.S.) on the value of economic equality. We do find small differences among subgroups within politician elites and within administrators (e.g., for age cohorts), but basically there appears to be a high level of value homogeneity for all politicians and administrators in all three countries. As already observed, this is in sharp contrast to bureaucrat-politician value findings at the national level.

The implications of the finding that politicians and administrators agree on both the values of political participation and conflict is important to reflect on. At the local level there is no evidence as at the national level that there are "two types of democrats," one set believing in equality, citizen participation, or "populism," and another set believing more in liberty, contestation, and conflict. In the national study on these two dimensions we found that the proportion of politicians and bureaucrats who were medium or high in support of both liberty and equality were: MPs - 67%; Administrators - 39%. The analysis revealed further that 42 percent of the national bureaucrats did not support citizen participation at all (while another 40 percent were lukewarm supporters of participation). For the MPs these findings were 17 percent and 38 percent respectively. Such levels of negativism and ambivalence we do not find in our local elites. A solid majority of politicians and bureaucrats at the local level support both equality (participation) and liberty (political conflict). Even in the Netherlands where the support for conflict is only at the 62 percent level, politicians and bureaucrats reveal virtually identical levels of support.

The relevance of party as an explanatory variable is again different at the local level. It is extremely important for the value economic equality, but not useful at the local level for the two key values of participation and conflict. this is counter to the finding in the national study, which found "ideology" (equivalent really to our variable "party") as a very important discriminating factor. National MPs and bureaucrats on the "Left" were far more democratic than other leaders. "Right" politicians in the national study are distinguished by the fact that they support "pluralism" (or "conflict") while generally having little sympathy for increased participation (or "populism"). Centrist politicians were found to be basically "anti-pluralist," opposed to conflict. Hence large differences were found as one moved along the ideological continuum, Left to Right.

These national variations by ideology in elite political values are not found at all at the local level. Our test of this is by party. We array our parties in all three countries along an ideological Left-Right continuum as in the national study (Table 7.8). While party is very relevant (in Europe) for the economic equality value, it reveals no differences (in any of the three countries) for the participation and conflict values. None of the national observations can be made at the local level: the "Left" leaders in local governments are not more (politically) democratic, the "Right" leaders are not less democratic, and the Center placed leaders are not anti-pluralist. Thus there appears a considerable disjunction in elite partisanism as reflected in value orientations between national and local levels. As we explained earlier this may, of course, be a function of time when the studies were completed. Otherwise they suggest the low level of party integration between the two levels of these systems. Or, it may from a "developmental perspective" suggest that the democratic socialization process has been moving elites in these societies toward more politically liberal and egalitarian value perspectives at both levels, manifest most clearly and initially at the local level.

While party affiliation is not helpful to explain variance in elite participation and conflict values, it is a critical variable to demonstrate elite differences in economic equality beliefs. In Europe, elites from parties of the Left are strikingly more supportive of this type of equality than are Centrist and Right politicians and bureaucrats. Party, as well as family SES and respondent educational level, is a major determinant of economic equality beliefs in Europe. In the U.S., however, it plays a rather insignificant role, because 75 percent or more of elites of all partisan persuasions are anti-egalitarian. This finding emphasizes the socialization role of Left parties in Europe for this particular value. In a sense we find for economic equality that parties of the Left in Europe are having the same basic distinctive socialization role today at the local level which ten and fifteen years ago we found them having for the values of political equality and liberty at the national level.

Two other variables dealing with socioeconomic status are important in Sweden for their associations with the high level of elite support in Sweden for economic equality—father's occupation and respondent's level of education. Elites with working class backgrounds and limited education in Sweden have a much higher pro-economic equality scale score than other elites from higher SES backgrounds (Table 7.9). This is less true in the Netherlands, and not true at all in the U.S. Here is an example of the possible

TABLE 7.7   Comparison of Value Orientations for Politicians and Administrators

Value Scales (% Pro):	U.S.		Sweden		Netherlands	
	Pols	Adms	Pols	Adms	Pols	Adms
1. Economic Equality	22	22	59	54	44	39
2. Political Conflict	83	85	77	74	74	70
3. Political Participation	81	77	91	87	86	82

TABLE 7.8 The Linkage of Party Affiliation to Elite Value Orientations (Politicians only)

	U.S.			Sweden			Netherlands		
Value Scales(% Pro):	Dems	Reps	Inds	Soc. Dems	Center	Conser-vatives	Labor	CDA	VVD
1. Economic Equality	26	19	16	73	49	31	52	25	7
2. Political Conflict	81	88	86	79	75	73	72	65	67
3. Participation	77	82	80	86	85	78	90	82	80

TABLE 7.9 Socioeconomic Status and Education in Relation to the Value of Economic Equality (% of elites favoring)

	U.S.	Sweden	Netherlands
1. SES (Father's occupation)			
Working class	23	67	35
Middle class	21	51	36
Upper middle and upper class	23	39	23
2. Educational Level			
University	23	47	34
Middle school	18	55	31
Lower education	20	63	37

impact of early socialization in family and school, but it is not generalizable across all three democracies. It really applies primarily to Sweden.

Age, or generational, differences do not appear to be great in our findings when the data for all leaders in the aggregate are combined (Table 7.10). But when we distinguish the generations of elites by politicians and administrators separately we do find certain contrasts. We use two generations here—those leaders born and brought up before World War II and those brought up after World War II (including a small percentage who were born just before or during W W II). The proportions who fall into these two generations vary by country considerably:

	Politicians		Administrators	
	Pre-war	Post-war	Pre-war	Post-war
U.S.	36%	64	33	67
Sweden	63	37	64	36
Netherlands	42	58	34	66

One must keep in mind, then, these country differences in interpreting the findings.

The presumption in this generational approach to the analysis is that the younger set of leaders brought up after 1945 "should have acquired enduringly different perspectives in democracy" than the older pre-war group (Aberbach 1981, 202). It is argued that this should be true not only for regimes interrupted by an authoritarian interlude, but also for countries like the Netherlands and Sweden which remained liberal democracies despite the war period and, in the Dutch case, a period of Nazi occupation. This is attributable to the different democratic "atmosphere throughout Europe" after the war. The study of national elites seems to confirm this because the younger politicians and bureaucrats were 18-20 percent more favorable to democratic pluralism (favoring conflict) and nine to twelve percent more populist (favoring citizen participation) than the pre-war set of elites.

In our local study we do not find strong evidence in support of this theory (Table 7.11). There is a slight tendency for the older elites who are politicians to be less supportive of political conflict and participation. But the difference on the average is small and both young and old politicians are (close to) 70 percent or more strong supporters of conflict. But the theory fails completely for local administrators—the young post-war group reveal a support for conflict at the 77 percent level on the average, while the older administrators support conflict at the 74 percent level. Indeed for two countries, Sweden and the U.S., there is no real difference at all. The same basic generalization is true for the values of citizen participation: there is no significant, striking difference for local elites between the pre-war and post-war sets of elites in their democratic value orientations. The contrast with the national elite study is clear. Only in the Netherlands do we find a meaningful differential. And even for the Netherlands elites support for democracy is much higher for local leaders. For example, on citizen participation only 30 percent of pre-war national bureaucrats were supportive (50% of pre-war MPs) while for local elites 77 percent of pre-war administrators were supportive (80% of pre-war MPs).

Why should this basic differential exist? It cannot be attributed to the differences in the proportions of elites in these two studies who were brought up in the pre-war period: 48 percent for the local study, 46 percent for the national study. Although the questionnaire approach in the two studies differed they both were tapping the same values. To attempt an explanation one must begin with the assumption that a large majority of these elites brought up in the pre-war period were indeed skeptical of political conflict and of increasing citizen participation. After the war, there developed a different level of acceptance of democratic values at the elite level and hence this was reflected in the recruitment of new leaders as well as some re-socialization of older leaders. Those born in the Twenties and Thirties took governmental positions in the post-war period and then were exposed to the strengthening of democracy in their societies subsequently.

TABLE 7.10 Elite Variations by Four Age Cohorts

	U.S.				Sweden				Netherlands			
Age:	21-39	40-49	50-59	60+	21-39	40-49	50-59	60+	21-39	40-49	50-59	60+
Value Scales (% pro)												
1. Participation	75	83	80	77	91	91	89	85	91	87	79	80
2. Conflict	85	84	86	82	78	79	76	72	85	82	68	64
3. Economic Equality	22	23	19	24	56	58	60	64	45	35	34	33

TABLE 7.11 Support for Democratic Values by Generations

	Politicians		Administrators	
	Young(under 50) "Post-war"	Older(50+) "Pre-war"	Young(under 50) "Post-war"	Older(50+) "Pre-war"
A. Political Conflict (% favoring)				
U.S.	80	78	83	85
Sweden	84	74	72	73
Netherlands	87	67	77	65
B. Citizen Participation (% favoring)				
U.S.	82	79	79	74
Sweden	93	87	91	86
Netherlands	90	80	85	77
N's				
U.S.	68	39	82	41
Sweden	99	170	40	72
Netherlands	116	84	66	36

Some evidence of this exists if we compare over time the value positions of the leaders in the American cities in 1966 with 1984. Using the earlier Jacob study findings of 1966 as our base we see a considerable change in these U.S. elites for the same cities, as follows:

	Elite Support for Democratic Values	
	1966	1984
Participation	58%	79
Political Conflict	63	84
Innovative Change	60	75

These 1966 figures for local elites are close to the findings for 1970 for U.S. national elites so far as the value of participation is concerned. The local elite figure (1966) for the value of conflict is considerably higher than the national finding (1970). Thus, the puzzle is not completely solved. Further longitudinal analysis of these data is necessary to document this change in detail and to explain the national-local difference. But there is evidence that the 1966-1984 period was crucial for value change in the U.S., and probably in Europe also. This suggests that the Dutch and Swedish local elites might have appeared much less democratic in the Sixties, and on the other hand the national elites would look even more supportive of democratic values today than twenty years ago.

To summarize the findings on "determinants" at this point may be helpful. We can generalize across systems on certain variables. Role differences are not great, nothing like the national study revealed. Party differences (and SES differences) are only significant for the economic equality value, particularly relevant for Sweden and the Netherlands. Otherwise there are no party differences for the "contestation" and "participation" values, again quite different than the national study. Age and generational differences are minimal for the U.S. and Sweden, but somewhat more relevant for the Dutch local elites. Nevertheless, for all three countries the generational analysis reveals a much higher level of support for democratic values for elites brought up under pre- and post-war conditions than we found in the national study. On three variables then—role, party, age—there is high congruence for local elites on the two democratic values of conflict and participation, no matter how one disaggregates them for analysis. There is clearly evident a pattern of cross-system political cultural "homogenization" for these two key values. Even if one looks at the ranges in the level of support by city, we find that cities with "low support" percentages are usually in actuality not very low, for the values concerning conflict and participation. There appears to be a "Western" elite democratic culture pattern which is generalizable across systems at the local level. This does not, of course, apply to economic equality. The three systems vary greatly on this value.

The Linkage of Elite Values to Other Orientations and Actions

Throughout this book we have referred off and on to the association of values to elite perceptions, evaluations and behavior. Usually we have discovered that values help explain other phenomena best if combined with other types of variables. Rarely is there a direct unilinear relationship of elite values and some other aspect of elite behavior. An example of this is the relationship between elite values and their contacts with other leaders (local or higher up) and their contacts with community groups. These were reported in Chapter VI. In all countries we found that those leaders who were strongest in support of participation and economic equality reported the highest level of contacts with community groups and other actors in the political process. But by itself this relationship was not strong. When the analysis was done by cities we found that there were two variables which together explained a great deal about the contact behavior of elites—the pressures on elites from community groups, and their strong belief in citizen participation. While the pressures on elites were a more important variable than the participation value by itself, the combination of the two led to the following finding:

	Average % of Elites High in Contact with Community Groups
In cities high in both pressures "from below" and in support for "participation"	33
In cities low in both pressures "from below" and in support for "participation"	19

These data suggest that it is the frequency of group pressures on elites along with pro-democracy values which leads to elite contact activity, with pressures playing a major role and participation value orientations secondary.

The relationships of values to elite contact patterns raise another question: Are those elites with most contacts, and thus presumably more involved with the decisionmaking structure, more likely to reveal a different set of values than those who have fewer contacts and are presumably "isolated" from decisionmaking? The national study found the "cosmopolitans" much more supportive of pluralist and populist values than the "isolates" (Aberbach 1981, 204). They reasoned that this was probably due to different socialization and recruitment effects for these networks of contacts. In the local study we find this differential much less true for political values (Table 7.12). Those most involved are also inclined to be most democratic, but the differences are not great. At the local level of these systems the values of participation and political conflict are so commonly supported that associations with other elite actors does not strengthen very much the belief in such values. In Europe, however, those with the highest level of contacts are definitely more inclined to support economic equality.

It is interesting to note, that the most influential leaders in these two European countries are most inclined to support economic equality. A look at the relationship of influence perceptions and elite value positions on economic equality demonstrates this clearly:

	The value scale scores	% of Elites Who Support Economic Equality Believe that "rich people should pay more for community programs"
U.S. elites		
- Low in influence	10	76
- High in influence	12	63
Sweden		
- Low in influence	57	35
- High in influence	67	49
Netherlands		
- Low in influence	31	68
- High in influence	40	78

All the findings are in the same direction except one! American elites with low influence status want the "rich to pay more," while their colleagues with high influence are less enthusiastic. The reverse is true for Sweden and the Netherlands. In the two European systems local elites in the "power network" are the ones who are the most egalitarian!

There is one final type of linkage for values which is suggested by our data. Although there is little evidence that elite democratic values affect elite perceptions of their problems, the data do indicate that in cities where elites are committed to political conflict, including such beliefs as the need for the good leader "to get things done even if he must displease people"—in such cities elites are also more willing to accept responsibility for dealing with their problems. Unfortunately the responsibility question was asked differently in the Netherlands ("does local government have the responsibility") than in the other two countries ("should local government have the responsibility"). So the only proper comparison is for the U.S. and Sweden. If we analyze our cities we see these results:

| | % of elites who say local government should have the responsibility to deal with their problems | |
	U.S.	Sweden
In cities where elites strongly support political conflict	57	74
In cities where elites reveal less support for political conflict	45	66

Belief in political competition as more important than "communal harmony" thus seems functional to more responsible elite orientations to action.

Conclusions

The local leaders in these three Western democracies are obviously strongly supportive of the democratic political values concerning conflict and participation, much more so than in non-Western societies (based on findings from 1966 or more recently). They are also rather localist in their commitment and interested in innovative action. If we compare across the three systems these local leaders are congruent on these four values, a level of value consensus which in one sense at least is in accord with that early classical elite theory. These elites differ, however, on economic equality: U.S. local leaders are low, Sweden relatively high, the Dutch in between.

It is interesting to note the actual level of consistency for local leaders in their support of the twin values of conflict and participation (Table 7.13). We have summarized our data in a way similar to that used in the earlier national study (Aberbach 1981, 206). The overwhelming consistent commitment of these local leaders to these two values is clear—they are "wholehearted democrats" at the 85 percent level or above. Few (one or two percent) are "authoritarians." The specific contrasts with the national study are as follows:

	National Elites	Local Elites
	(1970-73)	(1984, 1989)
"Wholehearted Democrats"		
Politicians	67%	90
Bureaucrats	39	82
"Authoritarians"		
Politicians	11	1
Bureaucrats	21	2
Mixed Patterns		
Politicians	22	9
Bureaucrats	40	16

If we include the responses on economic equality, however, the picture changes. Less than 50 percent of the European leaders are egalitarian in both political and economic terms, and the American percentage is much lower than that.

Local leaders in these countries are more supportive today (in the Eighties actually) than the national leaders in these countries were in the early Seventies. The data demonstrate also that local leaders do not vary much by position, by party, and by age. An overwhelming majority support political democracy irrespective of party, age, or position. Or, to state the opposite of this—the small minority of nonbelievers among elites is distributed fairly evenly across age cohorts, politicians and administrators, and by party. The cohesion of these local elites despite expectations that they would vary by subgroups suggests there is a pervasive "Western" elite value culture at the local government level, that democratic politics has come to have the same meanings to these leaders despite their system differences in many other respects—in historical development, in types of political institutions, in economic and social system, in cultural experiences. In a really significant sense these similar value patterns indicate the "democratization" process has occurred in parallel ways to converge to the same elite values end-state.

Yet, there are important differences. When we analyzed the strength of adherence to these political values we found differences by country. European elites are more likely to take "very strong" value positions than is true for American elites. The reason for this escapes us in the analysis here, and

TABLE 7.12 Elite Support for Values as a Function of Elite Contact Involvement

Elite Contact Patterns:	U.S.			Sweden			Netherlands		
	High Level of Contact	Medium Level	Low Level	High Level	Medium Level	Low Level	High Level	Medium Level	Low Level
Participation Value (% supportive)	80	78	78	95	89	88	83	86	83
Equality Scale (% supportive)	17	15	14	66	59	55	42	34	29
Example: "Rich people should pay more in support of community projects than poor people"	71	67	62	51	43	31	83	73	72

TABLE 7.13 Consistency in Elite Political Value Orientations (Based on the analysis of the two values of conflict and participation)

Value Consistency Patterns (percentages)	U.S.	Sweden	Netherlands
1. "Wholehearted Democrats" (Pro Conflict and Participation)	85	88	87
2. "Authoritarians" (Reject both Conflict and Participation)	2	1	1
3. "Communal Harmony Populists" (Accept Participation but not Conflict)	5	5	9
4. "Non-Populist Pluralists" (Accept Conflict but not Participation)	8	6	3

our data throw no light on the origins for this difference. It is possible that the European "party culture" at the local level contributes to this.

A second difference emerged from our analysis of specific components. If we investigate the level of support by system for specific items in our value scales, we find that countries, while generally supporting a political value at the same level, will vary in support for specific elements in that value. For example, the American and Dutch leaders are more concerned about the consequences of citizen participation for generating conflict. Again, items within the conflict scale produce a range of responses. Swedish leaders are more inclined to feel that a leader "should modify his action to keep consensus" than the Dutch or Americans do, a result which earlier Swedish research indicated. On the economic equality scale the Swedish are very egalitarian but they seem less interested in progressive communal taxation than the Dutch and Americans in having "the rich pay more." Thus, one must be cautious in accepting all these items as validly reflecting a particular value orientation in a country, and one must be aware that a value scale as "political conflict" or "citizen participation" has different meanings when operationalized for each country, even in Western democracies.

Another difference emerged from our subgroup analysis. The party system and social class origins obviously play a significant role in shaping economic egalitarianism in Sweden. Party is also important for the Netherlands, but social class origin differences (particularly working class vs. middle class status of father) are not as marked. The existence of a "social welfare" culture in the two European countries and the relevance of this yet today for elite values toward economic questions is very apparent.

We noted also differences by cities within each country in elite values. These are not extreme differences but they do exist and do seem to be linked to the party control context within which elites function in their cities. This of course reflects the role of party generally as well as the "breakage" analysis used in previous chapters to explain within system differences by cities. There are elite subcultures by cities, a phenomenon which needs more research.

Our generational analysis reveals that at the time of these studies (1984, 1989) there was no such clash in value positions for those leaders maturing before World War II and those after the war, as was found in the national study (early Seventies). Reflection on the reasons for this suggests that possibly a resocialization to democratic values took place in the Seventies and Eighties which our pre-war maturing local leaders were subjected to but the pre-war maturing national leaders had not yet been subjected to when they were interviewed in 1970-73. Thus the time of the study may have been the critical variable. Otherwise one is confronted with a value disjunction between national and local leaders which is difficult to understand precisely. More recent studies of national leaders are necessary to clear up this puzzle.

Values are indeed linked to elite thinking about politics and to their status in the system and to their behavior. We had only a limited opportunity in this study to push such inquiries. But it is clear elite value commitments to some extent may influence their strategies for support mobilization by initiating contacts with community groups and with other political actors. There is also evidence that local elites who believe in the utility and propriety of conflict in order to "get things done" are more "responsible" types. They feel local governments have to assume responsibility for their problems. It is reassuring, then, to find that the elites with the most expansive contact networks and who also see themselves as influential are the elites who accept to a somewhat greater extent these basic democratic values.

Notes

1. The question used in the national study was: "There has been a good deal of discussion in some countries about increasing popular control over the activities of government and increasing citizen participation in governmental affairs. How do you feel about this?"

2. These are averages for the elites at each level for the three countries. The U.S. percentage for the national politicians had to be estimated based on a variety of responses, and may be low.

8

Path Models of Community Effective Action Using Elite Data: An Exploratory Approach

Much has been written by scholars of the city about how cities differ in their budget allocations, their level and pace of development (political, social and economic), their policy responsiveness to citizen preferences or interest group demands, their "community activeness" and their capacity for dealing with fiscal stress. In terms of the number of studies, the complexity of the analysis, and the comparative breadth of research, the study of the plight of the cities, or their success, has become in recent years one of the most important in social science. However, controversy persists. Scholars differ as to what factors are most relevant for explaining city differences in "outcomes." The size of the city, the character of the population, the political power structure, the social structure, the industrial and business environment, the financial resource base, the type of political leadership, the party system, the degree of citizen interest and participation—all these and more variables have been used in theorizing about the success or failure of city policy and city development, A major question is whether "politics" (political leadership, groups, forces, structures) is of secondary or primary importance, compared to social/economic/fiscal determinants. Often the question is whether political forces work together with social and economic forces to promote or hinder the city's development. One scholar of the American city argued that external controls and constraints on cities mean that "political variables no longer remain relevant to the analysis" (Peterson 1981, 12). A comparative scholar of cities claims: "Political variables have relatively less direct and independent impact than socioeconomic variables . . . somehow the nature of the socioeconomic environment seems more important than the nature of community politics in shaping community policies" (Fried 1972, 71). Such a position relegates to relative insignificance the roles of political elites, parties, elections, pressure groups, etc. Who controls city hall to these scholars is presumably of marginal importance.

There are scholars, however, who disagree. Here are some examples:

"The obstacles in the way of solving city problems are mainly political" (Banfield 1965, 3).

"Resource capability contributes relatively little to the variance in policy development" (Eulau and Prewitt 1973, 519).

"A fairly general consensus has emerged concerning the importance of linking urban leadership . . . to policy outputs" (Clark 1981, 94).

"It is not plausible to regard the decline of some of our cities . . . as the irreversible result of economic processes" (Gurr and King 1987, 190).

Two European scholars of the city argue that "politics matters," that "policy outputs do not spring automatically from the socioeconomic structure" (Sharpe and Newton 1984, 19). In a recent review of the many studies dealing with political variables, the conclusion was that "the mixed and sometimes contrasting results from existing literature [on the relevance of politics] provide a stimulus for additional research on these questions" (Aiken and Martinotti in Clark, Hellstern, and Martiotti 1985, 34).

In recent years major cross-national research efforts have been mounted to understand better the problems of the cities. Much of that research utilizes both political and socioeconomic theory. Perhaps the most extensive of recent projects is the "Fiscal Austerity and Urban Innovation Project" (FAUI) developed by Terry Clark and his colleagues, first in 1982 in the U.S. and subsequently expanded to other countries. The impetus for the project was a deep interest in how cities adapt to fiscal strain. Earlier a national sample of 62 U.S. cities provided a data base for which a variety of information was collected and analyzed. Under the FAUI project this was extended to 1,000 U.S. cities in 1983 and then to over 30 other countries. Sweden and the Netherlands have both been included in this project. In the Netherlands a recent study of urban responsiveness to fiscal austerity concluded that political institutional (central-local government) policies may "strangle" urban innovation (Spit 1993).

The research reported in this book on urban political elites in a sense runs parallel to and supplements the international research efforts of the FAUI project. The key question for us is: What aspects of political leadership are most relevant for explaining what action is taken in the city to deal with its problems? The data we have collected on the backgrounds, careers, perceptions, values, and behavior of local political leaders in three countries are valuable in their own right in helping us understand the nature of leadership in our cities from a comparative perspective. These findings are unique, and may also provide critical variables for explaining city "outcomes", to help us explain why cities vary in their efforts and success in solving their problems. It is this latter concern which preoccupies us, if only in a preliminary and exploratory way, in this section of our report. Our data emphasize the role of elites, while not necessarily neglecting social and economic capability in a community.

In linking our elite data to community "outcomes", we define our dependent variable differently than other studies. As noted earlier, studies have defined different types of dependent variables—the policy responsiveness of local government, cities' adaptation to fiscal strain, the level of expenditures for common governmental functions, "community activeness," etc. City governmental performance is indeed multi-faceted and there are a variety of ways to conceptualize it and attempt to measure it. In our study, we do have local governmental expenditure data, but there was skepticism about the use of such data, because of intra-system and inter-system reliability and validity problems. European scholars were particularly concerned about evaluating city performance comparatively, based on expenditure data. American scholars have also expressed reservations (Schumaker, Getter, and Clark 1979, 48). After much reflection it was decided to use here "a perceived effectiveness of action" measure as our primary dependent variable. This measure is based on the perceptions and evaluations of our elite respondents in the cities in our three countries. Our questionnaire posed 14 policy problems for our respondents. After asking them to tell us how serious each problem was in their community, we asked the following:

> "Would you please indicate whether (on each of these problem) you think effective action is being taken to deal with these problems, some action is being taken, or nothing useful is being done?"

Using these two questions (on the seriousness of problems, and on effective action) we then created our dependent variable. For the five problems (excluding poverty and unemployment which were seen as primarily national problems) which the elites in each city considered most serious in their own communities, we took the mean percentage of elites for each community who felt that effective action was being taken on these five most serious problems. This became our "effectiveness of action" variable. This, one should note, is an "ideology neutral" measure, that is, it does not in the form presented here distinguish "effective action" by the ideological *direction* of policy. We can of course disaggregate the measure by type of policy (social welfare, health, taxation, economic development, etc.). Our objective here initially is to arrive at an overall measure of elite perceptions of the effectiveness of policy action on the serious problems, whatever they are in each community.

One might well question, of course, whether the responses of these leaders would be useful for such a purpose, since it might be argued that the leaders would be self-servingly optimistic and affirmative. We found quite the opposite, in fact, suggesting that our elite informants were very candid, critical, and discriminating. In presenting the data earlier we noted that the average proportion reporting effective action in their communities for all 14 problems was surprisingly low. The averages were 27% (U.S.), 26% (Netherlands), 13% (Sweden). When we restrict the analysis to the most serious problems, we find a considerable range by cities, in elite evaluations of effective action, as follows:

	High City	Low City	City Mean
U.S.	50%	13	31.3
Sweden	22	2	11.9
Netherlands	55	29	42.7

Our effectiveness variable also can be criticized, of course, as too subjective, with no control over the criteria used in making judgments of effectiveness. Its virtue is that it relies on the evaluations of elite informants who presumably are close to the decisional process. It asks them not whether there is *action* on problems, but whether there is *effective action*.

We have, then, a "perceived effectiveness" variable, derived from apparently candid elite evaluations, linked to the most serious problems specific to each community, and manifesting considerable community variance. One must keep in mind that these evaluations are system specific, although the measure itself is the same across nations and cities. It is interesting to note that even in a highly unitary system as the Netherlands the variance by community is considerable.

In the development of an explanatory theory from which to specify the key factors linked to "perceived effectiveness of action," the findings from the analysis done in the chapters of this study were very useful. We have identified several classes of independent variables which may be relevant. These variables generated by our study for each city are: *Community structural Variables* (population, median family income, unemployment rate, etc.); *Political Context Variables* (party control pattern, pressure group activity, community conflict pattern); *Elite Background* data (age, education, social class); *Elite Orientations Variables* (level of concern about problems, sense of responsibility for action at the local level, perceptions of power to act, perceptions of own influence, value orientations); *Elite Contact Variables* (contacts with community groups in own city, contacts with other actors at higher levels of the system). In addition we do have available fiscal data for each city, such as per capita taxes paid and per capita expenditures. In all, we could use over 20 variables for each city in each country.

In exploring the utility of these variables to explain "effectiveness of action" certain of them take theoretical precedence for us. The first is the party control (dominance - competitiveness) context for each city. In each country the cities vary considerably on this variable. Two alternative hypotheses can be advanced. One is that cities clearly dominated by elites of the "Left", or "Centre" will be associated with effective governance. Our focus here is on the actuality and degree of party dominance, not the ideology of the party in control. Unfortunately we may not have all the data we need to test our proposition properly, because of the lack of reliable data over time on both party competition at the elite level, and effective action. Our data are very time-bound. We can explore this relationship, however, and see what the findings suggest. In our opinion the pattern of party system relationship is probably relevant.

A second critical variable suggested by our work is pressure group activity. We have good data from our respondents on the extent to which they were approached by community groups, contacts which were at unusually high levels even in Europe. As others have suggested (Verba and Nie 1972; Schumaker, Getter and Clark 1979), "communal" group activity is associated with elite responsiveness. Our analysis also suggests it is linked to elite perceptions, evaluations, and behavior.

A third variable central to our theory is elite-initiated contacts. We are interested in two measures here: the extent to which elites report contact with a fairly large number of interest groups in their community (five or more), which is a measure, in a sense, of behavioral "populism", or the felt need of elites to mobilize for their policy positions. The second is a measure of the extensiveness of elite contacts with others beyond the city, at the regional, county, and national level—a measure of elite "cosmopolitanism" in contact networks. We would test for the relevance of both of these. These measures can be construed as indicators of two different phenomena: (1) the extent of elite awareness of public support or discontent; (2) the extent of elite activity, competence, knowledge and hence, elite desire to act effectively. The first of these interpretations is probably more true.

Of course, the political orientations and perceptions of elites constitute a fourth type of variable which should be used in explaining effective action. In our previous analysis we have demonstrated both how communities differ in the degree of elite concern about their problems, and on elite perceptions of their responsibility and power to act. Their responses are often strangely inconsistent and perplexing. It is therefore important to test for the relationship between these orientations and our dependent variables. In communities where elites are very concerned about their problems, willing to assume responsibility for acting on these problems, and satisfied that they have the power to act—one might hypothesize that these are communities where elites do take effective action. Alternatively, one might hypothesize that where elites are most concerned they are less likely to report that effective action is, has been, and can be taken.

Similarly one is tempted to reason that elite value orientations would be linked to effective action, that communities with leaders strongly committed to citizen participation, political conflict, and innovation in policy would be more inclined to be successful communities in dealing with their problems. There are difficulties with such a theoretical explanation. In these democratic societies a very high proportion of elites support these values, although there is indeed some variance by cities. Further, it is likely that the relevance of values for effective city policy decision making may be difficult to demonstrate directly. Values may influence elite orientations to action indirectly, as well as elite inclinations to be in contact with the public, and thus values may be part of a complex syndrome of elite predispositions to action. Or, alternatively, value commitment may be linked to cynicism about effective action. Nevertheless, it is important to try to demonstrate the role of value in the community decision making process.

Finally a variable which may be useful is elite influence perceptions, and particularly the type of influence structure which exists in their communities. We have noted the great differences by cities in the proportion of elites who say they have much influence and very little influence. By identifying the contrasting "hierarchic" and "democratic" influence structures in cities we are in a position to test the usefulness of this variable for explanation of effective policy action. One would be inclined to propose that non-hierarchic influence structures would be most closely linked to perceptions of effective action, but an opposing position could also be well argued.

There are other variables which we naturally want to investigate, and which we explore here, although they are not central to our theoretical position. Population size, for example, has long been suggested as of importance. And certainly some such variable as median family income, as a measure of the potential financial capacities for a city, may be an important conditional variable. The unemployment level of a city is another possibly relevant community variable. Certain social background variables should also be considered, such as social class and education and age. We certainly want to explore the utility of such variables. Nevertheless, we place highest priority on the set of variables identified above. Effective community action is no doubt the product of a complex set of community forces which result in the selection of leaders of varying competence and which influence these leaders, and propel them to take action or to not take action on their community problems. We hope to identify some of these forces and conditions in this ensuing analysis.

As we explore the association of these variables with effective action, we find that some seem more strongly correlated than others. We focus here on the most relevant variables. In presenting our findings we should first note that our dependent variable, a very subjective one, is not strongly associated with the per capita budgetary expenditure levels for these cities, nor with per capita taxes paid. The correlations with perceived effectiveness of action are as follows:

	U.S.	Sweden	Netherlands
Per Capita Expenditure	– .228	.059	.130
Per Capita Taxes Paid	.077	.180	– .150
Population Size	– .342	.388	.047

Elite evaluations of the effectiveness of action do not seem to be strongly influenced by, or a consequence of, the fiscal resource or budgetary allocation levels of their communities. The variance in per capital revenues and expenditures is considerable by community in all three countries, but elites in fiscally affluent or fiscally generous communities are not likely (U.S.) or not much more likely (Sweden and the Netherlands) to positively evaluate action effectiveness than are elites in fiscally strained and impoverished communities. In a sense this may seem counter to expectations raised by other scholarship. Population size is also a variable which appears to be very differently related to effectiveness—positively in Sweden, negatively in the U.S., irrelevant in the Netherlands.

Political context variables seem to have a somewhat greater, and cross-nationally similar relevance to the explanation of elite perceptions of effective action. The variable we call "party dominance" or "party competitiveness" seems to work consistently as the classical theory hypothesized. That is, in all three countries the correlation was negative for party dominance—which means that the greater the dominance, the less the perceived effectiveness of action. Or, to put it conversely, the greater the party competitiveness, the more likely the elites are to report effective action. The correlations are not strong (particularly for the Netherlands), but they are consistent: U.S. - .274, Sweden - .199, the Netherlands - .037. If we use a variant of this measure (percent controlled by parties of the Left), as many scholars have, we find the same result—the greater Left dominance, the less effective action. Again, perhaps a surprising finding!

While this evidence is by itself admittedly weak, a much more important finding is that party competitiveness is linked to other community political characteristics which in turn have consequences for effective action. For example, a higher proportion of elites report frequent contacts by pressure groups in party-competitive communities. Elites are also more aware of conflicts among groups in the community where parties are more competitive. As we shall see later these variables are linked to elite perceptions of effective action.

The pattern of elite initiated contacts, and pressures by community groups on elites, differentiates communities significantly, as we reported earlier. Thus, the percentage of elites reporting a high level of pressure group activity ranges, by city, as follows: from 82% to 30% in the U.S.; from 83% to 32% in Sweden; from 77% to 44% in the Netherlands. Similar levels of variance are found by city for elite initiated contacts with community groups. These two variables are a key to understanding the level of effective action in communities. These two types of elite contacts are also linked to each other, and together are associated with a high level of concern about the problems they face in their communities. Note these correlations:

	Correlations with the Level of Elite Concern about Problems		
	U.S.	Sweden	Netherlands
Extent of Elite Contacts with Community Groups	.311	.604	.129
Extent of Pressure By Groups on Elites	.296	.329	.353

This is an important finding since "the level of concern" variable is in all countries associated directly with the dependent variable. Hence, we now discover this nexus of variables as an important part of understanding effectiveness of action:

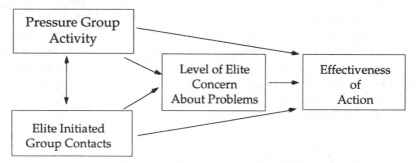

The actual correlations with effectiveness for these key variables are:

	U.S.	Sweden	Netherlands
"Populist Contacts"	− .229	− .211	− .286
Pressure Group Contacts	− .200	.349	− .225
Level of Elite Concern	− .445	− .252	− .129

The more elite contact behavior, linked to higher elite concern about the seriousness of the problems they face—the greater the feeling of negativism, frustration and ineffectiveness by leaders about their work.

Only one of these correlations (for Sweden) runs counter to this observation.

This leads to the question whether other elite perceptual and evaluative orientations are relevant for explaining perceived effectiveness of action, by themselves or because of their linkage to other variables. Aside from "level of concern", we considered the utility of the following elite orientations: (1) elite sense of responsibility for local government to act; (2) elites belief that they, at the local level, have the power to act; (3) elite feelings of influence in local government decisions, and (4) elite value commitments (citizen participation, political conflict, and economic equality). The "responsibility" variable revealed less relevance. Nevertheless, it does appear to fit in with our analysis in a peripheral manner. As for the "power" variable, it is more relevant for the U.S. than in Europe. The same is true for the "influence" variable. Thus, those cities in the U.S. where elites have a strong belief that they have power to act, and cities where a high percentage of elites claim to be influential—elites in these cities report a higher level of effective action. In Europe, possibly because of different central-local institutional relations, perceived "power" and "influence" seem much less relevant. Finally, the direct relationship between elite values and effective action is mixed, not uniform, and inconclusive. A summary of these correlations documents these observations:

| | *Correlations with Perceived Effectiveness of Action* | | |
Elite Orientations:	*U.S.*	*Sweden*	*Netherlands*
1. Responsibility to Act	− .002	− .079	− .150
2. Power to Act	.280	.098	.141
3. High personal Influence	.329	.039	.012
4. Value - Participation	− .213	.097	− .127
5. Value - Conflict	.070	.063	− .292
6. Value - Economic Equality	− .373	.224	.226

Earlier we hypothesized that certain of these elite orientations may have an indirect influence on effectiveness of action because of their linkage to other variables which are very relevant for the dependent variable. Illustrations of such associations, although the findings vary by country, are the following:

| | *Correlations with Value of Economic Equality* | | |
	U.S.	*Sweden*	*Netherlands*
Level of Concern about Seriousness of Problems	.391	.113	.437
Elite Contacts with Community Groups	.177	.345	− .022

Here we have a relationship between a value commitment (to Economic Equality) and an evaluative measure which is high for two countries (low for Sweden). We also have a test of the relationship between a value commitment and elite behavior (contacts with local groups)—positive in two countries, irrelevant for the Netherlands. As reported earlier the "Level of Concern" and the "Community Contacts" variables are closely linked to perceived effectiveness of action. It is such indirect and multipatterned sets of relationships which must be incorporated in attempts to develop explanations for effectiveness of action in communities.

On the basis of the type of data and analysis described here we have developed a set of "path models" to describe the configuration of variables related to effective action. A model is constructed separately for each country, although we use the same set of variables for each country. The reason for this is obvious from the correlational data already presented. However, the strength and relevance of variables for explaining effectiveness in the three countries varies considerably. The total set of variables for a country can be seen as constituting a highly suggestive, and possibly significant, conceptual model for the explanation of perceived effective action.

In presenting our models of explanation we should emphasize that the term "path model" is in a sense a misnomer. When the city is the unit of analysis, and we have only 15 to 20 cities, path coefficients for path models cannot be computed. So what we have done is used our Pearson correlation coefficients to construct an explanation of the factors related to the dependent variable (perceived effectiveness of action) in such a way as to suggest a probable "path model". We use the relationships between four types of variables to do this: elite backgrounds, community structure factors, elite attitudes and values, and elite contact patterns. These variables are operationalized for each city, as follows:

1. Population size for each city: U.S. census (1980); Sweden, 1984; Netherlands, 1989.
2. Party dominance: the percentage margin in party strength between the largest and next largest parties in our elite sample for each city.
3. Unemployment level for each city: U.S. census (1980); Sweden, 1984; Netherlands, 1989.
4. Racial composition (U.S. only): percentage of the city's population which was black in the 1980 census.
5. Elite age: the percentage of the city's elite sample which was under age 50.
6. Elite educational level: the percentage of the city's elite sample which had some graduate, or equivalent, education.

7. Level of elite concern: the mean percentage of elites in each city who saw the 14 listed problems as "serious" in their city.
8. Elite populist contacts: the percentage of elites in each city who initiated contacts with five or more community groups (such as business, union, civic, religions, ethnic etc. groups).
9. Pressure group activity: the percentage of elites in each city who reported contacts initiated by five or more community groups.
10. Economic Equality value: the percentage of elites in each city who responded favorably (pro the value) on the average, to the agree-disagree statements used in our economic equality value scale.
11. Participation value: the percentage of elites in each city who responded favorably (pro the value) to the agree-disagree statements in our participation value scale.
12. Sense of Responsibility: the mean percentage of elites in each city who, on a list of eleven problems replied that local government should have the responsibility to act. (Particularly relevant for Sweden)
13. Power to act: the mean percentage of elites in each city who on a list of eleven problems replied that they as local government leaders had the power to act on these problems.
14. Perceived effectiveness of action: the mean percentage of elites in each city who felt that, on the five most serious problems which they had identified for their city, they had taken or were taking effective action to deal with these problems.

We use only those Pearson correlations with a coefficient which is large enough, or comparatively relevant enough, to be useful as part of the explanation.

The models for each country separately are presented in Figures 8.1, 8.2, and 8.3. They each attempt to explain the key factors used in our study which are linked to (1) elite values, (2) elite contacts, (3) the level of elite concern about problems, and, most importantly, the direct or indirect linkage of all of these factors to (4) elite perceptions of the effectiveness of action in their cities. One must remember, as we stated earlier, that in our study elites had a low level of elite perception of effectiveness. And, thus, our objective is to try to explain why effective action is perceived as low in most cities, and high in a smaller number of cities.

A complex configuration of forces seems to be associated with perceived effectiveness, for all countries. We were selective in the variables used here, including those with the correlations which seemed most relevant. Examining the U.S. model (Figure 8.1) reveals the strongest linkage exists between the level of elite concern and perceived effectiveness (-.445). The most concerned leaders see the least effective action is taking place; the most sanguine are most likely to say effective action is occurring. This is some-what less true in Sweden, and much less true for the Netherlands.

At this point we must clarify the meaning of this correlation between "level of elite concern" and perceptions of effective action. These two variables co-vary negatively: i.e., as concern increases, less effectiveness is perceived; as concern decreases, more effective action is perceived. We find negative correlations in all three countries. One might feel that these two variables are tautological. But they are not. One is the measure of the extent to which elites feel their problems (a mean for 14 problems) are serious; the other is a measure of the extent to which elites feel effective action is being taken (a mean for the five most serious problems in each city). A negative correlation implies either of the following: (1) high concern about problems and no effective action on the serious problems, or (2) low concern about problems in the context of significant action on these problems. Thus, (1) high concern—no action; or (2) low concern—much action. Although causality is not directly demonstrated here, it is clearly implied: (1) high concern because no effective action, and (2) low concern because effective action has been taken or is being taken. The assumptions underlying this interpretation are clear, and in our opinion defensible. Other interpretations are possible, but probably less credible. In the larger sense what these data suggest is this causal chain: high concern by elites—associated with limited action—can lead to effective action—and then to a low level of concern. Alternatively the causal chain could be: no action on serious problems— high elite concern—eventual effective action—low elite concern. These two variables seem clearly interactive.

The U.S. model also reveals very high correlations between elite values and effectiveness perceptions: the greater a belief in economic equality and participation, the less likely elites are to report effective action. Elite values are in turn linked to elite contact behavior, which in turn is linked to low levels of effective action perceptions. That is, the more elites are involved in initiating actions with community groups, or are the targets of pressure group activity, the less likely are they to see that effective action is occurring. In addition, community structural variables in the U.S. are linked indirectly and directly to the dependent variable. The larger the city, the more dominant a party in that city, the higher the proportion of blacks in the population, the greater is the level of elite concern over the problems they face and the less likely they are to say effective action is occurring. (Not shown for the U.S. are the correlations of unemployment level and racial composition with perceived effective action, which are - .294 and - .397 respectively.) Finally, elite age plays a significant role: the younger the elites, the greater the concern, the more a commitment to economic equality, the more likely elites are to contact community groups, and the less likely the elites are to report effective action. Elite education level is primarily relevant in its association with elite belief in political participation.

FIGURE 8.1 Path Model for Explaining Perceived Effectiveness of Action: United States (20 cities) (Pearson Correlation Coefficients)

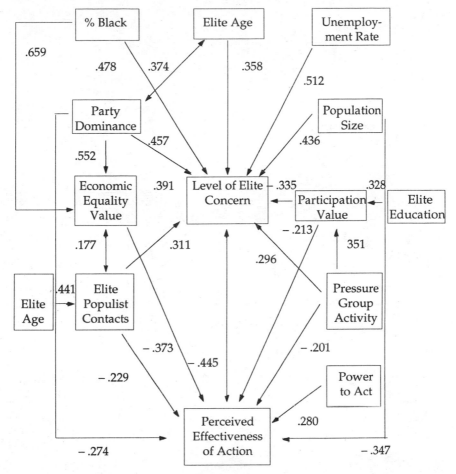

All the variables are calculated "high" to "low" except for "Elite Age" which was operationalized as "% of elites under age 50".

In Sweden, a similar configuration of forces seems relevant, but they are not identical, and they do not work in the same way as in the U.S. Population size is important, but the unemployment variable plays no role in Sweden, despite some evidence of elite concern about even its low level in that country. The party dominance pattern is less related to elite concern about problems, but is linked to elite contact patterns and perceived effectiveness of action. Elite age is a variable which is differently associated in Sweden,

FIGURE 8.2 Path Model for Explaining Perceived Effectiveness of Action: Sweden (15 communes) (Pearson Correlation Coefficients)

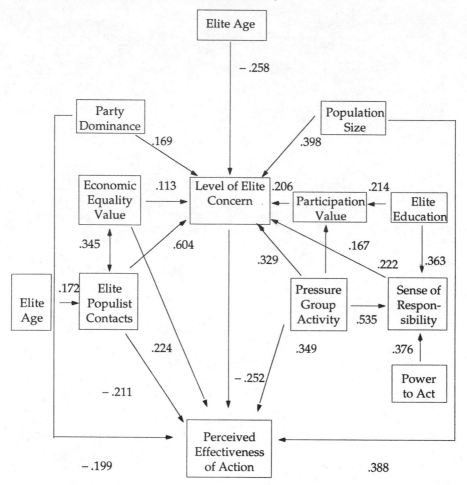

All the variables are calculated "high" to "low" except for "Elite Age" which was operationalized as "% of elites under age 50".

directly and indirectly, probably because such a high proportion of Swedish elites are over age 50, in contrast to the U.S. and the Netherlands. It is the older elites in Sweden who are very concerned about their problems, while the younger elites engage in the contacts with community groups. Elite age is not closely correlated with perceived effectiveness (.060), while in the U.S. it is (- .479). Most important for the Swedish explanation is the role of the

FIGURE 8.3 Path Model for Explaining Perceived Effectiveness of Action: The Netherlands (20 cities) (Pearson Correlation Coefficients)

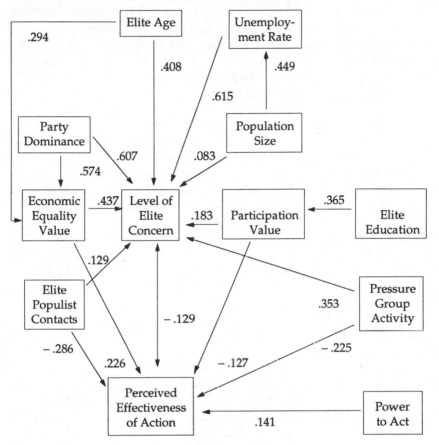

All the variables are calculated "high" to "low" except for "Elite Age" which was operationalized as "% of elites under age 50".

"responsibility" and "power to act" variables. A sense of responsibility by elites is related to the level of concern (.222) while in the U.S. and the Netherlands it is not a positive relationship. Finally, we should note that the elite contact and value variables are associated, but somewhat differently. In Sweden (and the Netherlands) the more elites support economic equality the more they felt their communal governments are engaged in effective action; in the U.S., the opposite is true! This is perhaps evidence of one consequence of a welfare-state system and elite culture.

The Dutch configuration of forces has its own character, but for most relationships it is closer to the U.S. Unemployment has a role as in the U.S., but population size no significant role at all, probably due to the limited variance in the size of the Dutch cities in our sample. The "elite age" variable functions similarly to the U.S., in its strong link to level of elite concern and to the economic equality variables. The party dominance variable has a strong link to the level of elite concern, as in the U.S., but has no significant direct relationship to effective action perceptions, contrary to the U.S. As mentioned already, elite belief in economic equality is positively related to effectiveness, as in Sweden, and contrary to the U.S. And the contact variables work very similarly to the U.S. in their association with both the level of elite concern and elite perceptions of effectiveness.

It is clear from a study of these "path models" that the variables we identified and described in our study are useful if one wishes to understand why cities vary in their elites' perceptions of effectiveness of action. It is a complex set of structural, attitudinal, behavioral, and elite background variables which are involved. It is also clear that the factors which have an impact vary by country and by type of system. The age of elites and their educational level are to some extent relevant in all systems. Community structural variables are relevant, but differ in particular ways as to their role in an explanatory effort such as this. Population size is not important in the Netherlands, the level of unemployment not important in Sweden. In all countries elite contacts and pressure group activity appear very much a part of how these local political systems function. And elite values, varying as they do by system, are relevant for explaining, in different ways, how elites judge the effectiveness of action at the local government level. Other "path model" configurations can be utilized, of course, to explain the phenomenon of effectiveness of action. The validity and utility of this structure of explanation, above all, should be apparent.

We have also done a regular path coefficient analysis using the data for individual respondents, and we emerged with similar findings (see Figure 8.4). Pressure group activity is linked to elite initiated contacts which, together with the participation value, influence the level of elite concern over problems. Concern plus some small impetus from a positive feeling about the power to act appears strongly related to perceptions of effective action. For this latter path the multiple R's are strong in the U.S. and the Netherlands, weaker for politicians in Sweden.

A Path Model Using Elite Data to
Explain Variance in City Expenditures

We can now use this "path model" approach to attempt, despite considerable skepticism by some scholars, an explanation of the variance in per capita expenditures, using our political leadership variables as well as

FIGURE 8.4 Path Models Explaining Levels of Elite Concern and Perceived Effective Action (Based on Individual Level Data)

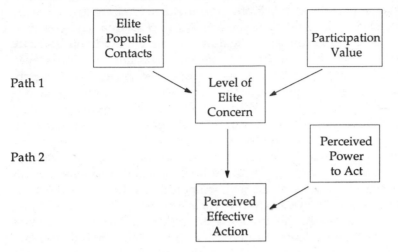

	Multiple R's			
	Path 1		*Path 2*	
	Politicians	*Administrators*	*Politicians*	*Administrators*
U.S.	.188	.167	.529	.213
Sweden	.147	.125	.042	.277
Netherlands	.159	.239	.446	.668

community structural and fiscal policy variables. There has been considerable interest in expenditure and fiscal strain analysis in recent years (Clark and Ferguson 1983; Clark, ed. 1981; Clark, Hellstern and Martinotti 1985). None of these studies, however, has combined elite background, attitudinal, and contact behavior variables with community structural and fiscal variables as we do here. The key question for us in this explanatory effort is not just whether "political leadership" is important, but what aspects of leadership may be important in explaining variations in fiscal policy. The variables we used are drawn from the earlier list presented, but are a smaller subset which revealed the largest correlations. The dependent variable, per capita expenditures, varied considerably in the three countries:

	U.S.	*Sweden*	*Netherlands*
High City	$1,019	20,900 (Kronor)	5,044 (Guilders)
Low City	342	13,600	2,152
Median	609	16,600	2,676

The range was greatest in the U.S. and smallest in Sweden. One must remember that municipal funds expended in the Netherlands come largely from higher authorities, while in the U.S. and Sweden local governments generate a much higher percentage of their income. (See Chapter I.) Further, in the two European countries the central government holds cities strictly responsible for providing a variety of services at a fairly uniform level. Nevertheless, local governments in the European countries have the right to raise some revenue locally (particularly in Sweden), and in addition, they have certain discretionary authority over expenditures. This helps explain the probably unexpectedly large variation in local government expenditures in Sweden and the Netherlands.

The basic model which emerges from our scrutiny of all the available correlations leads to one key elite attitudinal variable which emerges for each country: elite views about their responsibility to act on the local governmental level in order to resolve their problems. (See Figure 8.5) As discussed at length earlier, in the U.S. and Sweden the question asked was whether they "should have" responsibility; in the Netherlands the language was "have" responsibility. Despite this difference, and keeping it in mind, it seems to be a useful variable in each country separately. The Pearson coefficients are as follows:

	Correlation with Per Capita Expenditures		
	U.S.	*Sweden*	*Netherlands*
"Responsibility to Act"	.389	.319	.223

This responsibility variable was not found to be as useful in the earlier analysis, but was the most cross-nationally relevant among elite attitudinal variables linked to per capita expenditures (exceeded only by the "power to act" variable in the Netherlands). This finding, that responsibility oriented elites report higher expenditures for their cities, is significant. Other value and attitudinal variables, except for the "power to act" variable, show no such association to expenditures. And the question then becomes one of searching for the sources for such elite assumption of responsibility. Certain variables were indeed associated with this sense of responsibility, although they were usually not the same for each country. The most important are:

	Correlations with Elite Sense of Responsibility		
	U.S.	*Sweden*	*Netherlands*
Community Structural Variables			
1. Population Size	- .192	.300	.161
2. Median Family Income	.462	.480	.416
3. "Left" Party Dominance	.271	.301	- .096

	Correlations with Elite Sense of Responsibility		
	U.S.	Sweden	Netherlands
Attitudinal and Value Orientations			
1. Perceived Power to Act	.059	.376	.133
2. Pro Participation Value	.181	.575	-.090
3. High Influence Perceptions (% of			
elites scoring high on influence index)	.412	.219	.200
4. Pro Conflict Value	.226	.603	.247
Educational Level of Elites	.052	.363	.513

FIGURE 8.5 Path Model for Explaining Variance In City Per Capita Expenditures

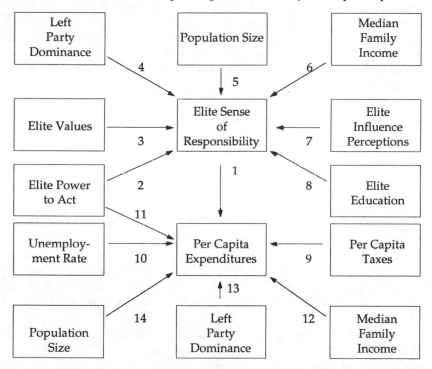

Countries for Which the Correlations Appear Relevant—By Type of Relationship

	Correlations with Responsibility							Correlations with Per Capita Expenditures						
	2	3	4	5	6	7	8	1	9	10	11	12	13	14
U.S.		x	x	x	x	x		x	x	x	x		x	x
Sweden	x	x	x	x	x	x	x	x		x		x	x	x
Netherlands	x	x		x	x	x	x	x		x	x	x	x	x

The "ideal-type" city of responsibility-oriented elites which emerges here is fairly clear. It is a city of relative affluence and, except for the Netherlands, with elites affiliated to parties of the Left. It is a city where elites are quite strongly committed to political participation (except Holland), and put a high priority on political conflict (rather than on community consensus and harmony). It is a city which in terms of its political influence structure is "democratic" rather than "hierarchic" (i.e., cities where a large proportion of elites feel they have influence in many policy areas). It is a city where elites tend to be more educated (except for the U.S.), and where elites also tend to feel they have the power to act (although, again, this correlation is not high in the U.S.). There are, thus, strong commonalties here in these three countries. However, the strength of these associations varies by country. Sweden fits this ideal-type image of elite responsibility best, and the Netherlands perhaps least well.

Returning to our aim of linking these variables to a model explaining city per capita expenditures, we can conceive of a "path model" which has some equivalence cross-nationally. The key relevant variables, aside from the sense of responsibility variable, are the following:

	Correlations with Per Capita Expenditures		
	U.S.	Sweden	Netherlands
Community Structural Variables			
1. Population Size	−.655	.152	.534
2. Party Dominance	.267	−.411	.201
3. Unemployment Level	−.438	.471	.537
4. Per Capita Taxes	.554	.017	−.195
Perceived Power to Act	.191	−.193	.531

It is clear that there are striking differences by country in the role which these conditions and influences have on local government expenditure policy. The U.S. is unique on population size, unemployment level, and the relationship of tax policy to expenditures. Sweden is very unique in the strong relationship of party dominance or competition to expenditures, as well as in the negative correlation for the power to act. The Netherlands surprisingly reveals that population size, even for these medium sized cities, may be an important factor. And both Sweden and the Netherlands, probably as expected, demonstrate that tax policy is not linked to per capita expenditures. Differing structural and institutional conditions, thus, have to be understood in explaining the variance in city per capita expenditures.

Yet, the uniformities in the overall "path model" for all three countries must be kept in mind. The common finding that "sense of elite responsibility" is linked to expenditures, and that this responsibility orientation is in all countries linked to influence perceptions, a belief in political conflict, and a tendency to agree that they have the power to act—these correlational uniformities stand out. "Responsibility" combined with special community economic and political conditions in each society together play significant roles apparently in explaining whether communities are governed by elites with expansive or restrictive expenditure policies and strategies.

Conclusions

Any effort to explain why cities vary in performance and outcomes is almost inevitably elaborate. It is a multifaceted theoretical problem. This is so particularly if one introduces a variety of variables concerning leadership behavior, values, and perceptions, as we do here, in addition to the community structural variables normally utilized. Our research strongly suggests that such leadership variables are probably relevant for explaining variance in city outcomes. Along with the economic status of the community and its political institutions such as the party system and pressure group complex, our findings indicate that the type of political leadership, in its broadest meaning, must be considered as playing a central role. However, one should always be cautious and quizzical, no doubt, while research explorations such as these continue.

The basic conceptualization which emerges here is that in between community structural conditions and effective action there are a set of intervening leadership variables which are influenced by the economic, populational, and political institutions of the city, and which in turn influence the level of effective action. We have identified several of these leadership variables as more or less relevant for all three countries. These are: elite contacts with community groups, elite sensitivity to the seriousness of their problems, elite value commitments, elite belief in their having the power to act on problems, and elite recognition of, and response to, pressure group activity. These variables seem to explain, together with community structural variables, why some communities are run by elites who report a low level of effective action and others report a higher level of effective action. In addition, another key leadership variable—the extent to which elites have a sense of responsibility that their problems should be or can be handled at the local level—seems to be linked to the per capita expenditure levels of these communities. Obviously the type of community is still very relevant—its population size, party control pattern, economic character. But the strong implication of these data is that a certain type of community with a certain type of leadership conduces to a certain level of effective action.

Finally, there is enough similarity in our "path models" across systems to reinforce the observation that this theoretical and conceptual configuration of forces has close equivalence for Western democratic systems. True, these three countries are by no means identical. Examples are close at hand. Elite values work differently in Sweden and the Netherlands in these models than in the U.S. The power to act variable seems irrelevant in Sweden, while the sense of responsibility variable carries more weight. But despite such exceptions the basic character of the models seems remarkably similar across these systems. While one remains skeptical of such elaborate models, as one should, it may be that, despite scholarly efforts to the contrary, the nature of political leadership is very relevant for explaining effective action in communities, whether conceptualized in subjective evaluative terms or in the hard realities of real expenditures.

9

Comparative Perspectives on Local Leadership in Western Democracies: Concluding Observations

Democracies differ and local elites within, as well as across, democracies differ, sometimes greatly. That is certainly one major realization which emerges from our study. There is great diversity, and the problem of generalization has been most acute for us throughout our analysis. The fact that elite differences exist at the national and subnational level alongside elite equivalencies has compounded our problem. How difficult it becomes then to identify an "elite political culture" for a system!

Comparative research is always demanding, of course. Yet, moving from the macro-national level of analysis to the local government level of analysis while retaining the goal of making macro-level theoretical generalizations, increases the difficulty. It then becomes necessary to specify the local system conditions which are responsible for explaining both variant and invariant local elite behavior and attitudes in more than one national system. The desire, and hope, is to arrive at theoretical propositions, or as some say, "general laws," which are valid for several countries at two system levels, national systems and local systems.

The central, organizing ideas directing our research can be expressed by reference to several underlying assumptions. One assumption was that if we were to understand our individual systems at the national level better, we should systematically and comparatively study the political and governmental leadership of the cities or communes, a long neglected area of inquiry. Two, we operate with the conviction that the positional elites in cities and communes, such as councillors, chief executives and mayors, administrators of city departments and major committees, and political party leaders—these actors are top decisional elites whose orientations and actions had to be carefully observed, understood, and compared. While there are many other aspects of city and communal life to study (groups, institutions, policies, media, etc.), the study of these elites is critical for understanding the political life and development of these nations at the sub-national level. Further, our study focused on particular aspects of these elites, on which information was necessary—their personal and political careers and social backgrounds, their perceptions about the problems of their communities, politically-relevant values, their preferred strategies for action, and their evaluations of their power, responsibility, influence, and the effectiveness of their actions in dealing with their community problems. Out of all that might be studied, these were the areas of substantive knowledge about local elites that we felt were most important for our objectives.

The study was done in three Western democracies. The practical reason for selecting these three was that in the U.S., Sweden, and the Netherlands there was a convergence at a particular time of scholarly interest and research resources. The intellectual reason lending credibility was that these systems all had a long history of the development of democratic local government, while at the same time being considerably different in the types of local government they used and in the relationship of local governments to their national governments. Such a three-country study could help us understand our individual systems by learning cross-nationally from other democratic systems.

Harold Lasswell and his colleagues said forty years ago: "The leadership of a society is a criterion of the values by which that society lives... By learning the nature of the elite, we learn much about the nature of the society" (Lasswell, Lerner and Rothwell 1952, 1). This should be particularly true in democratic societies where elites are popularly selected and can be periodically replaced. One aim for us was, then, to describe the amount of variance in local elite behavior and attitudes in these three different democratic systems. And after such a description the objective was to explain such variance (and conformity) in system relevant terms. Finally, on the basis of such analysis we hoped to be able to assess comparatively the state (or the effectiveness) of local government leadership today in these systems.

We have found these objectives rather difficult to achieve. This is not due primarily to the method employed, that is, the type of elite interview utilized. The survey in fact provided us with most of the basic information we sought, the responses were of high quality for the most part, and with few exceptions the respondents satisfactorily provided adequate data. Indeed the respondents tended to be rather candid and open in what they told us, and more modest than might have been expected. The data, then, permitted a great variety of unique and special types of analyses.

The problem has been, rather, with the extreme variation in elite orientations and behaviors *within* systems and *across systems*. The variations by cities and communes, particularly, complicated efforts at generalization. In their early reflection on political culture a quarter century ago Lucian Pye and Sidney Verba emphasized the need to understand the "community culture." Pye: "every community and national society seem so spontaneously capable of producing its own distinctive and persisting style, manner, and substantive forms of politics." And Verba: "most of what an individual believes about [the] political process is learned from observations about that process." And where learned? Obviously for local elites much of it is in their localities! And Verba added another observation helpful for comprehending the variations we find by cities and communes and some subgroups: "Not all cultures are well integrated and consistent. There may be sources of strain . . . sets of beliefs that are incompatible with other beliefs, sets of beliefs held by one segment of society and not another, or unmanageable incongruities between belief and reality" (Pye and Verba 1965, 3, 520, 550-51). Our study reveals such contrasts among elites, probably because we disaggregate elites by locality as well as by other variables (party, social class, age, etc.). One might have expected greater "integration" and fewer "incongruities" perhaps in these three democratic systems. Discovering the opposite taxes the attempt to explain these contrasts. In the ensuing summary of findings we will demonstrate both the respects in which we have integrated polities and in what respects not. We will extract the most important findings which are uniform and not uniform. And then try to make theoretical sense out of them.

Uniform Findings Across the Three Systems

We should expect certain common characteristics of local elites in these systems, and indeed that is the case. They may constitute a set of findings which could be considered "benchmarks" for such democratic systems. The explanations for these uniformities vary, however. They may suggest that system characteristics are irrelevant, but the opposite may be more true.

First, we find that many aspects of social and political backgrounds for local leaders are somewhat similar. In all three countries they are relatively well educated, only a small proportion are female, sizable numbers (but less than a majority) come from families with working class backgrounds, and a significant minority had parents who were involved in politics and government. Thus "social bias" persists at the local level of government although less so, considerably less so, than at the national elite level. While 90 percent or more of national legislative and administrative elites have a university education this is true of only 40 percent to 55 percent of these local leaders. Nevertheless, the chances for a person of working class background and no university education to achieve a local leadership position is only 6 percent for administrative positions and 16 percent for city councillors. This corroborates the classical doctrine that social status is indeed linked to political power, in these democracies as in other systems. Further, one should point out that bureaucracies in all these systems maintain relatively long tenures in public service, from 70 to 90 percent holding public positions for over 10 years. While this indicates competence, or perhaps at least experience, it also reaffirms another doctrine, that he who secures political power or status, at least in the bureaucracy, becomes habituated if not entrenched.

A second major uniformity is that local political leaders and administrators seem to work closely together and to share many perspectives. The data on interactions indicate that from 70 to 80 percent report that they initiate contacts with each other. However, in no country do administrators perceive that they have the degree of influence over policy that the political elites do. They are much more inclined to see themselves as policy specialists. Above all, these two sets of leaders reveal remarkable agreement *within their systems* on a variety of perspectives—on the seriousness of their problems, on perceptions of their power to act, on whether they should, or do, have the responsibility to act, and on their evaluations of effective action. *Within systems* the legislative and administrative elites are highly congruent. This seems counter to what was found in the comparative study of national elites and refutes in a sense the Weberian proposition of the inevitable disagreement and even hostility between bureaucrats and politicians. In local government these two sets of leaders act as very agreeable, mutually accepting, partners in the local governmental enterprise. Is this because of the nature of local government throughout the world, or democratic local government, or only a special feature of these three systems? It is certainly not a finding which holds true comparatively at the national level. More comparative research will eventually answer that question.

A third finding is that to a certain extent urban problems as perceived by local elites in all three countries are similarly identified and given relatively similar levels of priority. There is great concern over revenues and financial resources, as well as economic development, public safety, unemployment and poverty. From 60 to 70 percent or more see those as the most salient problems, in contrast, for example, to health, which in all three countries is rated much lower. The level of overall concern for problems, however, is not the same (the U.S. is low and the Netherlands is high), but the priority problems which are singled out are very similar. This is an observation which pertains exclusively to the aggregate proportions for all elites in each nation. When we disaggregate the data by cities we find great variation in elite problem perceptions. (More discussion of that aspect of the study will be undertaken later.) What these nation-to-nation findings suggest is that quite a few problems are common for local leaders in "the West," irrespective of certain distinctive system characteristics. For example, one might have hypothesized that in strong welfare-state (and unitary) systems like Sweden and the Netherlands local elites would be less concerned about health, unemployment, and poverty problems than in the U.S. But our data demonstrate that this conjecture is untrue! The level of concern is similar, and the U.S. is not usually high in the proportion of local elites who say these are serious problems. This may be one of the "incongruities" that Verba was thinking about (a conflict "between belief and reality"), or a consequence of urban conditions (as perceived by local elites at least) in all modern democratic societies. On the basis of our research this latter generalization perhaps for the time being is the most tenable.

Fourth, there is for the elites in all these countries a uniform disjunction between their perceptions of power and their reports on effective action. Many more leaders say that they have the power to act (on the 11 problems they were all asked to respond to) than they have taken effective action. The ratios are (average for all problems):

	Power	Action
U.S.	55	26
Sweden	44	12
Netherlands	44	26

While the Netherlands may be a special case (as explained in the text) because of its more circumscribed central government-local government fiscal relationship, the general point still holds. Large numbers of local leaders are saying "we have the power to act but have not acted (or can not, will not, act)." This is true for even some of the most serious problems they cite. This raises a series of important questions which we deliberated on in detail in the chapters of this study. How can we explain the variation in power perceptions (another "incongruity")? Why would local elites be so negative, self-demeaning, hopeless? Is this an expected pattern of response for all systems, all democratic systems, all systems with historic patterns of local self-government? Or is it time-bound, relevant particularly for this period of the Eighties when resources were low for urban development, neglect by national governments was high, and/or controversy over the capacity of local governments to provide services was deep? One is inclined to the latter interpretation until we secure more data over time. In the meantime before accepting that easy rationale it should be pointed out that the city-by-city data in each of these three countries reveals that there are cities whose elites report very high levels of performance on many of these problems. More about that when we summarize the data for individual cities later.

Fifth, one of the interesting by-products of this research is the information we secured on the level of political group activity in these cities in all countries, and the possible consequences of that activity for elite behavior. We asked all respondents to tell us in detail who they turned to for support (including such community groups as business, union, ethnic or racial, religious, civic and reform, neighborhood, and, of course, local party groups). And we also asked whether these groups contacted them as leaders. We found on the average 40 to 50 percent of the leaders reported "pressures" on them from community groups. Pressures from citizens were even more frequent. In the U.S., business, civic, and neighborhood groups were high. In Sweden, local party, civic, and public employee groups were high. In the Netherlands, local party, business and civic groups were high. If we can believe these leaders, they operate in a context of considerable group activity and group interest in political decisionmaking. This is quite contrary to the image conveyed in a report on American cities, contending that "local politics is groupless politics" (Peterson 1981, 116). These data by no means support such a proposition. Although the types of groups which function in local government vary by system, the fact of group activity and pressure emerges clearly from these leaders' responses. Further, as the analysis in the text reveals, the pressures on elites generated "from below" have a strong relationship to the strategies used by elites to mobilize support for their positions. The correlation between these two variables is significantly high in all three countries. What do we make of this? Although in the U.S. the pressure of interest groups in cities has to many observers seemed considerable for a long time (despite disclaimers by others), the same may not have been so true in Sweden and the Netherlands. Yet, as democracies develop, and community political life develops, the probabilities that local interests will organize, will develop political objectives, and will attempt to influence certain types of public policy, and thus will initiate contacts with local leaders, is very likely. That is clearly what appears to have become an important phenomenon of local government in these three systems. It is particularly significant that those leaders who tell us that they are "influentials" (who scored highest on our influence index) are in all three countries much more pressured by these community groups than the "peripherals," as this summary indicates:

	U.S.	Sweden	Netherlands
% pressured by 5 or more community groups:			
Influentials	68	80	83
Peripherals	35	38	43

Such data certainly attest to the targeted activity of local interest groups, if not to their relevance for elite action.

As for our three basic value scales—Political Participation, Conflict Resolution, and Innovative Change—we found very high support and similar levels of support. The local elites in these systems support these key components of the democratic process at the 70 percent level or higher. Again, we will find variations at the individual city level and must then identify the conditions which lead elites to deviate in support of these values. Generally, in the aggregate the support for these three values is so high, equally for bureaucrats and politicians, that one is inclined to attribute this to the existence of similar recruitment and socialization processes in each country. Which socialization agents are primarily responsible for this in each system is impossible to determine from our data—whether the early family, early school, later school, the political party, other political groups, the media, or socialization in position. There is some evidence that the agents may differ, with the exposure to party more important in Europe than in the U.S. Basically, however, it is significant that such a high proportion of local elites come to local office committed so definitely in all countries to these values. The democratic character of their institutions and processes seems presumptively responsible. On another value, economic equality, there is no such uniformity. An examination of that follows later in the discussion.

Finally, our path models explaining effectiveness of action demonstrated that with certain exceptions the same configuration of forces seemed linked to perceived effectiveness of action. Above all these models suggested that certain leadership orientations and behavior were similarly critical in explaining both subjective evaluations of action and, objectively, per capita city expenditures.

System Differences In Local Elites

The expectation that as democracies mature they will reveal a convergence in patterns of elite behavior (or "homogenization") is not borne out by our analysis. The uniformities already discussed are important to note. But in other characteristics and perspectives and values elites diverge across these three systems. The first point is that despite common tendencies to social bias in representation, the background characteristics are to some extent considerably different, in four respects: age, social class, education, religious activity. In religious affiliation the American leaders stand out from Europeans. They also have higher education. The Swedish elites are much older and come much more from the middle and upper class. The Dutch leaders are younger, and more representative of the lower and working classes (as are the Americans). Two of these differences—religion and education—may be considered to be linked to populational characteristics. The American public is much more religious in its affiliation and church attendance than in Europe, and 20 percent of the U.S. public over 25 years of age has completed college (compared to less than 10 percent in Europe).

But the other two credentials seem linked to the elite recruitment process, to the openness of that process and to the degree of rigidity in the criteria for political and administrative office. The Swedish system appears least open, the Dutch and the American more open.

A second set of differences appears in the way these leaders define their roles and responsibility in dealing with the problems which confront them. Aside from the identification of which problems are serious which we already noted revealed a considerable uniformity of response, elite orientations concerning the seriousness of problems and their opinions in dealing with them vary. A single recapitulation of these system differences is as follows:

	U.S.	Sweden	Netherlands
% seeing problems as serious	49	58	67
% stating they have the power to act on problems	55	66	44
% say they "should have" the responsibility to act on their problems	53	70	(34)

(As for the responsibility question one should remember here that in the Netherlands the question asked was whether local elites "have" the responsibility to act)

Clearly there are "incongruities" again her, and the explanation is not an easy one to come by. The Americans are, relatively, very sanguine about their problems, are confused on the issue of "power," and tend to be split on their responsibility. The Dutch are very worried about their problems but, perhaps incongruously, do not feel they have the power nor the responsibility. The conflict with reality for both sets of elites, U.S. and the Netherlands, is puzzling. The Swedish elites take positions which seem reality oriented (except perhaps for the nearly unanimous view that they had a serious unemployment problem), and reflect a basic commitment to responsibility. As our analysis demonstrated these orientations for the elites of all countries persist when we analyzed the elite subgroups (by party, position, and age). Hence one is inclined to see these orientations as pervasive and differential manifestations of the elite cultures of these systems. One is also tempted to say there is not only much rejection of reality here but also of normative commitment.

A third observation is that the elites in these systems also differ in their conflict perceptions. The Swedish elites are most concerned about the existence of conflict in their communes (73%), the Dutch much less concerned (43%), the Americans almost as concerned as the Swedish (66%). But when asked whether these conflicts interfere with community development, the Swedish are very low in level of concern (24%), the Americans and

Dutch much higher (67% and 53%). And these aggregate findings for all elites persist if we analyze the elite subgroups again. There is remarkable homogeneity within systems despite party, age, education, position. Hence, there are special aspects of these elite cultures or special system conditions which must be relevant for any explanation of such differences. The historic Dutch concern for the consequences of group conflict if it should develop again is probably relevant here. One should note that it is not differences in religious beliefs in the Netherlands which are of concern to these elites today—only 25 percent say they exist. Rather it is differences in political beliefs, in views about social change, plus generational, and income differences which are more salient—recognized by over 50 percent of the Dutch elites. Yet the incidence of all of these is lower than for the U.S. and Swedish. The greater preoccupation with the negative impacts of conflict in the Netherlands and the U.S. must be founded in the system's experience with conflict and awareness of the difficulty in handling it. It does not mean, however, that these leaders reject the necessity and inevitability of conflict in a democratic society. Our conflict orientation value scale reveals that they accept conflict as central to the democratic decisionmaking process. For example, when confronted by the statement "preserving harmony in the community should be considered more important than the achievement of community programs," over 80 percent of the leaders in these countries disagree. Thus, while operating with a conflict model of politics, which varies somewhat by system, the majority of these leaders refuse to capitulate to the pressure for consensus in making decisions.

Elite contact patterns reveal a fourth set of differences across these countries. In both European systems local elites have much more contact with national administrators than U.S. elites do. The close central-local state relationships are reflected in such data. European leaders are also more in touch with party leaders at the local and national levels. In Europe, for example, over 80 percent of local councillors report that they initiate contacts with the local party organizations (93% in Sweden, 83% in the Netherlands, compared to 27% in the U.S.). In addition, approximately one third of European councillors are in touch with national or provincial party leaders. Thus, there is a strong vertical structuring of party relationships in Europe among policy leaders, from the bottom to the top of the system, unlike in the U.S. This is achieved only in part in the U.S. through the contacts local leaders have with state legislators and Congressional representatives. The role of the political party as a very relevant, powerful, integrative institution for the entire system is very distinctive in Europe, in contrast to the U.S.

A further difference in contact patterns is found in the greater incidence of U.S. elite contacts (which they initiate) with a wide variety of community groups (business, civic, and neighborhood groups particularly). One sees elites in Europe doing much less of that. Media and public contacts are also reported more frequently in the U.S. The suggestion implicit in such data, combined with our observation of the extensive pressure group activity reported in European cities, is that European elites may be on a trajectory leading to more elite-initiated group contacts in the future, eventually paralleling the American pattern of contacts of such types. Already 40 percent of the Dutch elites report business group contacts, no doubt linked to the 68 percent who report pressures *from* business groups on them. The gap between pressure group activity and elite-initiated group contacts, however, remains relatively high in Europe. There elites still reveal reluctance to feel the need to go to such groups in order to mobilize support for their policies.

A fifth system difference emerged from our analysis of personal influence perceptions. When these leaders were asked in which policy areas they had "very much," "some," or "no" influence, they provided information revealing two key differences. First, in Europe many more of these leaders see themselves as influential in "social" policy areas such as housing, health, culture, recreation, and social welfare, than in the U.S. The contrast was striking: 82% (Sweden), 71% (Netherlands), 40% (U.S.). This is a significant indication of the difference in focus of interest and attention for these systems, no doubt linked to the strong "welfare state" system in these European countries.

Another difference which struck us was in the overall patterns of influence revealed by these responses. More European elites feel they have little or no influence. Using an "index of influence distribution" for the total sample as well as for individual cities we could construct the "influence structure" by nation and city. The analysis suggested that the "pluralist democracy" structure (a relatively high proportion of elites with much influence, a relatively small proportion with little influence) was the dominant American structure in cities. European cities varied, however—in Sweden the "hierarchical" pattern was most prevalent (few elites with much influence, many with no influence), but both the Dutch and Swedish also revealed mixed types of influence structures. While such attempts at modelling influence may have limited utility, the fact that elites do feel they have "much" or "no" influence turned out to be a useful analytical tool. The characteristics of the "influentials" in contrast to the "peripherals" are very sharp, and the differences between the two categories within each system are consistent on certain variables across systems. The top "influentials" are the politicians (mayors and councillors really), pressured much more by community groups, and much more in touch with prestigeful authorities than is true for the "peripherals." Thus, although the influence structures vary by system, the phenomenon of "political influence" *per se* links up similarly with other power-relevant correlates in all systems.

A final basic difference across these systems as we mentioned earlier is in the commitment of local elites to the values of economic equality. There is a wide difference between Sweden and the U.S., with the Dutch leaders closer to the Swedish, but in the middle. The average level of commitment for the items in our value scale are: 23% (U.S.), 41% (Netherlands), and 57% (Sweden). This difference is greater on certain tests of the value than on others. For example:

	(% of elites who agree)		
	U.S.	Sweden	Netherlands
"Rich people should pay more for the support of community programs than poor people" The Swedish version was: "Communal taxes should be progressive"	67	42	73
"There should be an upper limit on income so that no one earns very much more than others"	4	21	24
"In every situation poor people should be given more opportunities than rich people"	3	64	25
"Discrepancies in salaries should be continually reduced"	32	69	27
"Government has the responsibility to see that nobody lives well when others are poor"	3	88	57

While few of these leaders are interested in an upper limit on income, and while all three countries have elites willing to tax the rich more heavily, the Dutch and the Swedish leaders are obviously more willing to see government assume a redistributive role than the Americans are. This point has been made in other, earlier, studies. This elite equalitarianism in Europe seems clearly linked to social class origins plus party affiliation. The leaders with fathers with working class backgrounds and who were brought up in the Social Democratic or other "Left" parties are the most egalitarian, an excellent example of the link between personal backgrounds and belief. In the U.S., however, the low level of support for economic equality seems pervasive and holds up for all age groups, social class backgrounds, educational levels, and party affiliation. It seems thus to be a function of a general pattern of political socialization throughout the U.S. society. This is not so in Europe *apparently*. Yet, when one examines the values of elites by city in each country one finds considerable range in the commitment to this value of economic equality. In the U.S. it is a range in average level of commitment by city of 16 to 44 percent, in Sweden 44 to 68 percent, and in the Netherlands 31 to 67 percent. Hence even in this *apparently* striking cross-system difference, one must remember that there is a subnational elite socialization process taking place within each community. That is, the reality is that particular cities may have elites with quite distinctive value orientations. Elite values seem to vary by urban subcultures.

Theories To Explain System Differences and Uniformities

Throughout this book in the interpretations of our findings we have utilized different types of theories. The question to be asked in comparative analysis is: Can one identify one or more key factors, or conditions, or processes, which are linked to, and help explain, the differences we find across systems. Is there a Factor A, or Factor B, which if modified in System X would have made the elites in System X more like the elites in System Y? Also, of course, when the finding is the same for all systems can one identify what factors are responsible for that uniformity?

Institutional explanations seem to be very attractive and useful in this study. Central-state relationships in our three countries differ and one might quickly assume that is certainly a help in explaining power and responsibility perceptions. This appears particularly true in the Dutch case. But even that is not clear. The Dutch have a low sense of their power to act— a 44 percent average on all problems compared to 55 percent for the Americans and 66 percent for the Swedish leaders. Is it logical to connect that to the special central-local relationships in the Dutch system? We need much more precise knowledge of the frames of reference of the leaders to see that as a necessarily acceptable explanation. If it means "discretionary power to initiate" policies, it could be a logical interpretation, but if it means "power to act," probably not. Further, how explain the high Swedish percentage in these terms, since they also operate under a unitary system? In addition, how explain the variance in power perceptions by cities and among elites in terms of this institutional difference?

On the other hand, the centrality and basic nature of the party system in Europe *is* an institutional condition which seems clearly relevant to elite orientations and behavior. The contacts between local elites and party organizations are much more evident in Europe. The socialization role of parties in Europe is, thus, more probable, as well as the role parties seemingly play in the recruitment of different social class types to local positions (particularly in Sweden).

Also, the strong welfare state systems in Europe could be used as an explanation of the differences in concern for "social" policy areas, and the greater emphasis by European elites on those areas when they are asked to discuss their policy areas of greatest influence. To sum up, one can well say that if a system X (say, the U.S.) would be party-oriented and more welfare-state oriented one might indeed find local elites in system X to manifest certain different attitudes and behaviors.

A second type of theory we have explored is reflected in the "subgroup analysis" we have engaged in throughout the book. The subgroups we focused on were positional, partisan, social class, generational, and educational. In a sense we have continually asked whether it is possible to explain the differences and uniformities across systems in terms of the differential or similar types of familial or political or age-cohort environments to which these leaders were exposed. Another term for this is "lifepath socialization" influences on elites. We found it to be very difficult to find evidence of the utility of this theory for many elite orientations. For example, the difference between the U.S. and Swedish elites on their willingness to be held responsible for action on their problems (a 20 point differential) is not explicable with such theory. If we break our samples by age (generation), position, party, etc., we find the same basic differential across systems. Whether young or old, "left" or "right," politician or bureaucrat, etc., the Swedish local leader is always more likely to feel a sense of responsibility than the American leader! The same is true for evaluations of effects of conflict on their communities. So for both types of orientations the consistency by subgroups within each system suggest a pervasive set of elite norms and beliefs which differ at the national level. This suggests that possibly different historic traditions and cultural predispositions are operative. Unhappily this seems a weak explanation until there is adequate evidence of how such traditions and cultural norms emerged and why so differently in the U.S. and Sweden.

Subgroup analysis, as indicated, is more useful in explaining elite values for particular systems like the Swedish and possibly the Dutch. But it is important to realize that for U.S. local elites age, party, education, position, tenure in position, gender, father's occupation, religious activity—all these "independent" variables are not useful in explaining the incidence of elite belief in, for example, economic equality. No differences emerge by such variables! It is only when we get to "the city" as the independent variable that we find important differences.

A third theoretical exploration attempted to link the population characteristics of cities to elite problem perceptions. In the data presentations on this substantive area it was clear that cities and communes do vary considerably in elite perceptions. For example, the question on whether housing is a serious problem, or pollution, or health, or unemployment, evokes proportions in elite responses by city which vary from 12 to 100 percent. Again, the question concerning the power to act (on housing, pollution, etc.) evokes also widely different responses by elites by city in all countries, ranging from 23 to 95 percent. Clearly there is great diversity by city in all countries in elite beliefs that there is a need for action and the possibility of action. We secured aggregate data for each city on population size, median family income, unemployment level, and for the U.S. the poverty rate and the racial composition of the city. These objective indicators have relevance, i.e., they are associated with elite problem perceptions, particularly in the U.S. and Sweden, but by no means consistently. Median family income, for example, is correlated with elite perceptions of the seriousness of problems in all countries, but unemployment rate correlated well in the U.S. and the Netherlands, but is not associated with problem perceptions in Sweden. Population size seems clearly relevant in the U.S. and Sweden for many problems, but not in the Netherlands. Population size is also linked to elite conflict perceptions in the U.S. and Sweden (larger cities: more conflicts), but not in the Netherlands. One must conclude that these objective community indicators are under certain conditions relevant for understanding elite differences in problem perceptions, but they are only a partial explanation in two countries, and of very marginal relevance for the Netherlands.

Our preoccupation with understanding city-by-city differences within and across political systems pushed us to test the utility of another, fourth, theoretical formulation. This is the concept of a "dominant elite" culture which emerges in each city or commune, and to which political elites of all types tend to gravitate. If there is a dominant elite *and* its position is clearly articulated in a particular direction (e.g., that problems are very serious, or that local government leaders should be responsible for solving problems) then opposition leaders will be inclined to "join the bandwagon" and support this dominant elite position. But when there is no clear dominant elite position, opposition support will drop off. Further, the theory argues, the opposition's support for the particular position will be greater in a "dominant elite" context than is true generally for the opposition. Finally, when there is no dominant elite and political control is divided or split in the city, there may also be considerable concurrence since close political competition can lead to a convergence in elite positions. This theory follows on the work of other scholars, going back to Tingsten's "clustering effect" concept in 1937, Berelson and his colleagues in 1954, and others we have referred to in the text. The basic assumption is that there is a locality elite culture and that elites relate to a dominant norm or value in that culture, depending on the clarity with which that norm or value is articulated.

To test this it became necessary then to identify the existence of the dominant elite (Elite A), *and* its position on a particular perceptual or evaluative question, followed by an identification of the position on this matter by the opposition elite(s) (Elite B). A comparison is necessary then of elite positions in that context with (1) a context in which the dominant elite's (Elite A's) position is ambivalent, and (2) with a context in which the opposition (Elite B) is now dominant and has a position, as well as (3) a context in which no elite is dominant and political control is split. Such comparative data over the three systems was necessary if we were to demonstrate whether this theory is tenable.

In the analysis of problem perceptions (seriousness, power to act, and responsibility) we tested this theory with three alternative propositions: (1) the dominant elite will prevail, (2) competition or split party control leads to convergence also, and (3) elite dominance is irrelevant because local elites adhere to a basic political party position which transcends the city. We find strong support for both propositions 1 and 2. There may be other possible uses for this type of analysis. We found it particularly useful in explaining city differences in elite problem, power and responsibility perceptions. The data do not seem to indicate that such a theory or analysis will explain elite personal value orientations.

While this type of theory and analysis clearly has utility, our study suggests that it is a "configuration" of forces and factors for each city which must be analyzed in order to understand why elites differ in elite perspectives. These include, as we have indicated, certain social and economic characteristics of the population of each city, the pattern of conflicts which persist in that city, the "problem environment" as seen by elites, the nature and direction of party control, the structure of perceived elite influence (whether hierarchic or democratic), the group pressures on elites, and the values to which elites are committed. Our study has demonstrated that all of these may have an influence on elite views of their problems, their power to act, their responsibility to act, their strategies for action to mobilize support, and their evaluations of the reality of effective action in their community. We have developed suggested profiles for our cities revealing that there are indeed contrasting types of cities for each country (Chapter 4). And our analysis of group pressures on elites suggests that the political infrastructure of a city—the types of groups and the extent of their activity— is linked to elite attitudes and behavior.

Elite Political Culture or Cultures?

One of the major questions posed in comparative research is the existence of distinctive political cultures—their character, sources of origin, and relevance. Our paraphrase of that interest at the outset was: Are there clusters or syndromes of local political elite perceptions, orientations to power, and value perspectives which really distinguish systems like the U.S., Sweden, and the Netherlands at the national, macro-system, level? From time to time in our analysis we have found evidence on particular questions which suggest that a case might be made. The closest to such cross system cultural differences in our data would be: (1) the heightened sense of responsibility which Swedish local leaders, in comparison to American and Dutch leaders, are willing to accept for the solution to their problems; (2) the much greater emphasis in the U.S. on elite contacts with community groups and the public, contacts local leaders initiate to mobilize group and mass support; (3) the greater commitment to the personal values of economic equality by Swedish and Dutch elites; (4) the relatively "democratic" elite influence structures in American cities in contrast to the "hierarchic" and "bifurcated" influence structures in Sweden and the Netherlands; and (5) the partisan nature of local government in Sweden and the Netherlands revealed in strong affiliations local leaders have with parties, very frequent contact patterns with local party organizations, and the relevance of this for value perspectives. Using these five types of differentia one is tempted to generalize as follows about these systems based on the analysis of local elites:

U.S.: peripheral role for parties, low sense of responsibility, democratic elite influence relationships, close elite-mass linkages, yet uncommitted to economic equality.

Sweden: central role for parties, high sense of responsibility, somewhat undemocratic elite influence relationships, limited elite-mass linkages, but very committed to economic equality.

The Netherlands: central role for parties, low sense of responsibility, mixed patterns of elite influence relationships, limited elite-mass relationships, moderately egalitarian in commitment to economic equality.

One senses anomalies in these cultures of elite orientations and behaviors. Perhaps the central anomaly is between elite political and economic patterns of belief and behavior. Using these two dimensions, we can place our countries as follows:

Political Democracy In Elite Influence and
Mass-Elite Patterns

		High	Low
Belief in Economic Equality	Strong		Sweden Netherlands
	Weak	U.S.	

Theoretically, in the abstract one might not expect these constellations. Yet they appear to exist, and these systems continue to function as democracies despite the anomaly. To oversimplify, the point seems to be that political democracy, in terms of elite belief and behaviors, does not lead to economic democracy, and vice versa. And why? Among other reasons, because the cultural expectations and requisites for elite behavior differ, at the elite level *and* at the public level. And why such different cultural expectations, that is, what processes are responsible? A profound question our study cannot answer.

Interesting though these generalizations are, they really break down to some extent when we look at city-by-city patterns. Whatever the national patterns are, they are modified, if not reversed, by what we find at the level of the city and the commune. On all five dimensions of apparent "national culture" difference used above, we find evidence of many exceptions at the subnational level. Here are illustrations on those five dimensions:

	U.S.		Sweden		Netherlands	
	High City	Low City	High City	Low City	High City	Low City
1. % of elites having contacts with local party leaders	60	14	79	41	88	60
2. % of elites with a commitment to responsibility	63	46	80	60	46	30
3. % of elites who feel they have much influence ("democratic" influence structure)	57	0	33	16	57	13
4. % of elites initiating con- tacts with community groups	73	9	40	11	33	0
5. % of elites committed to the value of economic equality	44	17	68	44	67	31

One notices, of course, that a comparison of "highs" and "lows" across those systems reveals the Swedish and Dutch "highs" are higher than the U.S. "highs" on elite commitment to economic equality, and for the partisan interaction dimension. And, on the other hand, the American "high" on contact with community groups overshadows the Dutch and Swedish "highs." Nevertheless, the fact of considerable variation on these five crucial dimensions remains. The average *within system* differences for the five dimensions are:

U.S.	—42%
Sweden	—25
Netherlands	—31

While the contrasts in the U.S. are greater, the variance in all systems belies the consistency of national norms at the local level. Rather than a "national culture," then, we seem to have a diversified mosaic of "local cultures."

The State of Local Leadership in Western Democracies

What final observations can be presented about the condition of city and commune leadership in these democracies? How democratic? How effective? If we cumulate all our empirical information from these 900 leaders in 55 cities in three democracies what light do these data shed on the nature of local government leadership? We know that national reports of the state of the cities in these countries are in some respects pessimistic, and that there is a continuing debate on the resource capability and level of national (and state) support for cities. The 1991 report of the National League of Cities in the U.S. revealed that in 61 percent of the cities revenues were less than expenditures, that 48 percent of the cities had cut services, 59 percent had laid off employees, and 71 percent were less able to meet financial needs in 1991 than in 1990 (Pagano 1991). Mayor Flynn of Boston, President of the U.S. Conference of Mayors in 1991 said there is "a growing crisis in hometown America... something is very wrong" (*New York Times* December 18, 1991). The Conference asked President Bush and the Congress for $35 billion immediately for urban aid, which the President and Congress rejected.

In the Netherlands the 1990 Report of the Scientific Council for Government Policy called "Institutions and Cities: The Dutch Experience," concludes that Dutch cities, particularly the major cities, are also in a period of decline since the 1970s.

> "The major cities' growing social and economic problems since the 1970s are reflected in virtually every kind of statistic ... what is especially disturbing is that the cities are falling behind not only in manufacturing . . . but also in services . . . What is striking in international terms is that the relatively high level of social provision (which prevents poverty becoming extreme) hides a deteriorating social structure ... and high level of unemployment and economic inactivity." (Netherlands Scientific Council For Government Policy 1990, 149, 182-83)

Retrenchment in national government support is illustrated by the cuts in grants to Amsterdam of 180 million guilders between 1982 and 1989. The report recommends a major restructuring of the fiscal support relationship between the national government and the cities. Comparable analyses of the state of Swedish cities is also available. Recently several scholars have mentioned a variety of problems which Swedish communes face. One study emphasized the growing tensions between "equal service delivery" and "local self government" and noted that "there are greater demands for local government services than money available" (Gustafsson 1991, 256-59).

The responses from our interviews in a sense underline these reports of the problems of the cities. From the leadership perspective there are many serious problems and effective action is difficult to achieve. Only 25 percent report effective action in the U.S. and the Netherlands, and only 12 percent in Sweden. Both the candor and modesty of our respondents are impressive!

If one reflects on the evidence from our study certain insights stand out. Clearly these leaders in all countries are struggling with serious problems. In addition, many of them are confused or uncertain about what can be done and what should be done by them. Further, many have no feelings of personal influence. Yet, most are experienced and presumably competent; they are not neophytes. They have been active in politics or administration and in their communities for long periods of time, and continue to be pressured by community groups, as well as superiors, for action. Their value orientations reveal that most are anxious for change, they believe in democracy, and the importance of progress despite tolerating conflict. While not all of them are democrats, and not all are effective leaders, and not all are perceptive leaders, or reality-oriented and influential leaders—most of them are. What then is the problem? Part of it is cognitive—they are ambivalent on what they can do, what to do, what power they have, what responsibility they should assume. This may well be linked to a type of cynicism about their role as local leader in a large political system which expects much but provides less assistance than they think is necessary. But it is also for some more than a cognitive problem—it is a matter of volition—lack of will, of drive, of commitment to act. In democratic systems, even in unitary democratic systems, there is great permissibility for inaction by leadership. Finally, it is a matter of belief, or lack of belief, in two senses—no commitment that action should be taken primarily at the local level; rather, action is preferred at some other government level or through non-governmental agencies; and weak commitment to the goals of governmental policy. That becomes particularly clear in the responses to the economic equality items in our study. Only 22 percent of American leaders believe in that goal, but 43 percent of the Swedish leaders do not either, nor do 58 percent of the Dutch. Thus problems of cognition, volition, and belief seem to be elements in this overall picture of leadership inactivity in these systems.

This is a too pessimistic recapitulation of our evidence, to be sure. To counter it we should point out that the "saving grace" of our study is that we do find that *there are some cities with leaders who claim they are making progress!* The following data illustrate this point:

	% of elites reporting effective action		
	U.S. "City X"	Sweden "City Y"	Netherlands "City Z"
Problem Area:			
Housing	92	39	65
Pollution	75	27	75
Education	69	54	71
Economic Development	70	27	75
Race (Immigration)	46	28	72

These are not phantom cities! These are live data and live cities! Here is evidence from leaders reports (leaders who have been candid but modest) that despite system constraints policy action can occur. Perhaps that is the most important observation. In all our discussions of "city cultures" perhaps the most important distinction is between the city with elites who are "action-oriented" and the city with elites who embrace passivity. In the former, elites feel their problems are serious, but that they have power to act, and, as innovative leaders pressed by an active public, they do act. In the latter category of elites, the "passive" nonbelievers, one finds leaders apparently succumbing to a sense of powerlessness and ambivalence and limited sense of pressures to act. We do find effective urban leadership, elites committed to action, leaders who despite conflict and tensions within their systems, do act. Many, obviously, do not. What we probably need more of, which this study does not provide, is precise research on the particular processes of leadership recruitment and socialization, as well as the conditions of community life, which may help explain the emergence of local political leaders optimistic about their ability to act and committed to effective action. If cities are to become more successfully governed, the transformation requires change at national and local levels. At the local level it requires the development of political elites in cities (as a result of careful selection, training and socialization) who are motivated to work confidently on their problems in partnership with state (province, county) and national authorities. For some cities in all three countries this is happening; in many cities not.

Appendix

A. Selection of the Sample of Municipalities

Since the U.S. study in 1984 was purposely intended to be a "retake" of the cities studied in 1966, one must keep in mind the sampling process followed in the earlier study (Jacob 1971, 213-218, 366-375). The objectives of the 1966 study and the requirements for international comparison emphasized the need to select municipal units which were structurally and functionally equivalent, and feasible to study. A major decision was made to select middle-sized cities through a random and stratified selection process, distinguishing cities by size and economic development level. In the U.S. the universe of middle-sized cities between 25,000 and 250,000 in population was identified and divided into three categories by size: 25,000–50,000; 50,000–100,000; and 100,000–250,000. The cities in each size category were ordered by economic development level using five indicators: income, employment, retail trade, housing, and traffic. Cities then were selected randomly in each of the population size categories. Thirty cities were taken in the sample (out of 714 cities in these population strata), with a population median of 82,000. These cities, then, were in 1966 a representative sample of all U.S. cities in these three population strata. In 1966, 28 percent of the population living in urban areas above 2,500 population were living in cities in the population strata 25,000–250,000. A final point to be made is that as a result of random selection these 30 cities were regionally well distributed.

In 1984 we were successful in completing interviews in 25 of the original 30 cities. The population range for these cities was then (based on the 1980 census) 30,000–541,000. In the development of the comparative design in conjunction with the Swedish project, it was decided to use only 20 U.S. cities for comparative analysis, excluding the three largest cities in the original sample, and two medium sized cities for whom the "retake" was not properly completed. The population range for these cities was 30,000–160,000, and the median was 65,000. The cities in this population range in 1980 included approximately 35 percent of the U.S. population. Thus it must be understood that the U.S. city sample in 1984 was selected for purposes of longitudinal analysis and was not a new city sample selected for purposes of representation of all cities in the given population range in 1984. In a sense the 1984 sample of 20 cities used here may be considered representative of cities in the smaller population range indicated.

For the Swedish study the selection of communes was done to maximize comparison with the American study. A total of 20 communes was selected from four population strata, but the smallest group of communes was excluded, those below 25,000 in population. The three strata used were: 25,000 -50,000, 50,000–100,000, and 100,000–250,000. Five communes were selected from each stratum. Level of economic development was then used in the random selection of communes in each of the strata. The actual population of the 15 communes ranged from 31,000 to 151,000. The median was 51,000. Thus, the Swedish communes used in this study are representative of all communes with a population of 25,000 and above, except for Stockholm, Göteborg, and Malmö.

In the Dutch study, initially 40 municipalities were selected from four population strata, but the two strata with the smallest cities were excluded for the analysis here. The two population strata which were used are: 30,000–50,000, and 50,000 to 100,000. Ten cities were selected from each of these strata. These cities are medium-sized and are considered comparable to the Swedish and American samples used here. One difficulty with the Dutch sample for the lower population stratum is that most of the cities are clustered at the 30,000 to 35,000 population level.

B. The Selection of Leaders

In Chapter I we explained the nature of the leadership sample selection and the procedures used for making certain that the leadership samples are equivalent. That is, our goal was, first, to select positional elites which were similar in both position and function; second, we wanted a leadership which was properly representative of the "leadership structure" of local government (political and administrative) in each community in each country. We feel we have done that fairly well. However, this has meant leadership samples which are proportionally varied in the number of politicians and administrators in each sample. As the figures in Chapter I reveal this selection strategy resulted in the Swedish and Dutch samples including larger percentages of politicians (67% and 66% respectively) than in the U.S. (49%).

We should report here that the response rate for the studies varied also: Sweden, 72%; U.S., 57%; and the Netherlands estimated as less than, but close to, the Swedish response rate.

C. Community Structural Variables

Securing a common set of community structural data for each city or commune in all three countries was more difficult than we anticipated. Certain variables were more relevant for one system than for the others. In addition the availability and reliability of the data varied considerably. We finally developed a set of six common variables which we are relatively confident about. These are:

	U.S.	Sweden	Netherlands
Population Size	1980	1984	1989
Population Change	1970-1980	1969-1983	1978-1988
Medium Family Income	1980	1983	1984
Unemployment Rate	1980	1984	1989
Voting Turnout	1984	1982	1986
Party Strength	1984	1982	1986

Even for these variables the data were not completely or perfectly comparable. The voting and party strength data for municipal elections in the U.S. were not available for all cities, despite repeated collection efforts. We thus resorted to Presidential election data for comparable information. In Europe the precise and detailed data on local elections, by city, is available at the national level. On the other hand, the data on rate of unemployment was not provided for certain Dutch cities, which control the release of such data. Despite these problems, these community data were adequate enough to permit the analyses we felt were important to do.

In addition to these common community variables, for each country additional types of data were available, and to some extent necessary. For the U.S., cities were distinguished by the type of city government and whether they used a partisan or nonpartisan system of election. Also, the racial composition of the population was an important variable, and the percentage of families below the poverty level. The Swedish data set provided the following additional data by city: per capita tax base, per capita revenues, and per capita expenditures (1984), the educational level of the population, and the change in the political majority of the city council 1979-1982. The Dutch also provided tax and expenditure data as well as the percentage of immigrants from abroad. Difficulties in getting all such data for all three countries and/or concern over their comparability limited our use of such data.

D. The Value Scales

Since the approach to the study of elite values followed in our book is directly connected to the 1966 Jacob study, *Values and the Active Community*, it is well to keep certain key points in mind, which were the points of departure for the earlier study (Jacob 1971, 385-399, and Chapter 5). The 1966 study followed closely the theory and methodology of contemporary scholarship at that time, exemplified by Allen Barton, William A. Scott,

Adam Przeworski, and Henry Teune (Barton 1965; Scott 1965; Przeworski and Teune 1966-67).

The objective was to secure a set of value scale items which were comparatively useful and also valid for each of the four countries: U.S., Poland, India, and Yugoslavia. The scales were based on specific forced-choice statements to determine "the respondent's degree of commitment to, or repudiation of," items which were considered to be important components of each value. The respondent was presented with a four-point set of response options for each statement: Strongly Agree, Agree, Disagree, Strongly Disagree. These were treated as scores on an interval scale under the assumption of equidistance. Initially in 1966 two sets of such items were prepared, one set which was a core list of items which were "semantically uniform" and valid for all four countries. The other set was country-specific, adapted to the conditions and experiences of each country. Factor analysis of these responses "demonstrated the homogeneity and independence" of the value scales.

The development of the scales took about two years, and involved the identification of items used by others as well as the creation of many new items. All items were then pre-tested twice in all countries, with a total of 830 pre-test respondents. A statistical analysis was made of all pre-test responses. The reliability of all value scales was then reported. After the factor analyses the final sets of items to be used in each country for each scale were determined and agreed upon.

There was very effective cross-country cooperation among the scholars of the four national teams, in planning the research, creating the scales, and in the analysis. There was some dissent over the utility of some of the value items, their meaning as differently translated for each system, and in the construction of the value profiles. The Yugoslavian team was most concerned on these matters. However, all teams worked together in the production of the final report.

In 1966 nine value scales were operationalized: Participation, Conflict Avoidance, Economic Equality, Innovative Change, National Commitment, Selflessness, Honesty, Economic Development, and Action Propensity. In the current study we focus on the first five of these values as most appropriate for our purposes. In constructing these scales we have used the same procedures used in the 1966 Jacob study. At the outset we included 31 items. Two were dropped from the Swedish study because they were considered inappropriate and had low factor loadings. For few others the language had to be changed considerably. And a few new items were added to test different value components in Sweden. In the final construction of the scales, however, 25 of the 31 original items were retained in all three countries. We do utilize also average percentages of support for the items in each scale as a second measure of the degree of value commitment.

Further, reference is also made in Chapter VIII to value items excluded from the scales as illustrative of the range of support for value components.

The actual value items included in our study are found in the questionnaire and some of them are discussed in detail in Chapter VII.

E. The Questionnaire

Section I. Meeting the Problems of Your City

1. What do you think are the most important problems facing your city now?
2. Are any of the following issues a problem for your city?

PLEASE CHECK	VERY SERIOUS	SOMEWHAT SERIOUS	NO PROBLEM
(1) Quality of education	[ ]	[ ]	[ ]
(2) Unemployment	[ ]	[ ]	[ ]
(3) Poverty	[ ]	[ ]	[ ]
(4) Health services and conditions	[ ]	[ ]	[ ]
(5) Housing	[ ]	[ ]	[ ]
(6) Public improvements (transportation, streets, water, sewage, sanitation)	[ ]	[ ]	[ ]
(7) Recreation and culture (parks, libraries, theaters, music, art)	[ ]	[ ]	[ ]
(8) Public safety (prevention of crime and delinquency)	[ ]	[ ]	[ ]
(9) Pollution (air, water, noise)	[ ]	[ ]	[ ]
(10) Social services and welfare	[ ]	[ ]	[ ]
(11) Race relations	[ ]	[ ]	[ ]
(12) Economic development	[ ]	[ ]	[ ]
(13) Cost of local government	[ ]	[ ]	[ ]
(14) Migration of aliens into the city	[ ]	[ ]	[ ]
(15) Other (please specify)	[ ]	[ ]	[ ]

3. Would you please indicate whether you think—effective action is being taken to deal with these problems? Some action is being taken? Or nothing useful is being done?

PLEASE CHECK	EFFECTIVE ACTION	SOME ACTION	NO ACTION
(1) Quality of education	[ ]	[ ]	[ ]
(2) Unemployment	[ ]	[ ]	[ ]
(3) Poverty	[ ]	[ ]	[ ]

PLEASE CHECK	EFFECTIVE ACTION	SOME ACTION	NO ACTION
(4) Health services and conditions	[ ]	[ ]	[ ]
(5) Housing	[ ]	[ ]	[ ]
(6) Public improvements (transportation, streets, water, sewage, sanitation)	[ ]	[ ]	[ ]
(7) Recreation and culture (parks, libraries, theaters, music, art)	[ ]	[ ]	[ ]
(8) Public safety (prevention of crime and delinquency)	[ ]	[ ]	[ ]
(9) Pollution (air, water, noise)	[ ]	[ ]	[ ]
(10) Social services and welfare	[ ]	[ ]	[ ]
(11) Race relations	[ ]	[ ]	[ ]
(12) Economic development	[ ]	[ ]	[ ]
(13) Cost of local government	[ ]	[ ]	[ ]
(14) Migration of aliens into the city	[ ]	[ ]	[ ]
(15) Other (please specify)	[ ]	[ ]	[ ]

4. Regardless of how things are being done now, who in your opinion should have primary responsibility for—

PLEASE CHECK	FEDERAL GOV'T	STATE GOV'T	LOCAL GOV'T	NON-GOV'T	LEAVE TO THE PEOPLE
(1) Quality of education	[ ]	[ ]	[ ]	[ ]	[ ]
(2) Unemployment for everyone	[ ]	[ ]	[ ]	[ ]	[ ]
(3) Poor People	[ ]	[ ]	[ ]	[ ]	[ ]
(4) Health services	[ ]	[ ]	[ ]	[ ]	[ ]
(5) Housing problems	[ ]	[ ]	[ ]	[ ]	[ ]
(6) Public improvements	[ ]	[ ]	[ ]	[ ]	[ ]
(7) Recreation and culture	[ ]	[ ]	[ ]	[ ]	[ ]
(8) Crime and delinquency)	[ ]	[ ]	[ ]	[ ]	[ ]
(9) Pollution	[ ]	[ ]	[ ]	[ ]	[ ]
(10) Race relations	[ ]	[ ]	[ ]	[ ]	[ ]
(11) Economic growth	[ ]	[ ]	[ ]	[ ]	[ ]

5. In which of these areas do you think that your local government has enough power and
 autonomy to act effectively?

PLEASE CHECK	HAS POWERS	LACKS POWERS
(1) Quality of education	[ ]	[ ]

PLEASE CHECK	HAS POWERS	LACKS POWERS
(2) Unemployment for everyone	[ ]	[ ]
(3) Poor People	[ ]	[ ]
(4) Health services	[ ]	[ ]
(5) Housing problems	[ ]	[ ]
(6) Public improvements	[ ]	[ ]
(7) Recreation and culture	[ ]	[ ]
(8) Crime and delinquency)	[ ]	[ ]
(9) Pollution	[ ]	[ ]
(10) Race relations	[ ]	[ ]
(11) Economic growth	[ ]	[ ]

6. In many communities there are conflicts which interfere with effective action to meet community problems. Are there some major conflicts that interfere with getting things done in your community?
[ ] YES
[ ] NO
If YES, would you please name one or two?

7. To what extent do these conflicts come in the way of the development of your community?
[ ] VERY MUCH
[ ] SOME

8. To what extent do differences such as the following tend to divide people in your community?

PLEASE CHECK	VERY MUCH	SOMEWHAT	NOT AT ALL
(1) Differences in education	[ ]	[ ]	[ ]
(2) Differences in income	[ ]	[ ]	[ ]
(3) Differences in religious beliefs	[ ]	[ ]	[ ]
(4) Differences in political views	[ ]	[ ]	[ ]
(5) Differences between city residents and suburbanites	[ ]	[ ]	[ ]
(6) Differences between manager and employees	[ ]	[ ]	[ ]
(7) Differences between those desiring social change and those opposing it	[ ]	[ ]	[ ]
(8) Differences between the young and old	[ ]	[ ]	[ ]

9. In general, do you think that conditions have changed in the last 10 years
for the better?
For worse? Or remained about the same?
[ ] FOR BETTER
[ ] FOR WORSE
[ ] REMAINED THE SAME

10. We would like to get an overall impression of life in your city. All in all,
how satisfied are you with your city these days?

PLEASE CHECK ONE BOX BELOW

Completely   Completely
Dissatisfied   Satisfied

   1   2   3   4   5   6   7   8   9

Section II. Your Role As A Local Leader

We now turn to questions about your own role as a leader in your city.

11. We would like to know how much influence you feel you have on what
is accomplished in your city in the following areas. Please check the areas
where you feel you have a great deal of influence, only some, or none at all.

PLEASE CHECK	GREAT INFLUENCE	SOME INFLUENCE	NO INFLUENCE
(1) Economic development	[ ]	[ ]	[ ]
(2) Agriculture	[ ]	[ ]	[ ]
(3) Housing	[ ]	[ ]	[ ]
(4) Public improvement	[ ]	[ ]	[ ]
services and utilities	[ ]	[ ]	[ ]
(5) Health	[ ]	[ ]	[ ]
(6) Culture, recreation and sports	[ ]	[ ]	[ ]
(7) Education	[ ]	[ ]	[ ]
(8) Political organization activity	[ ]	[ ]	[ ]
(9) Collection and distribution of public revenue (tax collection and budgeting)	[ ]	[ ]	[ ]
(10) Public order and safety	[ ]	[ ]	[ ]
(11) Social services and welfare	[ ]	[ ]	[ ]
(12) Employment and labor relations	[ ]	[ ]	[ ]

12. When you as a public official or community leader need support from others, to whom do you usually turn among the following?

PLEASE CHECK
[ ] (1) Local party leaders
[ ] (2) Higher level party leaders (outside the city)
[ ] (3) Local elective officials
[ ] (4) State elected (legislative) officials
[ ] (5) U.S. Congressmen or Senators
[ ] (6) City administrative officials
[ ] (7) State administrative officials
[ ] (8) Federal administrative officials
[ ] (9) Business leaders
[ ] (10) Trade unions
[ ] (11) Ethnic or racial groups
[ ] (12) Religious leaders
[ ] (13) Civic and reform groups
[ ] (14) Neighborhoods
[ ] (15) Public employee unions
[ ] (16) Local media
[ ] (17) Close friends and supporters
[ ] (18) Other (please specify)

13. Do any of these contact you about their interests and views?

PLEASE CHECK
[ ] (1) Local party leaders
[ ] (2) Higher level party leaders (outside the city)
[ ] (3) Local elective officials
[ ] (4) State elected (legislative) officials
[ ] (5) U.S. Congressmen or Senators
[ ] (6) City administrative officials
[ ] (7) State administrative officials
[ ] (8) Federal administrative officials
[ ] (9) Business leaders
[ ] (10) Trade unions
[ ] (11) Ethnic or racial groups
[ ] (12) Religious leaders
[ ] (13) Civic and reform groups
[ ] (14) Neighborhoods
[ ] (15) Public employee unions
[ ] (16) Local media
[ ] (17) Close friends and supporters
[ ] (18) Other (please specify)

Section III. Values and Goals

The following are statements about issues often faced in the daily life of community leaders. Would you please indicate by checking in the appropriate column to what extent you agree or disagree with each of them? (Please feel free to comment on any of these statements)

PLEASE CHECK	STRONGLY AGREE	AGREE	DISAGREE	STRONGLY DISAGREE
1. If there is disagreement about a program a leader should be willing to give it up.	[ ]	[ ]	[ ]	[ ]
2. The complexity of modern day issues requires that only the more simple questions should be considered publicly.	[ ]	[ ]	[ ]	[ ]
3. National goals should not be obtained at great costs to local communities.	[ ]	[ ]	[ ]	[ ]
4. Rich people should pay more for the support of community projects than poor people.	[ ]	[ ]	[ ]	[ ]
5. Public decisions should be made by unanimous consent.	[ ]	[ ]	[ ]	[ ]
6. Widespread participation in decisionmaking often leads to undesirable conflicts.	[ ]	[ ]	[ ]	[ ]
7. Although national affairs are important, people should first worry about their own community problems.	[ ]	[ ]	[ ]	[ ]
8. Community progress is not possible if national goals always have priority.	[ ]	[ ]	[ ]	[ ]
9. Most decisions should be left to the judgment of experts.	[ ]	[ ]	[ ]	[ ]
10. There should be an upper limit on income so that no one earns very much more than others.	[ ]	[ ]	[ ]	[ ]
11. Only those who are fully informed on the issues should vote.	[ ]	[ ]	[ ]	[ ]

PLEASE CHECK	STRONGLY AGREE	AGREE	DISAGREE	STRONGLY DISAGREE
12. We should not worry so much about national problems when we have so many in our own community.	[ ]	[ ]	[ ]	[ ]
13. The government has the responsibility to see that nobody lives well when others are poor.	[ ]	[ ]	[ ]	[ ]
14. Local leaders should always be prepared to adjust their programs to national goals and policies even if it is disadvantageous for the community.	[ ]	[ ]	[ ]	[ ]
15. The people in this community must continually look for new solutions rather than be satisfied with things as they are.	[ ]	[ ]	[ ]	[ ]
16. Leaders who are over concerned about resolving conflicts can never carry out community programs successfully.	[ ]	[ ]	[ ]	[ ]
17. participation of the people is not necessary if decision making is left in the hands of a few trusted and competent leaders.	[ ]	[ ]	[ ]	[ ]
18. It is necessary to forego development of one's own community to help the development of the rest of the county.	[ ]	[ ]	[ ]	[ ]
19. Preserving harmony in the community should be considered more important than the achievement of community programs.	[ ]	[ ]	[ ]	[ ]
20. In every situation poor people should be given more opportunities than rich people.	[ ]	[ ]	[ ]	[ ]

| | STRONGLY | | | STRONGLY |
PLEASE CHECK	AGREE	AGREE	DISAGREE	DISAGREE
21. A good leader should refrain from making proposals that divide the people even if these are important for the community.	[ ]	[ ]	[ ]	[ ]
22. Changes are desirable even if they do not seem to contribute as much as one might expect.	[ ]	[ ]	[ ]	[ ]
23. A leader should modify his actions to keep consensus.	[ ]	[ ]	[ ]	[ ]
24. Avoiding spending on luxuries is necessary to minimize distance between social groups.	[ ]	[ ]	[ ]	[ ]
25. A community should not accept programs which upset the settled ways of doing things.	[ ]	[ ]	[ ]	[ ]
26. On the whole, questions of national importance should come first in the minds of local government officials.	[ ]	[ ]	[ ]	[ ]
27. It is important for a leader to get things done even if he must displease ppeople	[ ]	[ ]	[ ]	[ ]
28. There is nothing inherently superior in the past.	[ ]	[ ]	[ ]	[ ]
29. Discrepancies in salaries should be continually reduced.	[ ]	[ ]	[ ]	[ ]
30. Only those who are competent on an issue should speak about it.	[ ]	[ ]	[ ]	[ ]
31. If society is to progress, newer solutions to problems are essential.	[ ]	[ ]	[ ]	[ ]

Section IV. Background Data

Finally, we would like to ask some questions about yourself to help us interpret the results.

1. Present position: _____

2. How many years have you held this position? _____

3. How many years have you held a public position? _____

4. Have your father or mother held governmental or political positions, or performed functions
 such as yours?
PLEASE CHECK
 [ ] FATHER
 [ ] MOTHER

5. What political party do you usually support?
PLEASE CHECK
 [ ] DEMOCRATIC
 [ ] REPUBLICAN
 [ ] INDEPENDENT
 [ ] OTHER (Please specify)

6. What has been your principal occupation during your life?

_____

7. What were the principal occupations of your parents?

_____

8. How many years have you lived in this city? _____

9. Were you born in this city? ____ If not, somewhere near? ____ Or farther away? ____

10. How old are you? _____

11. Did you complete high school? ____ College or university? ____
 Do you hold a graduate or professional degree? ____

12. Sex:
 [ ] MALE
 [ ] FEMALE

13. Race or ethnic origin:
[ ] CAUCASIAN
[ ] BLACK
[ ] HISPANIC
[ ] AMERICAN INDIAN
[ ] ASIAN AMERICAN

14. Religious preference, if any: _____

15. Do you attend church weekly?
[ ] YES
[ ] NO

References

Aberbach, Joel, Robert Putnam and Bert Rockman. 1981. *Bureaucrats and Politicians in Western Democracies*. Cambridge: Harvard University Press.

Aberbach, Joel and Bert Rockman. 1977. "The Overlapping Worlds of American Federal Executives and Congressmen." *British Journal of Political Science* 7:40-52.

Aiken, Michael and Robert R. Alford. 1970. "Comparative Urban Research and Community Decision-making", *The New Atlantis* I.

Aiken, Michael and Guido Martinotti. 1985. *Does Politics Matter?* New York: Oxford University Press.

Almond, Gabriel. 1956. "Comparative Political Systems." *The Journal of Politics* 18(3): 391-409.

Almond, Gabriel and G. Bingham Powell. 1978. *Comparative Politics*. Boston: Little, Brown.

Andeweg, Rudy B. 1982. *Dutch Voters Adrift*. Leiden, Netherlands: Leiden University.

Anton, Thomas. 1980. *Administered Politics: Elite Political Culture in Sweden*. The Hague: Martinus Nihoff.

——. 1987. "The Political Economy of Local Government Reform in the U.S." Providence, R.I.: Brown University, Alfred Taubman Center for Public Policy and American Institutions.

——. 1989. *American Federalism and Public Policy*. Philadelphia, PA.: Temple University Press.

Banfield, Edward C. 1965. *Big City Politics*. New York: Random House.

Banfield, Edward C. 1968. *City Politics and Public Policy*. New York: John Wiley.

Banfield, Edward C. and James Q. Wilson. 1963. *City Politics*. Cambridge, Mass.: Harvard University Press.

Barnes, Samuel. 1988. *Politics and Culture*. Ann Arbor, MI.: Center for Political Studies, The University of Michigan.

Barton, Allen. 1965. *Measuring the Values of Individuals*. New York: Columbia University, Bureau of Applied Social Research.

Berelson, Bernard, Paul Lazersfeld and William N. McPhee. 1954. *Voting*. Chicago: University of Chicago Press.

Birgersson, Bengt-Owe. 1975. *"Kommunal sjalvstyrelse-kommunal indelning: Nagra forskningsresultat fran kommunalforskningsgruppen."* Stockholm: Ministry of Communal Affairs.

——. 1977. "The Service Paradox: Citizen Assessment of Urban Services in 36 Swedish Communes," in Vincent Ostrom and Frances Pennel Bish, eds., *Comparing Urban Service Delivery Systems*. Urban Affairs Annual Review. Berkeley, CA: Sage Publications.

Brantgarde, Lennart. 1971. "Political Decision-making in a Risk-taking Situation: Swedish Local Councils in the Face of Amalgamation," *Scandinavian Political Studies* 6 :54-86.

Clark, Terry N. eds., 1981. *Urban Policy Analysis.* Beverly Hills, CA: Sage Publications.

Clark, Terry N. and Lorna C. Ferguson. 1983. *City Money.* New York: Columbia University Press.

Clark, Terry N., Gerd M. Hellstern, and Guido Martinotti. 1985. *Urban Innovations As Response to Urban Strain.* Berlin: Verlag Europaische Perspectiven.

Daalder, Hans. 1988. "English Language Sources for the Study of Dutch Politics." *West European Politics,* (Special Issue on "Politics in the Netherlands: How Much Change?") 12:162-85.

Dahl, Robert. 1956. *A Preface to Democratic Theory.* Chicago: University of Chicago Press.

———. 1961. *Who Governs?* New Haven, CT.: Yale University Press.

———. 1967. *Pluralist Democracy in the United States.* Chicago: Rand McNally.

———. 1971. *Polyarchy: Participation and Opposition.* New Haven, CT.: Yale University Press.

Eldersveld, Samuel J., Jan Kooiman and Theo van der Tak. 1981. *Elite Images of Dutch Politics.* Ann Arbor, MI: University of Michigan Press.

Eldersveld, Samuel J. and Renata Siemienska. 1989. "Elite Conflict Orientations in Polish and U.S. Cities," *International Political Science Review* 10:309-329.

Eulau, Heinz and Kenneth Prewitt. 1973. *Labyrinths of Democracy: Adaptations, Linkages, Representation, and Policies in Urban Politics.* New York: Bobbs-Merrill.

Eyestone, Robert and Heinz Eulau, in James Q. Wilson, *City Politics and Public Policy,* 1968.

Field, G. Lowell and John Higley. 1980. *Elitism.* London: Routledge and Kegan Paul.

Fried, Robert. 1972. "Comparative Urban Performance," European Urban Research Working Paper No. 1. Los Angeles, CA: University of California.

Gottdiener, Mark. 1987. *The Decline of Urban Politics.* Beverley Hills, CA: Sage Publications.

Gurr, Ted and Desmond S. King. 1987. *The State and the City.* Chicago: University of Chicago Press.

Gustafsson, Agne. 1983. *Local Government in Sweden.* Stockholm: The Swedish Institute.

Gustafsson, Gunnel. 1991. "Swedish Local Government: Reconsidering Rationality and Consensus," in Joachim Jens Hesse, eds., *Local Government and Urban Affairs in International Perspective.* Baden-Baden, Germany: Nomas Verlagsgeschellschaft.

Holmberg, Soren. 1974. "Riksdagen representerar svenska folket." Doctoral dissertation, University of Lund, Sweden.

Hunter, Floyd. 1953. *Community Power.* Chapel Hill, N.C.: University of North Carolina Press.

———. 1959. *Top Leadership U.S.A.* Chapel Hill, N.C.: University of North Carolina Press.

Inglehart, Ronald. 1990. *Culture Shift in Advanced Industrial Society.* Princeton: Princeton University Press.

Irwin, Galen. 1976. "Party Accountability and the Recruitment of Municipal Coun-cilmen in the Netherlands." In Heinz Eulau and Moshe M. Czudnowski, eds., *Elite Recruitment in Democratic Polities*. New York: Halsted.

Irwin, Galen and J.J.M. van Holsteyn. 1989. "Decline of the Structured Model of Electoral Competition." *West European Politics* 12:21-41.

Jacob, Philip, ed., 1971. *Values and the Active Community*. New York: The Free Press.

Jones, Bryan. 1983. *Governing Urban America*. Boston: Little, Brown and Co.

Judd, Dennis and Michael Parkinson. 1990. *Leadership and Urban Regeneration*. Newbury Park, CA: Sage Publications.

Kaijser, Fritz. 1962. "1962 ars kommunalforordningar," in *Hundra arunder kommunalforfattningarna 1862-1962*. Stockholm: Svenska landskommunernas forbund.

Knoke, David. 1981. "Urban Political Cultures", in Terry Clark, ed., *Urban Policy Analysis*. Beverly Hills, CA: Sage Publications.

Kreukels, Anton and Tejo Spit. 1989. "Fiscal Retrenchment and the Relationship Between National Government and Local Administration in the Netherlands", in Susan E. Clarke, ed., *Urban Innovation and Autonomy*. Beverly Hills, CA: Sage Publications.

Lasswell, Harold D. 1936. *Politics: Who Gets What, When, How*. New York: Whittlesey House, McGraw-Hill.

Lasswell, Harold and A. Kaplan. 1950. *Power and Society*. New Haven, CT.: Yale University Press.

Lasswell, Harold, Daniel Lerner, and C. Easton Rothwell. 1952. *The Comparative Study of Elites*. Stanford: Stanford University Press, Hoover Institute Studies.

Lineberry, Robert L. and Edmund P. Fowler. 1968. "Reformism and Public Policies in American Cities," in James Q. Wilson, *City Politics and Public Policy*. New York: John Wiley.

Meisel, James H. 1965. *Pareto and Mosca*. Englewood Cliffs, N.J.: Prentice Hall.

Meisel, James H. 1962. *The Myth of the Ruling Class: Gaetano Mosca and the "Elite"*. Ann Arbor, MI: University of Michigan Press.

Mills, C. Wright. 1956. *The Power Elite*. New York: Oxford University Press.

Mitra, Subrata. 1992. *Power, Protest and Participation*. London: Routledge.

Mouritzen, Paul Erick and K. M. Nielsen. 1988. *Handbook of Comparative Urban Fiscal Data*. Danish Data Archives publication, Odense University.

Netherlands Scientific Council for Government Policy. 1990. "Institutions and Cities: The Dutch Experience," The Hague, Netherlands.

Norell, P. 1989. "De Kommunala Administratorerna," Doctoral dissertation, University of Lund, Sweden.

Pagano, Michael. 1991. "City Fiscal Conditions in 1991." National League of Cities Research Report.

Page, Edward C. 1985. *Political Authority and Bureaucratic Power*. Knoxville, KY: University of Kentucky Press.

Peterson, Paul E. 1981. *City Limits*. Chicago: University of Chicago Press.

Pitkin, Hanna F. 1967. *The Concept of Representation*. Berkeley, CA.: University of California Press.

Presthus, Robert. 1964. *Men at the Top: A Study in Community Power.* New York: Oxford University Press.

Prewitt, Kenneth. 1970. *The Recruitment of Political Leaders.* New York: Bobbs-Merrill.

Przeworski, Adam and Henry Teune. 1966. "Equivalence in Cross-National Research." *The Public Opinion Quarterly* 30:551-68.

Przeworski, Adam and Henry Teune. 1970. *The Logic of Comparative Social Inquiry.* New York: John Wiley.

Putnam, Robert. 1973. *The Beliefs of Politicians.* New Haven, Ct.: Yale University Press.

——. 1976. *The Comparative Study of Political Elites.* New York: Prentice Hall.

Pye, Lucian and Sidney Verba. 1965. *Political Culture and Political Development.* Princeton: Princeton University Press.

Rochon, Thomas. 1987. "The Dutch", in *The Wilson Quarterly* (Spring):53-69.

Rose, Lawrence E. 1990. "Nordic Free-Commune Experiments: Increased Local Autonomy or Continued Central Control?" in Desmond S. King and Jon Pierre, eds., *Challenges to Local Government.* Beverly Hills, CA: Sage Publications.

Schumaker, Paul David, Russell W. Getter, and Terry N. Clark. 1979. *Policy Responsiveness and Fiscal Strain in 51 American Communities.* Washington, D.C.: The American Political Science Association.

Scott, William A. 1965. *Values and Organizations.* Chicago: Rand McNally.

Sharpe, L.J. and Kenneth Newton. 1984. *Does Politics Matter?* New York: Oxford University Press.

Spit, Tejo. 1993. *Strangled in Structures: An Institutional Analysis of Innovative Policy by Dutch Municipalities.* Utrecht, Netherlands: Drukkerij Elinkwijk.

Strömberg, Lars. 1974. *Valjare och valda. En studie av den representativa demokratin i kommunerna.* Unpublished dissertation, Statsvetenskapliga institutionen, Goteborgs universitet.

——. 1977. "Electors and the Elected," in Vincent Ostrom et al., eds., *Comparing Urban Service Delivery Systems,* Urban Affairs Annual Review 12:243-302..

——. 1990. "Det svenska frikommunforsoket 1984-1989" in Krister Stahlberg, *Frikommunforsoken i Norden,* Abo Akademi.

Strömberg, Lars and Per-Owe Norell. 1982. Kommunalförvalt-ningen. Ds kn.

Strömberg, Lars and Jorgen Westerståhl. 1984. *The New Swedish Communes.* Lerum, Sweden: Lerums Boktryckeri AB.

Tarrow, Sidney and V. L.. Smith. 1976. "Crisis Recruitment and the Political Involvement of Local Elites: Some Evidence from Italy and France." In Heinz Eulau and Moshe M. Czudnowski, *Elite Recruitment in Democratic Polities.* New York: Halsted.

Thompson, Michael, Richard Ellis and Aaron Wildavsky. 1990. *Cultural Theory.* Boulder, Colo.: Westview Press.

Tingsten, Herbert. 1937. *Political Behavior: Studies in Election Statistics.* London: King.

Toonen, Theo A.S. 1987. "The Netherlands: A Decentralized Unitary State in a Welfare Society," *Western European Politics* (Special Issue on "Tensions in the Territorial Politics of Western Europe) 10:108-129.

Verba, Sidney and Norman Nie. 1972. *Participation in America.* New York: Harper and Row.

Verba, Sidney and Gary R. Orren. 1985. *Euality in America.* Cambridge, MA: Harvard University Press.

Wallin, Gunnar, Hentry Båch, and Merrick Tabor. 1981. Kummunalpolitkerna.Ds kn.

Westerståhl, Jörgen. 1971. "The Communal Research Program in Sweden." *The New Atlantis* II:124-32.

Wildavsky, Aaron. 1989. "A Cultural Theory of Leadership." In Bryan D. Jones, ed., *Leadership and Politics.* Lawrence, Kansas: University Press of Kansas.

Williams, John A. 1976. "Determinants of Governmental Administrative Capacity." Doctoral Dissertation, University of Pennsylvania.

Index

About the Book and Authors

What kinds of leadership do we have today in the cities of the U.S. and other Western democracies? At a time of widespread urban crisis, with worsening social and economic conditions and shrinking resources, the character of local leadership is a major concern. Because local leaders' decisions affect the lives of most people more immediately than those of presidents or monarchs, we need to know who these leaders are, what they believe in, what they do, and how effective their actions are in community problem-solving.

Through an extensive and original comparative analysis of mayors, council members, department heads, and party leaders in 55 middle-sized cities, this internationally renowned author team gives us a clear, candid picture of our leaders' political and social backgrounds, their perceptions of problems, their political values, and their past and current experience in mobilizing support for their policies. Anyone concerned about "the problem of the cities" on a global scale will find here unique urban profiles that are both disturbing and reassuring. And for all who are interested in democratic theory-testing, this book provides a benchmark of empirical and normative analysis.

Samuel J. Eldersveld is emeritus professor of political science at the University of Michigan. Lars Strömberg is professor of political science at the University of Göteborg, Sweden. Wim Derksen is professor of local government at Leyden University, the Netherlands.